# Pirates

# Pirates

Truth and Tales

## HELEN HOLLICK

AMBERLEY

The author and publisher would like to thank the following people for permission to use copyright material in this book:

Helen Hart *The Black Banner* ISBN 9781906236465
James L. Nelson *The Only Life That Mattered: The Short and Merry Lives of Anne Bonny, Mary Read, and Calico Jack Rackham* ISBN 9781590130605
Janis Pegrum Smith *The Book Ark – Black on White* ISBN 9781511885157
Anna Belfrage *Like Chaff In The Wind* ISBN 9781781321690
Phil Berry: weapons and fighting skills
John Fitzhugh Millar: sea shanties and the *Bachelor's Delight*
Cathy Helms: www.avalongraphics.org graphics and photographic images

Every attempt has been made to seek permission for copyright material used in this book. However, if we have inadvertently used copyright material without permission/ acknowledgement we apologise and we will make the necessary correction at the first opportunity.

First published 2017

Amberley Publishing
The Hill, Stroud
Gloucestershire, GL5 4EP

www.amberley-books.com

British Library Cataloguing in Publication Data.
A catalogue record for this book is available from the British Library.

ISBN 978 1 4456 5215 3 (hardback)
ISBN 978 1 4456 5216 0 (ebook)

Typesetting and Origination by Amberley Publishing.
Printed in the UK.

*To Jesamiah, for becoming as real as a fictional character
can become real*

# Contents

# Timeline

| | |
|---|---|
| 1677 | William of Orange marries Mary, daughter of James II |
| 1680 | Edward Teach born |
| (–90?) | Charles Vane born |
| 1682 | Jack 'Calico' Rackham born |
| | Bartholomew Roberts born |
| 1683 | October: Henry Morgan removed from Port Royal Council |
| 1685 | Charles II dies; succeeded by his brother James |
| | 11 June: Duke of Monmouth lands at Lyme Bay |
| | 6 July: Monmouth defeated at Sedgemoor |
| | Judge Jeffries' Bloody Assizes: hundreds of rebels hanged or sold as slaves |
| 1684 | Alexandre Oliver Exquemelin's *The Buccaneers of America* published |
| | Tortuga deserted by pirates |
| | The term 'buccaneer' widely adopted |
| 1687 | Dr Hans Sloan and Duke and Duchess of Albemarle arrive in Port Royal |
| 1688 | Stede Bonnet born |
| | Pirates using Port Royal, Jamaica |
| | James II flees to France |
| | 25 August: Henry Morgan dies |
| | 5 November: William of Orange lands at Torbay |
| 1689 | War with France |
| | Sam Bellamy born |
| 1690 | William of Orange defeats James II at Battle of the Boyne |
| | Howell Davies born |
| 1691 | William Dampier completes his first circumnavigation of the world |
| 1692 | 7 June: Port Royal devastated by earthquake |
| | Thomas Tew active as a privateer |
| 1693 | Fictional pirate Jesamiah Acorne born |
| | William and Mary College, Virginia, founded |
| 1694 | Bank of England founded |
| 1695 | Death of Queen Mary |
| | Death of Thomas Tew |
| 1696 | William Kidd active as a privateer |
| 1697 | End of war with France |

1699    William Kidd arrested for piracy
        William Dampier commissioned for a second
        circumnavigation
1700    Death of Charles II of Spain
        Anne Bonny born
1701    War of Spanish Succession declared
        James II dies
        17 May: William Kidd hanged
        William Dampier returns to England
1702    William II dies
        Anne becomes Queen
        Founding of first daily English newspaper, the *Daily
        Courant*
1703    Work begins on building Buckingham House (Palace)
        William Dampier sets off on another expedition
1704    The English capture Gibraltar
        Battle of Blenheim
1706    Building of the Governor's Palace in Williamsburg begins
1707    Act of Union (Scotland and England to form Great Britain)
        William Dampier returns to England
1708    Planned Jacobite rebellion, with French landing in
        Scotland, abandoned because James (III) catches measles
        William Dampier joins Woodes Rogers' circumnavigation
        expedition
1709    17 February: Andrew Selkirk rescued by Woodes Rogers
1710    St Paul's Cathedral completed
        Alexander Spotswood appointed Governor of Virginia
1711    14 October: Woodes Rogers' expedition returns to
        England
1713    War with Spain over, privateers expect full pardons for
        acts of piracy
1714    Bahamas raided by French and Spanish
        Nassau sacked three times
        Death of Queen Anne
        Accession of George of Hanover
        End of the War of Spanish Succession
1715    31 July: Spanish treasure fleet wrecked
        Death of William Dampier

1717    Stede Bonnet active as a pirate
        *Whydah Galley* wrecked
        17 November: Blackbeard captures the *Queen Anne's
        Revenge*
1718    Woodes Rogers arrives in Nassau
        Calico Jack Rackham active as a pirate
        May: Blackbeard blockades Charlestown harbour
        June: *Queen Anne's Revenge* runs aground
        July: Howell Davies active as a pirate
        September / October: Blackbeard meets other pirates on
        the beaches of Ocracoke
        November: Governor Spotswood sends Lt Robert Maynard
        to capture or kill Blackbeard
        22 November: Blackbeard killed
        10 December: Stede Bonnet executed
1719    March: Blackbeard's remaining crew hanged at Williamsburg
        19 June: Howell Davies shot dead
        War with Spain
        Royal pardon extended to 1 July
        *Robinson Crusoe* published by Daniel Defoe
        Anne Bonny and Mary Read become pirates
        Charles Vane arrested
        Benjamin Hornigold disappears at sea
1720    Governor Woodes Rogers hangs all pirates who refuse to
        give up piracy
        Edward England active as a pirate
        South Sea Bubble bursts; financial ruin for many
        Robert Walpole becomes the first Prime Minister of Great
        Britain
        February: Battle of Nassau
        18 November: Calico Jack Rackham hanged at Port Royal
1721    Pirate community in Madagascar coming to life again
        Bartholomew Roberts of the *Royal Fortune* killed in battle
        Edward England dies
        Woodes Rogers returns to London
        March: Charles Vane hanged
1722    Edward Lowe active as a pirate
        February: Bartholomew Roberts dies

1723   Charles Johnson's *A General History of Robberies and Murders of Notorious Pyrates* published
1724   Edward Lowe disappears, probably drowned at sea
       Governor Spotswood returns to London
1727   Death of George of Hanover (George I)
       Succession of George II
1732   15 July: Woodes Rogers dies
1740   7 June: Governor Spotswood dies

# Weigh Anchor!

Arrrr! Pirates!

Even that single word, 'pirates', conjures up vivid scenes of derring-do and exciting adventures at sea. We are fascinated by pirates – real pirates, not the romantic, swashbuckling heroes of the Errol Flynn and Johnny Depp kind – because pirates were, are, sea-based criminals, robbers, thieves, rapists and murderers. You could easily add a few more adjectives to the list. They have been around for a long time, even before the Greek and Roman empires. Wherever goods worth the effort of stealing were being transported along regular, predictable trading routes, there would be the pirates.

Back in those early days, the pirate was the hunter seeking a way to supplement his family income by plundering goods that did not belong to him. In the ancient world of the Greeks he was respected, admired as a brave warrior; the word pirate comes from the Greek verb *peiran*, which means to attack. The pirates thumbed their noses at danger, and at law and government, which is probably why they remain admired today.

Pirates were tolerated, even encouraged, when they plundered the ships of countries seen as enemies – as Spain was to the English for so long, for instance. In such cases it was acceptable, even applauded and rewarded, to steal from others. However, when they started hitting the pockets of the merchants who were rapidly becoming rich through trade in tobacco, rum, sugar and slaves, that was their death knell.

We tend to think of pirates as rough men dressed in striped shirts and baggy trousers, wearing jaunty spotted bandanas and eyepatches, maybe with a hooked hand or a wooden leg and a parrot perched on one shoulder. Such is the impression given by films and fiction. The Jolly Roger as the flag, a pretty ship, adventure, usually with a trim-waisted, full-bosomed, curly-haired wench in tow. Most of these common images are, alas, fiction.

Modern pirates of today – Somalian ones in particular – prefer small speedboats and attack cargo vessels that have few crew aboard; these ships are big, but the crews are not. Modern pirates pose many challenges to international communities for they, just like pirates of the past, are hard, even impossible, to eradicate and they are nothing like their fictional counterparts.

The Romans had their problems with pirates. So did the Anglo-Saxons. The term 'Viking' comes from *i-viking*, meaning 'to go raiding'. Move on to Tudor times and we meet Grace O'Malley, an Irish pirate and a thorn in English Queen Elizabeth I's side. The Tudor period was the start of the age of privateering, which was the same as piracy except you carried a Letter of Marque from your government that gave you permission to attack, loot and destroy ships of countries at war with your own. The concept was quite ambiguous and not always cheerfully accepted as being 'legal' by the crews of ships on the 'other' side. Sir Francis Drake was a privateer, as were Sir Walter Raleigh and Henry Morgan, but even with government (and royal) blessing they were still looters, killers and thieves.

However, these men were clever; they shared the spoils with the reigning monarch of the day, who needed the gold, silver and gems to pay for the on-going wars that raged between variations of England and Spain, Spain and France, and France and England. Add the Dutch into the mix, then the American Colonies towards the end of the 18th century, and there was plenty of scope for an intrepid seafarer in search of a life of freedom away from the restrictions of authority.

Most of the Caribbean pirates of the 'Golden Age', the early 18th century, with the exception of a few (Edward Lowe, for instance) started out as honest seafarers – either as merchantmen or in the Royal Navy. A harsh, even cruel captain, poor food and poorer conditions easily led to discontentment and the final straw. Mutiny was easy and the lure of possible riches and a better life was enticing. The noose could end it all, but so what? Everyone dies at some point, one way or another. Better to meet your maker a free man rather than as a

miserable nobody. A small handful of pirates, those who were better
educated and therefore slightly more respectable, made their fortune
and retired to a quiet life, or at least a settled one – a pleasant prospect
when you had gold in your pocket. Some pirates sailed off across the
ocean and were never heard of again. Did they simply disappear to
start afresh somewhere under an assumed name? Or did they with
their crew and ship meet a tragic end at the bidding of Nature and the
Grim Reaper? Unless a wreck is found – highly unlikely for anything
at the bottom of the Atlantic – we will never know. Even with modern
technology, lost ships and aeroplanes are often never found.

Pirates were not particular about personal hygiene and were rarely
sober, but then neither were the men of the Royal Navy. Come to that,
nor were most of the Western populations from early times right up to
the end of the Victorian era. (In fact, when you take a hard look at the
homeless or the out-of-work, life today is not so different for some.) Port
Royal, Jamaica, was known as the wickedest town in the world. God's
retribution put a brief stop to the drunken debauchery in 1692 when
half the town sank into the sea during an earthquake, while the other
half was reduced to rubble. However, the halt was brief – the rich merely
upped sticks, moved to the other side of the bay and founded Kingston.

This is the reality of pirates – but who wants reality? The romantic
ideas portrayed in films, books and TV shows are far more appealing
because they are crammed with adventure and fun. The secret of a
good pirate novel, any novel come to that, is the pace of the action, the
larger-than-life characters, and how believable it all is. Even fantasy has
to be believable, regardless of how many dragons, dwarves, wizards or
vampires are included in the narrative – or how many pirates buckle
their swashes over a tankard of rum and a treasure chest brim-full of
golden doubloons.

Pirate movies and TV shows – novels as well – can initiate a certain
amount of controversy. There was a bit of a hoo-ha in the Caribbean
when Disney's *Dead Man's Chest* was to feature the Caribs, the natives
who gave the islands their familiar name, who were to be portrayed as
cannibals. Apparently, this scurrilous untruth was originally a wild and
fanciful rumour deliberately put about by Christopher Columbus and
his Spanish cronies *circa* 1492. A social media and press-related uproar
protested that Disney was trading on this dreadful slander, but the fact
that most of the islander descendants were willing and eager to take

part in the movie as extras was somewhat overlooked. Then various respected authorities on pirate history fired broadsides at Disney because the dastardly production team was not sticking to the facts or reflecting the truth about the lives of various seafaring blackguards.

The truth?

In the 17th and 18th centuries, pirates were the dregs of the Seven Seas. Most of those who were caught were hanged; only a few made their fortune and retired. Johnny Depp has reportedly said that pirates were the rockstars of their day; this isn't quite so, as more accurately they were the terrorists of the early 18th century, and, strictly speaking, the romanticism surrounding the general conception of what piracy was is nowhere near the truth. The major criticism, therefore, is that pirate tales do not reflect reality – but even the contemporary or near-contemporary accounts are not necessarily accurate. Things get exaggerated, tales get twisted. There are very, very few accurate accounts, even some of the court documents from various pirate trials and subsequent hangings, can be suspect.

The entertainment motive of movies and novels, however, means avoiding being too realistic. Unless you like violent horror films, why would you want to watch a movie about sordid louts pillaging, butchering and torturing when the alternative is fine-looking actors creating enjoyable, fun-filled stories designed to make you sit there smiling when the credits roll? In addition, has it not escaped the naysayers' attention that as far as the *Pirates of the Caribbean* franchise is concerned, skeletons do not live, Aztec treasure is not cursed and there is no such thing as a magic compass that does not point north? There is no Kraken, nor a *Flying Dutchman*, Davy Jones, a Fountain of Youth (although it is a bit of a shame that there was no real Jack Sparrow...). Fiction, especially fantasy fiction, is not meant to be believed or taken seriously. Especially where pirates are concerned, it is not intended to be a suitable replacement for a historical documentary or school history lesson.

As viewers or readers we do not want everyday reality; that is (often depressingly) what the news channels and daily newspapers are for. We want the fun, excitement and even the blood-pulsing danger of our fictional heroes and heroines.

Even if they are pirates.

# What We *Think* We Know
# about Pirates

Pirates. Mention 'pirates' to adults, even more so to children, and eyes begin to twinkle, a smile broadens and the clichéd '*Arrr*' erupts from the lips. Given the choice of dressing up as a pirate or a wizard for a fancy dress party the outright winner, more often than not, is the stereotypical pirate.

The romance of fiction, in the form of novels, TV shows and movies, influences our perception of pirates and piracy, specifically during the so-called Golden Age of the early 1700s. We have a romantic view of a life 'On The Account'. Say 'pirate' and we immediately think *Treasure Island*, Jack Sparrow, or Captain Hook from *Peter Pan*; some of us even remember the bumbling but lovable Captain Pugwash. Real pirates were not, on the whole, nice people. For 21st-century entertainment, though, who is going to sit through a three-hour movie about drunken, stinking-to-high-heaven louts pillaging and butchering? TV drama *Black Sails* depicts some of the rougher side of a life at sea in the early 18th century, but the storyline, especially in the first series, had to be buoyed up by quite a few (unnecessary in my opinion) explicitly sexual scenes to keep the interest and attention. Factual it was not.

Do we want accuracy for entertainment? Moonlit nights, calm seas, a gentle breeze rippling through swaying palm trees; that is the image conjured up in our minds. Do we care that the *Flying Dutchman* does not exist, or the *Marie Celeste* was probably abandoned because her crew thought the vapour escaping from the hold full of alcohol was smoke? Frightened, believing the ship was about to blow up, they hurried into a rowboat and abandoned ship. In their panicked haste, they did not do so wisely; leaving all sails set, the ship took off without them. In a good following wind, with the ship travelling at seven to nine knots, an oarsman in a small boat would not have been able to keep up. It must have been devastating to see your vessel, your home, your livelihood – your only way of staying alive – disappearing towards the horizon without you. The poor unfortunates, however, were not abducted by space-alien pirates, as fiction would have us believe.

Reality has its place, but so does the world of stories and the rose-coloured tint of pleasurable escapism. We like handsome heroes and pretty heroines. We enjoy the breath-taking alarm of danger and engrossing, adventurous romps. Pirate stories give us the (safe) dangerous excitement we crave. Pirates seek treasure – but don't we all? Maybe we do not go off to dig at 'X marks the spot' with our trusty, by-chance-discovered treasure map but several million of us do trot off to the local store every week hoping to buy that illusive winning lottery ticket.

Pirates were on a get-rich-quick mission and did not particularly care how they succeeded as long as they had silver in their pockets to spend in the taverns and brothels. We all know that pirates plundered their loot and then buried the heavily laden treasure chests on remote Caribbean islands. They made their captured enemies walk the plank at sword-point, leading to inevitable death by drowning or fiercesome sharks. Pirates went about saying things like, 'Shiver m'timbers,' and 'Where be tha' rum?' Their ships were all gloriously fast, and the flag fluttering jauntily – yet menacingly – from the masthead was always a pair of crossed bones beneath a leering skull set against a black background. Pirates, we know, wore a gold-hooped earring and had gold-capped teeth. They drank rum (a lot of it), had frequent swashbuckling fights with those sharp-bladed lethal cutlasses they carried, lusted after buxom wenches and died nobly on the long drop with a short stop.

Or did they?

Where does the fact end and the fiction begin?

## 2

# What We *Ought* to Know (Skip This Chapter If You Don't Want To Be Disillusioned)

Pirates were not born to a life of plunder on the high seas – they were usually driven into it by poverty, necessity and opportunity. They got together and mutinied if aboard a ship with a cruel, callous captain, or if they had seen no wages for months on end. They turned to piracy rather than face starvation, or, in some cases, in order to stay alive when the choice was 'join us or die'.

Only one of the more famous pirate captains, Edward Lowe, was known to be a criminal before he went to sea and began a new career of piracy. Many pirates were cruel, even downright evil men (especially Lowe). Some were women. All were thieves and murderers.

So what is it about pirates that attracts us? Is it the splendour of a Golden Age long past? The romantic dream of sun-kissed islands washed by a sparkling azure sea beneath a cloudless pale-blue sky? The bravado, the adventure, the sheer couldn't-care-less attitude? And what was the lure for them? Why become a pirate and face the more-or-less forgone conclusion of the noose? Was it the rum? The treasure? The freedom?

Freedom. Pirates were, apparently, a democratic lot, a concept that was almost unheard of in the 18th-century 'civilised' Western world. Pirates did not have high-ranking, often pompous, always well-off naval officers – admirals, lieutenants, midshipmen and the like – although a sailing master, boatswain and quartermaster would be on the deck of a pirate ship. If they were lucky enough, they might even have a surgeon of sorts. The crew elected their captain. If he turned out to be as useless as an ice cube in the noonday Caribbean sun, they demoted or marooned him. What a pity we do not have the same instant choice with some of our bosses!

The Spanish called runaway slaves *cimarrónes*; the English shortened the word to 'maroons', with 'marooners' eventually becoming a by-word for the Caribbean pirates because marooning was a favoured way to dispose of less-than-favoured personnel aboard a ship – walking the plank, sadly for fiction lovers, does not seem to have existed beyond *Peter Pan* and *Treasure Island*. Marooning was a salve for the conscience because it was not a deliberate killing; the victim had a chance to survive, albeit a slim one. Pirates were fussy like that. The unfortunate maroonee was put ashore with a keg of water, and a pistol and ammunition. Very thoughtful, that. When the drinking water was gone, he could shoot himself. Suicide was not murder; no one took the blame. All very tidy.

The entire crew, as a whole, discussed and voted on where their next piratical voyage would be. There were no weekly pay-slips. Wages were distributed by the plunder being scrupulously shared out and according to previously agreed set amounts, with the captain, surgeon, quartermaster and navigator (ship's master) getting a higher portion than the rest of the crew. This system was neatly and efficiently described as, 'No prey, No pay'. They also had an insurance scheme through which various injuries were compensated for on a guaranteed payment scale. They had rules, although it is not certain whether these were diligently followed by all piratical scallywags or were 'more like guidelines' to a mere few gangs. Just because we have evidence of the written 'articles of agreement' for some of the pirate ships, this does not mean they all had the same system in place.

Life in the 18th century was not an easy one for anyone, except perhaps the gentry and the merchants who were rising into wealth and who were starting to make money on the back of trade, in particular, the slave trade. The Industrial Revolution had not yet happened, the mills and factories had not yet been envisioned, and the population of the cities had not swelled into hundreds of thousands but nonetheless, squalor, poor food, dirty and cramped living conditions were the norm for the majority of the population of England. Work was not easy to find, and the convicted criminals who hanged within days of their trial were perhaps the lucky ones, for few who did not have money survived the horrific depravation of gaol or transportation to the other side of the world – to the new-formed plantations of the American Colonies in this period. Captain James Cook was born in October 1728 and he was not due to 'discover' Australia until a good many years later. Accepting the King's Shilling for service in the army or navy ensured clothing, a bed of some sort for the night and almost regular food, even if it was rancid and full of weevils. The wages were a pittance and there were the chances of being shot at and wounded or killed by the enemy, but it was still better, for many, than life as a poor civilian. Although the Royal Navy was very much in its infancy in the early 1700s, it was Monsieur Bonaparte and the outbreak of the Napoleonic War at the end of the century that increased its efficiency, assisted by that little hiccup of disagreement that took place between England and America over a shipload of tea in Boston Harbour ...

The navy was a better option than the army because you were guaranteed a tot of 'grog', the common name for rum. Admitted, it was heavily watered-down but life had never been a bed of roses.

The serenity of a calm sea belied the danger. Wooden ships could be unstable vessels. They pitched, rolled, sprang leaks, and sank. A fall from the masthead usually resulted in death – if you were fortunate, an immediate one.

The oceans were, for the most part, uncharted territory. Those early explorers – Ferdinand Magellan, Columbus, Drake, da Gama, William Dampier, Woodes Rogers, James Cook (to name but a few) – had little to no idea of what lay beyond the horizon. Compare them to Aldrin, Armstrong and Collins, the crew of Apollo 11. That spaceflight team, while indeed heroic men, knew where they were going, how long it would take to get there and back, and had almost continuous communication with Mission Control. Those early intrepid seamen, once out of sight of land, had nothing, not even knowledge of where there would be a chance to replenish their sour drinking water. We only know of them and their explorations because they, or at least some of the crew, survived the ordeal and returned to tell the tale. The dozens of bones rotting at the bottom of the Atlantic or Pacific will never have their adventures revealed, let alone told.

Before navigation took off with the means to reckon latitude *and* longitude, even an exact whereabouts was uncertain. Clockmaker John Harrison finally solved the problem of accurately establishing longitude at sea – he was rewarded for his Marine Chronometer in 1773. Not that his methods were instantly and widely adopted, that was not to happen for several more years. The only timepieces aboard a ship pre-1773 were the sun and an hourglass used with some good guesswork and the ship's bell.

Disease, illness and injury took their toll on foremast jacks and captains alike. If a ship had the advantage of a good surgeon, it was a lucky ship. But even surgeons succumbed to disease or injury. Few good surgeons – apart from Patrick O'Brian's *Aubrey-Maturin* nautical series – volunteered to serve in the Royal Navy because better opportunities, and higher profits, were to be had on the solid, expensive, ground of Harley Street.

Pirates, especially the most notorious, passed through each day of their lives with the same ferocity as they used when they preyed upon others. On the whole, pirates were not nice people to meet. The lure to go 'On The Account' was the opportunity to get rich quickly and relatively easily – give or take a skirmish or two, and providing you could dodge cannon fire, the Royal Navy and the noose.

The Golden Age, the end of the 17th and start of the 18th centuries, was a period of a mercantile explosion as new countries and new goods were being discovered. Gold and other riches from the collapsing Inca and Aztec South American empires funded the expanding wealth of Europe, although most of it was immediately spent on costly wars with other countries wanting a share of the same new trade and treasure. The embryonic North American Colonies, from the fishing grounds of the Canadian coast down to the emerging tobacco, sugar and cotton plantations of what is now the eastern United States, served England and France as well as Holland, Spain and Portugal. The Dutch originally settled New York in 1624 using what is now Lower Manhattan as a trading post for the seafaring colonists of the Dutch Republic. In 1626, after the area had expanded into a settlement, they named it New Amsterdam. When the city came under English control in 1664, King Charles II of England granted the land to his younger brother, James, Duke of York, and New Amsterdam became New York.

Dutch sailors and traders fared well from their equivalent of the English East India Company, with exploration around the Cape of Good Hope and into the Indian Ocean, and from there, eventually, to the China Seas where the bone china and tea trades began to expand. By the mid-1800s, the world's oceans had become busy trade routes with ships becoming bigger and faster, so the temptation to acquire ill-gotten plunder was an attractive prospect.

Florida was the first part of the vast continent of North America to be settled by the European explorers. Of course, the Vikings had arrived in the Canadian regions centuries before, and the Native Americans, of which there were many and varied tribes, had lived there across what we now call the United States of America for centuries. In April 1513, the Spanish conquistador, Juan Ponce de León, landed and named the area *La Florida* – land of flowers. The town of St Augustine, the oldest settlement in the U.S., was founded in 1565. With English and French settlements later expanding to the north and west, Florida began to shrink in area and St Augustine itself was attacked several times, mainly by the English. Cuba had been taken by English privateers during the Seven Years War and, in 1763, Spain traded it in exchange for Florida. Maybe the Spanish had a premature inkling that better cigars came from Cuba and while Disney is a popular tourist attraction, it does rather spoil the peace and quiet of the place?

The Carolinas, North and South, were also initially Spanish, but Spaniards did not bother to settle there, or even name the region. The French arrived in 1562 and took control, giving the name 'Carolina' after their king, Charles IX, but they had little use for the place so more-or-less also abandoned it. This was before the realisation that cotton, tobacco and sugarcane would soon be in high demand and vast plantations would be required. The English (maybe with insight about the value of land) took over during the reign of Charles II, with the name Carolina retained, but for the English king, not the French one.

Georgia was founded as a colony by the British in 1733, and named after King George II. It was to be administered by a group of trustees, with the vision of it being for the explicit use of yeoman farmers and, interestingly, slavery was prohibited. The grand plan failed, however, and Georgia became a Crown Colony in 1752. In 1776, Georgia was one of the Thirteen Colonies to initiate a revolt against British rule.

Back in 1583, Queen Elizabeth I of England granted a charter to Sir Walter Raleigh to establish a colony of settlers to the north of the Spanish-held land of Florida. The name chosen, Virginia, refers to Elizabeth, known as the Virgin Queen. The land originally covered the area from North Carolina to Maine and the Bermuda islands. The first settlement, founded in May 1607, was at Jamestown, on the James River, named for Elizabeth's successor, King James I of England. Many of those first colonists died of starvation in 1609, and in a Native American massacre of 1622. Only just over 3,000 of the original 6,000 settlers survived, but the demand for tobacco brought in new arrivals. A capital had been established at Middle Plantation, a short way inland from Jamestown, but it was renamed as Williamsburg, after England's new rulers, William and Mary, in 1699.

Much of New England was colonised by the Puritans, establishing their first settlement at Plymouth Colony in 1620, with the Massachusetts Bay Colony following in 1630. Modern Pennsylvania, New York, New Jersey and Delaware came into being through the rest of the century.

The establishment of settlements and colonies led to a need to trade various goods. With Europe several thousand miles away across the Atlantic Ocean that in turn meant the necessity for shipping to transport it all. There was stuff – all kinds of valuable stuff – for the taking. Not just gold and silver, but gems, ambergris, (a solid, waxy substance produced in the digestive system of sperm whales, highly prized and valued for making perfume,) rum and slaves, mercantile goods that were ripe for the taking, for the want of a fight or two, and available to be sold for high profit. No wonder that where there were trading ships, there were also pirates waiting to pounce on them. In addition to their cargo, the ships themselves were valued. No pirate came upon his vessel honestly, except for one, Stede Bonnet, who paid to have a ship built for him.

The Prize was the ultimate goal; a heavily laden East Indiaman on her way home from the East Indies, or a Spanish Galleon ploughing across the Atlantic from Mexico to Spain, her hold groaning with treasure. To gain the Prize involved the Chase.

Pursuit at sea could last from anything from an hour or two, to several days. See a pirate ship – and run. Pirates had weapons: muskets, pistols, grenados (an early form of hand grenade) and cannons as well as armed-to-the teeth men. Lots of them. Merchant ships had very few men as crew, and barely any weaponry. Cannons were heavy and took up space where goods could be stowed. Likewise, when it came to men, the basic requirement was the minimum number of hands required to sail a ship, not to defend it.

*'Sail ho!'*
*'Where away?'*

The shouts between masthead and deck would alert all crew, be they merchant or pirate, with one on edge, studying that approaching vessel and appraising whether it be friend or foe, with the other assessing whether that ship was lying low in the water from heavy weaponry or a hold full of precious cargo. Pirates rarely attacked anything that could put up a fight. They sought easy-pickings – the under-manned and vulnerable. Usually the give-away for a ship being worth plundering was if she set all sail and fled. A reason to run was a reason to hunt and capture.

The Prize had to be an easy target, preferably one that would heave to (stop) and surrender so the idea was to throw out as much intimidation as possible to achieve that aim. Pirates had fast ships, guns, and bravado by the bucket-load. They made a noise, a lot of it, and used a great amount of intimidation, shouting and jeering, banging anything that came to hand: 'Death! Death! Death!'

The wise captain of a pursued ship gave in quickly, showed where the goods were stowed, kept quiet and made no resistance. Have things changed much? When faced with a gang of scruffy youths intent on stealing your mobile phone and wallet, the official advice from the police is: 'Do not put yourself in danger. Do not resist, just hand over your phone and wallet.'

For vessels that put up a fight, pirates could turn nasty. Very nasty. They would inflict various forms of punishment such as stripping a captain naked and shoving him in a barrel of cockroaches (there were always plenty of those aboard ship). Or forcing him to run naked around the deck while being beaten with sticks or ropes; binding him (again naked) to the mast and throwing glass bottles at him, and these were the nicer tortures! Other victims had body parts cut off and roasted before their eyes, or were dropped from the height of the yardarm to the deck. Brutal times, brutal methods, but life back then was almost all brutality in one form or another. Was the Spanish Inquisition in which innocents, including women and children, suffered for their faith any different? Was the widespread practice of showing jailed prisoners off to the gawping public willing to pay a few pennies in order to witness the inmates deprivations any better? Were the streets of squalid towns where children starved, and rape and murder was rife, any safer?

Where did the pirates come from? When Bartholomew Roberts' crew of 272 men were captured off the coast of Africa in 1722, it was recorded that sixty-five were black (they were sold on as slaves). Forty-two percent of the crew were from Cornwall, Devon and Somerset, nineteen per cent were from London, and the rest came from northern England, Wales, Ireland, Scotland, the West Indies, the Netherlands and Greece. The Irish had given Roberts problems with threats of mutiny so he tended to avoid recruiting Irishmen, which merchantmen soon cottoned-on to as they tended to put on false Irish accents if captured. That plan seems a bit risky to me; did they not fear being shot outright by Protestant anti-Catholics instead of being forced into piracy?

With a hold filled to capacity with loot, the ultimate destination for any pirate crew was the nearest town that had an adequate harbour and with taverns and brothels a-plenty crammed with rum and prostitutes. Few pirates became rich because most of them spent their ill-gotten gains almost as soon as they ill-gottenly had gained them. There was rarely enough to bury, but often enough to get drunk and enjoy a night of pleasure with a woman or two. Many pirates were riddled with sexual diseases. Nearly all were permanently drunk.

It was a short life, but a very merry one.

3

# An Acorne, that 'Sparrer Feller', and a Few Other Old Salts

The timeless classic story of *The Life and Surprising Adventures of Robinson Crusoe,* written by Daniel Defoe and published in 1719, concerns a man surviving on a desert island as a castaway. The tale was based on a Scotsman from Fife, Andrew Selkirk, a real man in real history enduring real circumstances – although, strictly speaking, he was not marooned and he was a privateer, not a pirate, but that is nit-picking.

Born in 1676, as a young man Selkirk joined a buccaneering (legal piracy) expedition to the South Pacific under the overall command of privateer William Dampier. One of the expedition's ships was the *Cinque Ports,* captained by sailing master Thomas Stradling. After several adventures involving Pacific Islands, leaking ships, near mutiny and hostile Spanish galleons, Selkirk eventually had enough of exhaustive and increasingly alarming adventuring and voiced his disapproval of Stradling's incompetency. When they anchored to reprovision at the Juan Fernández Islands, off the coast of Chile, Selkirk stated his opinion that the ship was not seaworthy chose to disembark and took his chances ashore. He was right about the ship. It sank. But he had seriously miscalculated the voluntary marooning bit because it was to be four years before another ship sailed by, which – as fate would have it – was piloted by that same Mr William Dampier, who was now a part of a different circumnavigation expedition commanded by Woodes Rogers.

Back home in England, Rogers knew a fine chap called Daniel Defoe who eagerly seized the story, embellished it with a large dollop of poetic licence, and turned it into a very successful novel that is still going strong these several hundred years later. Archaeologists excavating the islands have found abandoned nautical instruments and discovered evidence of a campsite-like dwelling.

Written accounts produced shortly after his dramatic rescue relate that Selkirk had shot goats for their meat, and to use their skins as clothing. He diligently read his Bible and would sing psalms to cheer himself up.

He died of yellow fever off the coast of Africa on 13th December 1721 and was buried at sea. His fictional counterpart, Robinson Crusoe, is far more famous than the real person. Selkirk seems to have been a dour man with very little romantic appeal, whereas the goatskin-clad Crusoe and his trusty servant, Man Friday, spark a glow of imagination and excitement, even if their adventures on the island are all fiction.

Stories are a part of human nature, both telling them and listening to them. As far back as cave men, when language had developed enough to embellish the mundane into exciting adventures, it is probable that bearskin-clad men, women and children gathered around a blazing fire within their smoky caves on cold winter nights to listen to the elders, shamens, bards – or whatever they called their taletellers – to recount another awe-inspiring marvel. Sailors, too, told their richly embellished yarns about sea monsters, mermaids, the awful prospect of meeting Davy Jones, and fierce encounters with pirates.

Scientists have discovered that a good, well-told tale activates the release of endorphins, so becoming engrossed in an exciting adventure causes a chemical reaction resulting in a natural feel-good factor, like exercise or sex. Maybe that is why reading a book at bedtime aids restful sleep?

The limitless realm of the imagination when telling stories or writing fiction gives us leave to plunder reality as blatantly as those rascal scallywags plundered treasure. Whether the baseline of a story is historically accurate, or all of it made-up, the prime purpose is to entertain, and swashbuckling pirate adventures fit the bill nicely.

In addition to Defoe's story, Robert Louis Stevenson's *Treasure Island* and J. M. Barrie's *Peter Pan* remain firm favourites. Stevenson was born in Edinburgh in 1850 and he started writing when a respiratory illness affected his health. Barrie was also a Scotsman, born in May 1860; he wrote many other works but is best-remembered for his story about Peter, Wendy and the dastardly pirate, Captain James Hook.

These two stories were written a little over 100 years after the Golden Age of piracy, when tall ships ploughed the oceans and filled the dockyards, their towering masts seeming like a forest of leafless trees. It was also an age of ripening nostalgia for these writers. With the onset of the Industrial Revolution, those days of sail were rapidly drawing to a close and the age of steam was choking the air with the belch of smoking progress. Were their pirate novels a reminiscent nod to a time gone by? To when three-cornered hats, primed pistols and sharp-bladed cutlasses were disappearing due to the advance of oily rags and shovel-loads of coal?

Are pirate stories classed as historical fiction? For children and younger readers, no, as these tend to be fantasy and adventure, or just good fun for the new-to-books readers, while novels like the excellent *Pirates*! by Celia Rees, for teenage and older readers, is more of a 'reality' novel. There is debate about how 'historical' historical fiction should be; are the facts more important or should the interpretation and the story take priority? Historical fiction authors (and I am one of them) have a duty of care to our readers; it is no good writing about the 1066 Battle of Hastings and setting it in 1067, unless you are writing in the genre of alternative fiction. The author will soon be rumbled about inaccuracies and will figuratively be made to walk the plank on various social media sites. I wonder... has anyone thought of opening a Facebook-type Walk The Plank site for exposing inaccurate fiction or movie misdemeanours?

As for pirates, the majority of fiction about their lives and misdeeds is not accurate for the very reason that the entire genre lends itself to inaccurate, fun-based escapism. Do adults read pirate-based fiction for the facts? No, is the simple answer. There is also the more fundamental question of 'do adults read pirate fiction anyway?' Ask any publishing house or agent and you are likely to get a similar, firm 'no'. Publishing houses do tend to have an unfortunately myopic view of what readers read. A now very famous author had a hard time finding a publisher for her novel but, eventually, almost at the giving-up point, she came across one who realised the potential of a bespectacled boy wizard. Maybe one day I will stumble across a similar bright spark who can grasp the same potential for my pirate? My ex-agent insisted that I alter my draft manuscript of what eventually became *Sea Witch,* from an adult novel to something suitable for teenage boys. I had written it *specifically* for adults, not adolescent boys, and I refused to budge. We parted company. The future will show who was right, Agent or Author. At the time of writing this, the Author is winning by several furlongs.

To be fair, even the Disney organisation did not realise exactly what they had in Johnny Depp's portrayal of Captain Jack Sparrow. But he knew how to play the character to interest a wider audience than families attending the Disney rides at the theme parks. The first movie of the franchise, *Pirates of the Caribbean: the Curse of the Black Pearl,* was intriguing from the instant we saw a bold, somewhat dishevelled pirate perched atop the mast of his boat that was drifting into harbour. The fun started a shot later when we discovered the boat was rapidly sinking. As Jack Sparrow blagged his way ashore, and filched a bag of coins in the process, the agog fan-base erupted with enthusiasm. Will Turner, played by Orlando Bloom, was supposed to have been the hero and the main focus of audience attention and participation. Like all true pirates, though, Jack Sparrow walked in, stole the plot, pilfered the praise and Johnny Depp walked away a very rich man.

Not surprisingly, the movie is not historically accurate – even leaving out cursed treasure, living skeletons, a magic compass that does not point North and the fact that Port Royal had been abandoned after an earthquake in 1692. What the heck? Who did not enjoy that first movie adventure? Let's be honest here: the plot was somewhat thin, bits of it were a little silly but so what! The movie was fun. A tongue-in-cheek, swashbuckler brim-full of entertainment for kids of all ages, from nine to ninety. No one took it seriously and it was not meant to be serious.

The American TV series *Black Sails* is scripted as a prequel to *Treasure Island,* although this story is most definitely for adult viewing. Created by Jonathan E. Steinberg and Robert Levine for *Starz,* it was first screened in 2014, with a second, third and fourth season soon following. Real-life pirates such as Jack Rackham, Anne Bonny, Charles Vane and Blackbeard join fictional Captain Flint, with the hunt for treasure being the prime plot. Is the series a little too gratuitous in violence and sex? Yes. But then, it *is* about pirates.

Pirates were a drunken, flamboyant lot of rogues who lusted after rum, treasure and the nearest strumpet. (Not necessarily in that order.) The Royal Navy, once it finally got its act together circa 1720 because lucrative trade was being disrupted (and therefore rich men's pockets were being emptied), hunted down the pirates and ruthlessly hanged them. 'Pyrates ye be warned!' Yet despite all that, we still love the thought of adventuring on screen or within the pages of a book with pirates as our companions. Nor is this a recent phenomenon.

The movies saw the very first pirate romp in 1908. Directed and written by D. W. Griffith and titled *The Pirate's Gold,* it was less than twenty minutes long, a black and white, silent film. *Treasure Island* followed next as the 1912 version, again black and white and silent, with several new versions weighing anchor in the years between then and now. Hollywood, while not finding buried treasure, had still struck gold and produced one pirate movie after another. Some films even starred women in the lead role: 1916 saw Lillian Gish in *The Pirate* and Gladys Hulette appeared in *Prudence the Pirate* but usually the star was a Hansome Hunk. In 1926, Paramount Studios' *The Black Pirate*, starred Douglas Fairbanks, which became the clichéd stereotype for most pirate adventures: treasure, walking the plank, man has to become a pirate to seek revenge/ the girl / his fortune.

In this film, the Duke of Arnoldo (Fairbanks) has been left to die on an island, after his ship had been destroyed by pirates. He is determined to seek vengeance and becomes The Black Pirate in order to do so. Typical piratical adventures follow, including an attack on ship which, by pure chance, is carrying the woman that the Duke has fallen in love with. Dastardly things happen with a lot of swashed buckles. He manages to rescue her before she is harmed but the pirate crew are not pleased by this so make him walk the plank. He, of course, survives and returns to put an end to the villains and gets the girl.

Next came Errol Flynn sailing over the horizon. He was the Johnny Depp of his age. He was born Errol Leslie Thomson Flynn in Tasmania, in 1909. His parents were native-born Australians of English, Irish and Scottish descent. Flynn maintained that his mother's family were seafarers, although subsequent claims that he was descended from the *Bounty* mutineers remain challenged. His first role as an amateur actor, however, was as Fletcher Christian in the Australian film, *In the Wake of the Bounty*. Moving to Hollywood, he took a role as Geoffrey Thorpe, an English privateer defending his country prior to the launch of the Spanish Armada in *The Sea Hawk* (1940). The movie was nominated for four Academy Awards.

*Captain Blood,* made in 1935 and directed by Michael Curtiz, anticipated the 2003 *Pirates of the Caribbean* movie. Set in England, in 1685, an Irish doctor, Peter Blood, (Errol Flynn) is falsely accused of treason against King James II because he had treated a wounded man after the disastrous failure at the Battle of Sedgemoor during the Monmouth Rebellion. Dr Blood is sentenced to hang but, at the last moment, is reprieved and sent to Port Royal, Jamaica, to work as an indentured slave. The Governor's daughter, Arabella Bishop, (the lovely Olivia de Havilland), purchases him for £10. Life is hard for enslaved men forced to work on the plantations so when opportunity strikes, Blood and his friends rebel and commandeer a Spanish ship. They become the most feared pirates in the Caribbean. When Arabella is taken prisoner, Blood gallantly returns her to Port Royal – only to find that it is now under the control of England's enemy, France. All of them must decide if they are to fight for their new French King or not. No spoilers but, of course, it has a happy ending. Although I wonder how a medical doctor could have come to know so much about sailing and navigating a ship? Nevertheless it is a delightful, if somewhat dated and predictable adventure on the High Seas. Full of exciting action scenes, with a well-written screenplay by Casey Robinson, the movie is based on the novel of the same title by Rafael Sabatini.

There are a few anachronisms for the eagle-eyed to spot: some of the uniforms of naval officers are incorrect for the time-period. Gunner Guy Kibbe places his foot on a cannon's gun carriage several times – no sensible man aboard ship (or even on land) would ever do this as the iron gets hot and the recoil would be a sure way to risk a severe injury. Arabella carries her pet dog, a Pekingese, which was unknown outside of China until the late 1900s – indeed China itself was barely known to the western world in the 1600s. Captain

Blood's ship would not have been square rigged on the mizzenmast in the 1600s, but maybe the biggest *faux pas* is hoisting the Union Jack ensign. The Act of Union joining England, Ireland, Wales and Scotland did not occur until 1707, while this scene was set in 1689 during the reign of William and Mary. To have been accurate, the colours flown should have been a red cross on a white background, the English Cross of St George. Do these things matter when the rest is a brilliant fun movie? Not in the slightest.

Flynn died in October 1959, and is fondly remembered as an excellent, and most handsome, pirate.

The 1940s and '50s saw more of the formulaic pirate adventures: *The Black Swan,* starring Tyrone Power; *The Princess and the Pirate,* a comedy with Bob Hope and Virginia Mayo; *The Buccaneer's Girl,* starring Yvonne De Carlo; *The Crimson Pirate,* with Burt Lancaster in the title role. In 1952 there was *Against All Flags* with Errol Flynn again and Maureen O'Hara, a remake of the 1916 *Prudence the Pirate.* 1958 yeilded *The Buccaneer* with Yul Brynner. More recently, *Cutthroat Island,* with Geena Davis, was made in 1995.

I met my own fictional pirate on a wet and windy beach on the English south coast of Dorset. To me, and most writers, our characters are very real, they just happen to live in the imaginary world inside our heads, not physically next door. I wanted to read a story similar to *The Curse of the Black Pearl*, a rollicking pirate adventure with a touch of fantasy and with adult content. Apart from some very good teenagers' novels and the various 'serious' nautical fiction series – *Hornblower*, Patrick O'Brian, Alexander Kent, and such – there was nothing available. Young adult novels are fine – they have lots of adventure – but they do not usually include adult content, if you get my drift. My hero pirate captain was to be a sexy charmer of a rogue, and adult scenes were to be included, although tastefully, I might add. That 'Sparrer' feller' had caught the attention of many a lady's eye, pirates were in vogue, but as I could not find the book I wanted to read, I decided to give up looking and write my own.

I spent most of that Dorset holiday researching the facts about pirates because the movie had sparked my interest. Several real events spurred my imagination into overdrive. The outline of a plot developed. I had my ship, *Sea Witch*, I had my secondary characters: Claude de la Rue, Toby Turner, Jansy, Finch, Jasper, and I had my accurate facts alongside the slightly re-arranged ones. For example, in *Sea Witch*, I place William Dampier at Cape Town a few months after he actually died, but to quote the wonderful English comedian, Eric Morecambe in one of his most famous sketches; 'I am playing all the right notes, but not necessarily in the right order'. So we have all the right historical facts, but not necessarily at the right time.

I had my novel planned out in my head, but I had not encountered my hero. I sat on a rock in the grey drizzle of an October afternoon looking out over a sullen slate-grey English Channel and pictured the sun-kissed Caribbean. (Proof that I have a vivid imagination.) I looked up, and there he was – standing a few yards away. A pirate in full pirate regalia complete with three-corner hat, cutlass, pistol, blue ribbons laced into his hair and a gold acorn earring dangling from his earlobe. He nodded, touched one tar-grimed finger to his hat in salute.

'Hello Jesamiah Acorne,' I said, and then he vanished, disappearing back into his own World of Imagination, I guess. And that, in case you have ever wondered, is how authors occasionally discover their lead characters; they find them when the boundary between real and unreal slips sideways like a parting curtain.

Excited, I started writing. I wrote solidly for three months, which included Christmas, although I did stop for Christmas Day. *Sea Witch, the First Voyage of Jesamiah Acorne*, wrote itself. I put my heart, soul and life into that story. Then, setback. My (now ex) agent did not like it. She insisted adults would not be interested in pirates and I refused to rewrite it for teenage boys, and in true pirate style, went my own way.

I wonder if Daniel Defoe had a similar uninspiring agent for *Robinson Crusoe*?

'Look Danny dahling, old chap, you have a good title and a good idea, but adults do not like this sort of thing. I want you to rewrite it for younger readers, something they will relate to and that will sell well, hmm? What about adding a wizard or two, and calling it *Robinson Potter*?'

'Nuff said?

4

# Captain Henry Jennings: A War with Spain, Wrecked Ships and Some Sunken Treasure

On a par with what had happened in England, a major conflict flared up in Europe triggered by the death in 1700 of the childless King of Spain, Charles II. With no heir, the unease over who would succeed him troubled governments throughout Europe. As Charles, the poor infirm old soul, lay dying he made the decision to settle the entire Spanish Empire on Philip, Duke of Anjou, who was the second-eldest grandson of King Louis XIV of France. Obviously, Charles II had some motive in mind, although probably not the resulting War of the Spanish Succession.

If Philip ruled Spain, Louis XIV could claim huge advantage for himself and his heirs, (not to mention the financial benefits). If the French royal house of Bourbon held such power, the rest of Europe could suffer (especially financially), as France and Spain united would dominate trade to the great detriment of Dutch and English merchants. That could not be allowed to happen – well, not as far as England and Holland were concerned, anyway. Something had to be done and that something turned out to be England, the Dutch Republic, and Austria, along with the Holy Roman Empire, forming a Grand Alliance in 1701 to support Emperor Leopold I's claim to the Spanish inheritance for his second son, Archduke Charles.

For privateers, the short war, which lasted from 1701 to 1714, was a delight as wealth-laden Spanish ships sailing from the gold-rich South Americas and Mexico could be attacked with impunity. Legal, government-backed impunity at that. However, for our seafarers, it did not last long enough. The various wars and skirmish between Spain, Holland, France and England – in different combinations with different allies and enemies, ground to a halt.

In the Caribbean, Port Royal, Tortuga and Nassau, and along the North American coast of the Colonies, men sat idle with no money to spend in the brothels and taverns, with nothing to do except watch the wind, weather and tide, while in the harbours ships lay at anchor, slowly rotting.

With the onset of peace, Spain assumed it was safe to sail the seas again – but the weather decided to interfere. In July 1715, a fleet of heavily laden galleons set sail from Mexico heading home to Spain after many months of delay. They never made it.

Initially sailing to Veracruz in Mexico carrying mercury, an essential substance for refining silver cobs, the *Flota de Nueva España* – the Fleet of New Spain – set out on the return voyage to Spain, rendezvousing in Havana, Cuba, with a second fleet, the *Escuadron de Tierra Firme*. The entire fleet was a floating treasure chest of silver and gold coin, gold bars, gold dust, jewels, tobacco, spices, indigo and cochineal, as well as emeralds and pearls. The combined value of cargo, not including any contraband that was likely to have been aboard, neared something like a modern equivalent of £1,500,000,000.

The *Tierra Firme* was under the command of Captain-General Don Antonio de Escheverz y Zubiza, and the New Spain Fleet was under Captain-General Don Juan Esteban de Ubilla. Confusingly (probably as much for them as it is for us) both flagships were called *Capitana*, one a captured English ship previously known as the *Hampton Court*. Other ships believed to have been in the fleet were the *Almiranta*, the *Nuestra Señora de la Concepción*, *Urca de Lima*, *San Miguel*, the *El Ciervo*, the *Refuerzo* and a smaller, unknown merchant vessel. Sailing with them was *Griffon*, a French ship under the command of Captain Antoine Dar.

All the Spanish ships were top-heavy, overloaded, and had delayed in harbour for too long, the convoy not weighing anchor until into the hurricane season. The route was to sail along the Florida coast, making use of the Gulf Stream, and then veer across the Atlantic, and so home.

One week after departure from Havana, just off the Florida coast, a hurricane blew in. With the exception of the *Griffon*, which sailed on unscathed, the entire fleet was wrecked. More than 1,000 seamen lost their lives, including Ubilla and his officers.

Some of the ships sank in deep water, most broke up in the shallows. The more fortunate ran aground close to the beach. About 1,500 men reached the shore, the survivors improvising makeshift camps while a party was despatched to fetch aid from St Augustine further along the coast. This was the 18th century. Disney had not yet been born, the American West was unknown and unexplored, the huge slave-labour plantations were only starting to expand. Florida was not the tourist attraction, heavily populated State that it is today. Apart from Native Americans and natural flora and fauna, there was nothing there. Many of the poor wretches who scrabbled ashore succumbed to exposure, thirst, shock and hunger before help arrived. Salvage ships were despatched from Havana, but not for the benefit of survivors. The prime concern was for the cargo.

Most of the treasure from the holds of the ships that had run aground in the shallows was recovered. A salvage encampment was built and a storehouse erected among the dunes, behind the beach bordering unexplored jungle.

Word spread and many of those bored men sitting around doing nothing had the same idea: get a boat, get rich. Like moths to a flame, they surged to the shallows in the hope of picking up a fortune – literally.

And then, in January 1716, Henry Jennings appeared on the scene.

Henry Jennings was an opportunist. Like so many privateers and pirates, little is known of Jennings' early life. (Were none of these men obliging enough to pen their memoirs?)

There is some evidence to support Jennings owning a vast amount of land in Jamaica, so the motivation for privateering against the Spanish was not primarily a lust for gold. It has also been suggested that he supported the Jacobites' struggle to restore James II and then James III to the British throne, but unless he was attempting to raise money 'for the cause' this does not make sense – Spain supported the exiled Stuarts, to the extent that they attempted a second Armada in March 1719. Like the first one during the reign of Elizabeth I, it failed.

For Jennings, commissioned by Jamaica's governor, Lord Archibald Hamilton, the privateering during the conflict had gone well but when it was over, he found himself kicking his heels and looking for adventure. (Aided and abetted, no doubt, by a surfeit of rum and a need to procure the funding to buy more.)

A merchant captain and a respected, educated land-owner, Jennings headed off, like everyone else, for the Florida coast with his ten-gun sloop *Barsheba* accompanied by a second vessel, *Eagle*, captained by John Willis, with a combined crew of between 150 and 300 men.

Scrabbling around in the shallows for mere handfuls of the lost treasure was not Jennings' intention, though. He was made of sterner – and brighter – stuff. He bided his time, let the Spaniards do all the work of collecting up the treasure, then sailed in, as calm as you please, and raided the piled-high warehouses. He got away with something like 350,000 pieces-of-eight, the equivalent of about £87,000 British sterling. The raid was illegal, an act of piracy – the war had ended, privateering was redundant: a small, inconsequential fact to these men.

Even so, Jennings might have got away with it, if it were not for a small indiscretion when sailing back to Jamaica. He compounded his piracy by attacking a French ship, the *Sainte Marie*, amassing another 60,000 pieces-of-eight. He reached Jamaica, where hitherto the governor had welcomed Jennings (and probably a share of the plunder) but this time things were different. The Spanish had (justifiably) complained, and Henry Jennings and his crew were no longer welcome. They were more likely to be hanged. Sensibly, Jennings went elsewhere.

The 'elsewhere' was Nassau, on New Providence Island, in the Bahamas.

At the start of this Golden Age in the area of the Caribbean, Florida Coast, Chesapeake Bay, Virginia and the Bahamas, many of the later infamous names sailed together, drank together, and probably sampled the delights of the street doxies together. That they then fell out – often to the point of vicious revenge – speaks volumes about the times.

For a while, Jennings had a young sailor in his crew, Charles Vane, and he also teamed up with 'Black Sam' Bellamy. Bellamy, who subsequently joined with Benjamin Hornigold, double-crossed Jennings. (Moral: Never trust a pirate.) Bellamy had run away to sea as a lad, escaping his life being bored on a farm. When he arrived in the American Colonies, between 1713 and 1715, he was in his late-twenties, and a penniless able seaman. Piracy seemed a good way to improve his financial status.

In early 1718, Jennings took advantage of King George of Hanover's Amnesty, overseen in the Bahamas by the new governor, Captain Woodes Rogers. Dozens of pirates surrendered and Jennings, being educated and well-to-do, soon found himself in a position of leadership as the unofficial mayor. With his pirating days behind him, Jennings retired as a Bermuda plantation owner, and became one of the rare ex-pirates who not only avoided the prospect of the noose to apparently enjoy a leisurely retirement.

His ultimate fate is uncertain; some speculate that he was captured in 1745 by the unforgiving Spanish, and died in a colonial Spanish prison cell; others have him growing old with his family on his plantation, pipe and slippers to hand. That is a better ending than a lonely one, disease-wracked in a Spanish prison, so we'll plump for the happier ending, shall we?

As for the treasure fleet: the Spanish continued salvaging what they could until 1719, then gave up. It is possible that around £300,000,000 still remains on the seabed, an occasional haul being found by professional marine archaeologists and treasure-hunters. No wonder Florida's beaches are such an attraction for holidaymakers.

5

# Turning Fact into Fiction

Fiction – whether in novel, movie, or TV-drama format – is made up; it is not meant to be taken as the truth, although the essence of the facts are often incorporated, especially where historical fiction is concerned. What makes good fiction, apart from the obvious good writing skills and engrossing story, is the believability of the characters and the plot that form the story as a whole.

Building on fact, or classic tales, can create an entertaining and enjoyable reading or viewing experience. The TV-drama series *Black Sails* is a prime example. For me, the sinking of the Spanish Fleet and Henry Jennings' derring-do adventuring inspired the initial idea for my novel *Sea Witch*.

'What if,' I thought, 'it wasn't Henry Jennings' idea to raid that warehouse? What if my pirate, a friend of his, was the brain behind the scheme?'

The idea took flight and became an exciting part of the first *Sea Witch Voyage*. I wanted a storm and a wreck – which fitted nicely with the actual events of the year 1715. My protagonist hero, Jesamiah Acorne, is in command of his first ship. Unfortunately, the hurricane that did for the Spanish fleet was not kind to him either and he lost both ship and many of his crew. Such things happened at sea. They still do.

Excerpt: *Sea Witch* by Helen Hollick:

*Their ship wrecked, disheartened and depressed Jesamiah and his first mate, and friend, Claude de la Rue, are kicking their heels in a Florida coast shanty town fishing village:*

'Rue! Rue? Wake up!'

Rue was stretched out beneath the shade of a palm tree, legs crossed at the ankles, the wide-brimmed grass hat he had fashioned pulled low over his eyes, arms folded across his chest. He shoved the hat from his eyes, stared at Jesamiah squatting beside him, closed his eyes again and resettled his hat.

'Go away.' He added something crude and explicit in French.

'Listen. I have news! Superb, gift from God news!' Jesamiah's excitement was unmistakable. Like a boy on his birthday.

'It 'ad better be,' the older man growled, removing the hat and waving it ineffectually at the irritating buzz of insects. 'I do not take kindly to being woken from my afternoon nap.'

'Three more survivors have straggled ashore, down in the next village.'

'*Très bon* for them! As long as they find their own shade, I am most 'appy for them.' Annoyed, Rue replaced his hat. Jesamiah snatched it, tossed it away.

'*Merde!*'

'Will you listen? They are Spanish.'

The Frenchman was unimpressed. 'Unless they are natives, so is everyone along this stretch of coast. In case you 'ad not noticed, we 'appen to be idling in Spanish territory.'

'They were from a Spanish vessel. One of a fleet.' Jesamiah ignored the sarcasm, and had his hands on Rue's shoulders attempting to shake sense into him. 'A convoy of galleons. Galleons, Rue. The entire fleet went down. Carrying gold from Mexico; packed to the fore-deck, great, treasure-carrying galleons!'

Interest was twitching. Rue uncrossed his legs. 'You are serious?'

The grin swept over Jesamiah's mobile face. 'As serious as a duck's quack, mate! Word is spreading as wild as fire in the hold; they were on their way to Spain from Havana, were hit by the same hurricane that did for us. All of them Rue, all laden with gold bullion and silver, precious gems and barrels of indigo. The wrecks are scattered along God-knows how many miles of reef.' Hunkered on his heels, he rested his forearms on his thighs, giving a moment of silence for the implication to sink in.

The wind scurrying in from the Atlantic was strong on the far side of the dunes, among the scrub and vegetation its bluster dropped considerably. Here, it was more of a whispering breeze, its voice a very quiet, continuous, *sssss,* a muted harmony whispering with the muffled restless sound of the ocean.

'A fortune's in the holds of those ships, Rue. A fortune run aground an' sitting there with only fish and crabs to look at it.'

Slowly the Frenchman smiled, a sweep that split his face from ear to ear. 'Or for someone with enterprise and skill to salvage it, *non?*'

Problem: They have no ship, but Jesamiah knows where he can commandeer one – moored alongside his half-brother's wharf at the Virginia tobacco plantation where Jesamiah grew up – and fled from a few months before his fifteenth birthday because of a falling out with said half-brother. Jesamiah became a pirate, the brother kept the estate and their father's fortune. The adventures that follow Jesamiah's bright idea to steal his half-brother's boat lead from one action scene to another; a fight between Jesamiah and his brother, a meeting with a lover from the past, all wrapped up with swash-buckling scrapes and a little bit of fantasy, courtesy of Tiola, a white witch, and the elemental spirit of the sea, Tethys.

For writers, inspiration comes in many guises although it is not always easy to tether the Muse, let alone find her in the first place. Many writers tend to spend as many hours gazing out of a window, lost in thought, as they do at actually writing the words down. Procrastination can be a common companion, even for the best of writers.

Pirate-based stories – whether in a novel, as a TV-drama or a blockbuster movie, need to keep the action going from scene to scene, chapter to chapter. We know the hero, or sometimes heroine, will escape the predicament he or she has landed in, will survive the noose, not drown as the ship goers down, dodge that pistol bullet ... but the fun is in not knowing how the lead character gets out of various predicaments. That is the skill of a good writer, to keep the swashes well-buckled and hurtling in, one after the other, like wind-tossed white-capped waves breaking in a great, gushing swoop of relentless excitement upon a wide sweep of a sandy beach. Excitement, adventure and derring-do, maybe with a pause here and there for a tender scene of romance, or a character's reflective thoughts. Tension wrapped within every chapter, the reader turning page after page, promising 'just one more', reading on and on, into the small hours of night, keeping going until that final scene, that final, satisfied fulfilment as the book closes. Knowing the next adventure is there, waiting, on the bookshelf to be opened, explored, and devoured with relish.

The writer's aim is to hook the reader with enticement at that very first page, that very first paragraph, that very first sentence. To hook, to draw in and entice from first page to last page. To leave the reader satisfied but wanting more.

The reality of facts entices the imagination as much as the pleasure of fiction can. That one spark, one sentence or one word discovered, perhaps by accident, while researching or reading something out of intrigue or interest, can cause an inferno of ideas that will not rest until it becomes the narrative filling a blank page.

That one idea expands, forming into scenes, and chapters, an entire plot. Characters emerge, take shape and life – and suddenly that one, small fact has become a simple or a complex novel.

So how did my character, Captain Jesamiah Acorne, after he had (illegally) acquired a ship sail into Spanish-held territory, go ashore, worm his way into favour and then abscond with a hold full to the hatches with chest loads of treasure?

Here's a taster. Maybe the real Henry Jennings swindled the Spanish by doing something very similar? Who knows?

Excerpt: *Sea Witch* by Helen Hollick:

*Disguised as a Spanish merchantman ordered to assist with salvaging the treasure scattered over the shallows off the Florida coast, and carrying forged documents, Jesamiah has dropped anchor and gone ashore ...*

Jesamiah had to admire the tenacity of the Spanish. All this, once the alarm had been raised, built and operational within a few weeks of the disaster. The Dons always were quick on their feet when it came to the matter of gold.

Speaking in fluent Spanish, Jesamiah affably greeted the man walking towards him. 'My regrets, Admiral, the tide is ebbing and I am not familiar with this shore.' Deliberately, Jesamiah promoted the man's rank, although it was doubtful he was anything above an ordinary captain. Playing to a man's vanity always established a quick, easy relationship. 'You surely could not expect me to risk running aground?' He laughed at his own jest, an expansive belly-rumble of mirth. 'All that gold on the seabed once-over already. Wouldn't do to have it snagged there again would it, Señor?'

He slid his arm around the officer's shoulders, steered him towards the hut he had emerged from. 'I am in no lather to return to those shoals, it's a devil of a job down there, you know – what with those scurvy pirates roaming on the edge of it all like basking sharks. Frankly, I do not know why I volunteered for the damned commission. If I had known it was to be like this I would have opted to go home and harass the British in Biscay instead.'

Inside the hut, a table, two chairs, a wooden chest, little else except piles of papers and ledgers. Jesamiah stood beside the open door, laid his right finger alongside his nose, his gold acorn signet ring glinting in the brief, vivid glow of an elaborate sunset. 'Now, a night ashore would be most welcome, especially if ...' He peered out at the distant tents and shanty buildings, keeping his attention from roaming towards the storehouse. 'Especially if there are any women here?'

Of course there were. They would have been brought in along with the supplies.

He nudged the Spaniard with his elbow, whispered, 'I have an itch needing a good scratch, if you get my meaning. What if I left my crew to lay alongside and we unload at first light? My ship will be safe, no?' Jesamiah sat on the nearest chair, made himself comfortable. 'I am not going anywhere, you are not going anywhere and the gold as sure as the sun shines, isn't. Stand these good, tired men of yours down, Señor, mine will take care of my ship. What say you?'

A little reluctantly the Spaniard set Jesamiah's gift of a bottle of brandy among the cluttered mess and seated himself on the far side of the table. Jesamiah handed over the ship's papers. They were authentic, with only the name of the vessel altered. The real carrier of the documents was at the bottom of the Atlantic with all hands, minus her load of gold, silver and casks of gems, which were now stacked snugly in Jesamiah's forward hold.

In the dim lamplight, the Spaniard frowned over every word written, Jesamiah prattling a continuous banter of nonsense. After a few moments he wavered, put his own brandy bottle in his pocket and stretched across the table to reclaim the other one. 'Of course, Señor, if you would rather get on with the work now? It will not take us long to rig tackle...'

'*Está bien, ningún problema,*' came the quick reply as the officer made a hasty grab for the brandy and unstoppered it; drank straight from the bottle. 'This appears to be in order. You can leave everything to your crew?'

'*Claro*. Of course.'

'*Bueno, bueno. Excelente*!' The Spaniard dropped the papers on to the pile, heaved himself up from his chair and gesturing to the doorway, invited Jesamiah to proceed outside. 'Come, let me introduce you to a friend of mine, she has sharp nails, ideal for getting into those places difficult to reach.'

With night settling and the stars showing bright against the darkening blue, Jesamiah rested his arm companionably along the duped officer's shoulders as they strolled, deep in conversation, towards the encampment. He lifted his hat, waved it in a circle, clamped it back upon his head and disappeared over the crest of the dunes.

Nodding satisfaction at the received signal the men took the longboat back to the *Inheritance* – renamed *Cariola* for this enterprise – and under Rue's direction added their weight to bringing her in and mooring alongside the now deserted jetty. By the time Jennings brought his vessel silently into the cove, with no lights showing and the least amount of noise – warping her in, towing from the longboats – it was late and the Spanish salvage teams were either drunk or asleep. No moon, only the clear brilliance of stars studding the sky with silver light.

Perfect.

Before they were even moored, Jennings' men were rigging hauling tackle to the main yard ready to sway the bullion aboard. Like a silent tidal wave men of both crews flooded ashore from the decks, knives and cutlasses drawn, bare feet padding. No pistols or muskets, there was to be as little sound as possible. The bray of drunken, boisterous pleasure-taking drifted from the encampment, drowning the choked-off grunts of the storehouse guards as their throats were cut, and the rustle of more than 200 men working their way to raking in an easy-made fortune. The only misplaced sound, the sharp-bladed axe striking twice through the chain securing the doors. The only suggestion something was amiss, the steady flicker of moving shadows in the shrouded lantern light, as with organised efficiency the men transferred chests containing fantastic wealth from storehouse to ship.

Strolling into the almost emptied storehouse two and a half hours later, Jesamiah was well pleased with himself. Just as he liked things, clean and simple. He would not be admitting to Jennings he had employed his time ashore in a three-some with a dark-skinned, slender-waisted beauty. What else could he have done? His new Spanish friend had insisted they share her, and afterwards it had taken both bottles of brandy to send the idiot to sleep.

6

# Captain Howell Davies

A pirate's career was often short. A few merry (or not so merry) months and the noose or a pistol shot put paid to the rum, the street doxies, and the delight of plundering property that was not his, or hers.

Howell Davies, (or Hywel Davis, the spelling varies) was a Welshman. No prizes for guessing that. His pirate days lasted a little over eleven months, from 11th July 1718 to 19th June 1719. During that time, he proved to be very successful at his chosen life, capturing fifteen ships of English and French origin.

He was born in 1690, at Milford Haven, Pembrokeshire, an essential supply point for voyages to Ireland that had once been a haven for Viking raiders. Several military operations were launched from the port; Henry II's invasion of Ireland in 1171 and Oliver Cromwell's in 1649. Shakespeare mentions 'blessed Milford' in *Cymbeline,* so it is an odds-on wager that Davies spent most of his youth messing around the harbour on or around various ships and listening to the talk of seafaring men.

He turned to piracy when the slave ship he was serving on, the *Cadogan*, was taken as a Prize by Edward England. Some pirates avoided slave ships because the holds stank; others sought them out because to sell the live cargo of shackled slaves brought a high, quick profit.

The African slave trade was in its infancy during the opening years of the 18th century. The American Colonies were only just starting to open up – and realise the potential value of the tobacco and sugarcane plantations. Cotton was still not the in-demand commodity it would very soon become. The practice of indentured slavery that had been in place during the latter half of the 1600s was not proving too successful in the Caribbean and the Colonies. For the most part, indentured work was for the drudgery of the timber and coffee plantations of Mexico and Brazil, but with the Colonies expanding, and tobacco in increasing demand, more workers were required.

Indenture was voluntary slavery, with people giving their labour free for an agreed, and contracted, period of years in return for the promise of payment or land at the end of it – a promise that was sometimes never met because death was the price paid instead. Occasionally, indentured service was offered as an option instead of a prison sentence. Whatever inducement it masqueraded under, indenture was still slavery and the men and women enduring their miserable lives through the term of the contract suffered horrific abuse.

Many of the early indentured men and women were Irish, taken prisoner by Cromwell, or from poor families whose only alternative prospect was to starve. Most were never to see their freedom again because they died in the harsh conditions of heat, disease, and exhaustion. When the slave trade subsequently burst into fruition, the financial gain for the landowners meant it rapidly became popular and was embraced by the rich men who saw a way to obtain cheap, expendable labour more suited to the hot and humid climate of the Bahamas, Caribbean, Carolinas and Virginia.

Slavery is abhorrent to us now and while not defending the morals of merchants and rich landowners who could not, or would not, see beyond the weight of their coin-purses, their attitude towards those of a lower rank or class, or different colour, or creed, was very different from our understanding and expectations of today. Africans were not regarded as having the same level of intelligence, culture or even humanity as Europeans did. Even so, the treatment and squalor those poor people endured was beyond appalling. And, by the way, despite its abolition, slavery still exists although it is now a hidden problem.

Slaves were taken from anywhere along the vast length of the African coast – usually they were captured by black people from other tribes. A good way to deal with your enemy: take him prisoner and sell him for gold to the white men with the satisfaction of knowing he would never be coming back.

A recent archaeological investigation of the wreck of a Portuguese slave ship has highlighted the horror suffered by these African wretches, who were shipped across the Atlantic to a perpetual life of hard labour and misery. In December 1794 a slaver, the *São José Paquete Africa,* left Mozambique bound for the vast plantations of Brazil. It would be a voyage of 7,000 miles and would take at least four months, unless they met storms or other adverse weather conditions. The 500 or so men, women and children were shackled in the depths of a dark hold, forced to lie side-by-side on their backs, pressed in like packed sardines, with only a once-daily chance of exercise or relief. For some, the dreadful journey was to end in drowning after only twenty-four atrocious days.

Rounding the Cape of Good Hope, in treacherous seas, the ship ran aground and broke up on reefs not far from Cape Town. An estimate of 212 slaves perished as the ship went down; the rest, with the captain and crew, managed to scrabble ashore. Although it is not known what happened to the African survivors, it can only be hoped, from our view in the 21st century, that they escaped to freedom, but it is more likely that they were recaptured and resold, only to face yet another dreadful journey across the Atlantic.

One of the interesting facts discovered by the diving teams that confirmed the ship was carrying slaves was the extraordinary amount of extra ballast that she was carrying. Unlike heavy barrels, casks, kegs, bales, timber or whatever a ship was carrying, a living cargo was not a stable, unmoving commodity. Human beings move about and they need a chance – even if only once a day – to exercise, relieve themselves, eat food, and drink water. Animate human life is not as heavy as a cargo of inanimate objects that, once correctly stowed, stays put. To keep a ship evenly balanced between what is above and below the waterline, ballast is used in the lowest part of the ship. If insufficiently, or inefficiently, weighted, a ship could tip, or 'heel' over, especially in rough seas, in high winds or when excessive sail is set, making the vessel top-heavy. Using cargo limits the need for artificial ballast. Stones, gravel, or iron ballast blocks, timber or bricks especially formed ideal ballast by doing two jobs at once, by providing ballast and then as a cargo to be sold and replaced once the destination was reached. Did the ballast shift, causing those poor unfortunates to be drowned? Or was it careless seamanship? Or plain and simple bad luck? The only good fortune that came from this was for the survivors who might have escaped and for the marine archaeologists who centuries later prospered intellectually from their rare find.

When Davies' ship was attacked by Edward England and his men, the crew of the captured ship were given a choice: become one of us, or die. Not much of a choice, really, as the possibility of acquiring riches was better than the prospect of death after being tortured. The captain and his officers were brutally killed by England's men, but Davies appeared to have been attracted to the lure of adventure and getting rich quick, although he initially showed excessive bravado by claiming he would rather die than go 'On The Account'. This impressed Captain England to such an extent that he offered Davies, being an experienced seaman, the command of the *Cadogan*. After accepting, Davies set off for Brazil with the intention of selling the ship and presumably her miserably wretched cargo. Maybe his crew were not tempted by the lure of Brazilian coffee or Brazil nuts because they mutinied and sailed to Barbados instead. Arriving there, Davies was put under arrest and imprisoned on a charge of piracy. However, without firm evidence to convict him, he was released. He then made his way to the notorious pirate haven of New Providence in the Bahamas, which turned out to be another short stay.

Governor Woodes Rogers was in control and in the process of installing law and order and cleaning up Nassau's somewhat tarnished image. Davies did not fancy the quiet life of going straight so, leaving on the sloop *Buck,* bound for Jamaica, he joined with six other scurrilous men and, somewhere near Martinique, took over the vessel. Elected as captain, Davies used his cunning to take easy plunder and captured two French merchant ships off the coast of Hispaniola. The second was heavily armed, but Davies duped the crew by hoisting pirate colours and forcing the prisoners of the first ship to brandish (unloaded) weapons as they posed like pirates. The Prize surrendered without a single shot fired.

He then crossed the Atlantic to haunt the Cape Verde Islands off the African coast. There, he took what was to become his flagship, the twenty-six gun *Saint James*.

Davies formed a partnership with a French pirate, Olivier Levasseur (*La Buse)* and Captain Thomas Cocklyn. The three of them formed a formidable pirate fleet, albeit a short-lived one because they had a drunken argument, fell out with each other and parted company. During their partnership, however, they seized the *Bird*, captained by William Snelgrave. Cocklyn's men treated the captured crew abominably and Davies, disapproving of the abuse, attempted to protect Snelgrave who later reported the kindness to the authorities. Maybe it was this moralistic act against violence that caused the disagreement between supposed friends?

Davies transferred to the thirty-two gun *Rover* and sailed south to capture more rich Prizes off the Gold Coast. One of his prisoners was fellow Welshman, Bartholomew Roberts, who was destined to become famous as a pirate in his own right.

Masquerading as a legitimate merchant, Davies duped his next victim, the commander of a Royal African Company slaving fort in Gambia. Looking to buy slaves, Davies was invited to dine, an honour he and his crew eagerly accepted, and repaid by taking the unfortunate, unsuspecting host prisoner and ransoming him for £2000 in gold coin – after locking up the soldiers, drinking all the rum and firing the fort's cannons, that is.

The dastardly plot had worked well, so Davies used it again on the Portuguese island of Principe by pretending to be a Royal Navy pirate hunter. He was again cordially invited to partake of a glass of wine at the fort, but unbeknown to him, his scheme had been rumbled. Making his way from the harbour to the fort on 19th June 1719, he was ambushed by Portuguese soldiers, and shot dead.

There is a moral in the tale somewhere.

Bartholomew Roberts was elected as his successor and he retaliated by raiding the island's main town later that night and inflicting great damage on property and people. Davies's outraged crew slaughtered the majority of the male population, raped most of the women, whatever their age, and looted everything of value. The assault marks one of the rare land attacks made by pirates in the 1700s, although it was more of a revenge raid than anything else. It was most certainly not an act of war, although I doubt that fact bothered Roberts and his crew, or lessened the traumatic impact on the island's few survivors.

7

# Keep to the Code

Privateers, Corsairs, Buccaneers, and Brethren of the Coast are all names synonymous with piracy, as well as to go 'On The Account'.

The Caribbean pirates were described by the French as *flibustiers*.

The term 'freebooter' is a corrupted version of the Dutch word *vrijbuiter*.

A *swashbuckler* is a 16th century word connected to the noise made by striking a sword sharply against a shield.

*Corsairs* were associated with the southern Mediterranean in the 16th-18th centuries, and menaced shipping with their oar-powered, fast and easily manoeuvrable galleys. Rather than gold, spices and gems, their main prey was people. Ransom demands (as with modern-day pirates) could be big business with the prospect of a fortune to be made for little expenditure of energy and effort. Prisoners who were not worth ransoming had the unfortunate experience of being sold into slavery. The Barbary

Corsairs ranged along the North African coast, operating from Muslim bases such as the Moroccan ports of Tangier, Casablanca and Salé, their main plan of action being to plunder European ships. By the 1700s, they roamed further afield attacking coastal villages as far away from the Mediterranean as Devon, Dorset and Cornwall, with the intention of acquiring much-prized white slaves to trade in the Middle East Arab states – the women wanted for their looks, the men for their strength.

*Buccaneers* originated on the Caribbean island of Hispaniola, now Haiti, and the Dominican Republic. The word comes from the French, *boucanier* and a Caribbean Arawak word *buccan*, which was a wooden frame for smoking meat, usually wild cattle and pigs, and from which we get the modern outdoor dining entertainment (on days when it is not raining) of a barbecue. So when The Man of the House, who barely has any idea of where the cooker is when dinner needs preparing, is more than happy to wave a pair of tongs about over a smoking charcoal fire, merrily burning sausages and pork chops, just smile because he is merely recreating a hidden memory of his pirate roots.

Buccaneers were a rough, rugged and burly lot with their numbers swelling when runaway slaves and navy deserters joined their ranks. Around 1630, some were driven out of Hispaniola by the Spanish and fled to the nearby island of Tortuga, from where the Spanish also attempted to evict them. But like moths to the flame, displaced English, French and Dutch seafarers settled there and retaliated by harassing the richly laden galleons that sailed between the Mexican coast and Cádiz.

The buccaneers' favourite method of attack was to use the cover of darkness to come alongside, then board the ship, and before an alarm could be raised, kill the helmsman and officers. They were ferocious, ruthless, and skilled, expert marksmen.

For land attacks, they relied on surprise and stealth, beaching their shallow-draught boats well outside populated areas and marching overland to their destination. The landward side of towns were less well fortified and therefore easily breached. A raid such as this was the successful 1683 buccaneer visit to Veracruz and, later that year, to Cartagena, which set a precedent for others to follow.

The English settlers of Jamaica soon began to associate 'buccaneers' with piracy and the term became widely adopted in 1684 when the English translation of Alexandre Oliver Exquemelin's *The Buccaneers of America*, relating the exploits of these seafaring ruffians, was published.

Maybe the best-known English buccaneer was Captain Henry Morgan, but more of him (and his rum) later.

With the various wars being waged between the French, English, Dutch and Spanish, privateering became legalised piracy as long as the captain carried a government-given Letter of Marque. In return for the Crown's protection, and even approval, the profits had to be shared with King and Country.

Thomas Modyford, Governor of Jamaica, cottoned on to this idea of easy money-making and invited buccaneer ships to drop anchor at Port Royal harbour, which soon overtook Tortuga as a favoured pirate base and rapidly became the most prosperous town in the entire Caribbean. Buccaneering was highly profitable, even if there was not a convenient war going on at the time.

The most notorious and feared buccaneering men were not always English: Jean-David Nau, also known as François l'Ollonais, and Daniel Montbars were French, while Roche Braziliano was Dutch.

Montbars slaughtered so many Spaniards that he came to be called 'The Exterminator', (and you thought the term only applied to Dr Who's Daleks?) He was born into a well-to-do family around 1645, was educated and had been expected to lead the life of a gentleman. Although based only on a legend, his disgust for the Spanish sprang from the Conquistadors' atrocities against the native populations in the New World of the Americas. Montbars served with an uncle in the French Royal Navy, fighting against Spain in the West Indies, where his uncle was killed and their ship sunk. Reaching Tortuga, Montbars joined the buccaneers, became a captain and earned respect and fear in a successful attack against a Spanish galleon when he appeared to relish the killing and mutilation of his enemies rather than having any interest in acquiring looted treasure. Attacks against Spanish towns followed, with the capture of Cartagena and Vera Cruz. He did not murder, as such, but gave no choice of surrender to his opponents and tortured Spanish soldiers he captured rather than inflicting a clean death. Skip this next bit if you are squeamish: his favoured method of execution was to slit open the abdomen of a victim, extract the large intestine and nail one end to a convenient post or mast. He would then force the prisoner to 'dance' by beating his buttocks with a burning log. What a charming man. His death is unrecorded but it is believed he was lost at sea in 1707.

Roche Braziliano used Port Royal as a base for his raiding. He was born in Groningen in the Netherlands; his parents emigrated to Brazil and his privateering took off in 1654. He led a mutiny, captured a highly valued Spanish ship, then was himself captured by the Spanish, but he escaped and returned to his buccaneering career. He sailed with François l'Ollonnais and Henry Morgan. Braziliano would shoot those who did not care to drink with him, roasted two Spanish farmers alive and treated his Spanish prisoners horrifically by hacking off their limbs and leaving them to die. His disappeared in 1671, probably lost at sea.

François l'Ollonais was an indentured slave in the 1650s, with his servitude ending by 1660. He ended up in Haiti, menacing Spanish shipping in the Caribbean. He was shipwrecked off the coast of Mexico and attacked by a group of Spanish soldiers, who murdered most of l'Ollonnais' men. He survived and took revenge against the Spanish, becoming a notorious murderer and torturer.

The Spanish, who bore the brunt of these attacks, thought differently about the apparent legality of the buccaneers. To them, they were heretics, thieves, louts and pirates, and if captured were hanged, or garrotted, without mercy and without any notice being taken of those Royal '007-type Licences To Kill' letters of marque.

As in all things when violence and the acquisition of riches are involved, legalised piracy soon got out of hand. The buccaneers who had fed the pockets of the wealthy soon began to drain that wealth. The profits from merchant shipping started being affected – and therefore the merchants back in England, France and Holland found their coffers and pockets were becoming lighter. Views changed and demands in various Parliaments for something to be done grew louder. With the change of attitude and support, by the end of the 1690s the buccaneers either opted for a legal life enjoying their ill-gotten gains, or joined other pirate crews plundering the Indian Ocean and the sailing routes to Mecca, the

North American coast, or the slaving areas off the African Coast. Semi-legal buccaneering was going out of fashion, while entirely illegal piracy was on the rise.

The height of piracy, at least in the Caribbean, was between 1716 and 1726 – a mere ten years. Documentation, mostly official court records made at various trials, recount the ages of about 170 pirates, ranging from as young as fourteen to the ripe old age of fifty, which was elderly for the 18th century. The average age, however, was twenty-five to twenty-seven. Old enough to 'know the ropes', young enough to want more, and fit enough to get it. There were French and Dutch pirates, along with Africans – usually escaped slaves – and no doubt several Spanish and Portuguese among the various pirate crews. But half of those recorded in the criminal trial ledgers had British connections, with a quarter originating from the West Indies and North American Colonies. There were also Chinese pirates but in the early 18th century, trade with the Far East was yet to be established. Australia had not yet been discovered, beyond a few rocky shorelines to the north of the continent, which were presumed by those early mariners to be islands. Master William Dampier discovered much of that early-found Australian coast, a remarkable man whom we will be meeting again later.

To be a pirate you needed one essential piece of equipment. No, not a parrot or a peg leg, a cutlass or an eye patch. Not even a bandana or tricorn hat, or the ability to snarl 'Arrr!' at every opportunity. You needed a ship. Ships were as expensive to acquire back then, as they are now, (although you can add a few more noughts after a £ sign today.) Apart from Stede Bonnet, no self-respecting pirate would *buy* a ship. They stole them.

The most daring potential pirate eyed-up a suitable vessel anchored in the harbour, whatever harbour, to wait his chance, steal aboard with a few well-chosen men and simply sail off with her. Alternatively, as with Howell Davies, they legitimately went aboard as crew, bade their time, mutinied or rebelled and took over a ship that way. The third option was to attack another ship with the small vessel you already had and simply upgrade to something bigger, better and faster. Oh, and to carry more guns.

All well and good, but someone was needed to take overall charge, someone was needed to navigate, and a surgeon was a desirable crewmate – even if he was not particularly happy about being forced aboard a pirate ship.

The crew elected the captain, with the man most suitable for the job gaining the most votes. He should be capable, bold and fearless. He would have skill in seamanship and fighting and be able to shoot straight. Modern election tactics such as shaking hands, broad grins and kissing babies did not come into it because popularity was the least important necessity. 'Is this man going to be able to capture Prizes without getting too many (if any) of us killed?' That was the priority. Votes came with respect for the ability to sail and navigate a ship efficiently, to keep order and discipline, and to find plunder as quickly and efficiently as possible.

Apart from a larger share of any plunder, there were few perks for the captain. He and his quartermaster received 1¼ to 2 shares of any loot taken; the master gunner, boatswain, and carpenter got 1¼ shares, while the rest of the crew were entitled to one share each. If he was lucky, the elected captain got the Great Cabin to himself. Otherwise, if he was not deemed superior to any other man, the crew were free to enter his cabin whenever they wanted, could swear at him, eat his food, swill his drink, and no doubt share his whores. There was no saluting or kow-towing, apart from when there was to be a battle, board a ship or evade capture. That was when their elected captain had to use his cunning and do a good job. If he did not fulfil his role, he would be replaced. One pirate crew worked their way through electing thirteen different captains in only a few months. Was that democracy or indecisiveness?

Second-in-command, although often more respected than the captain, was the shipboard peacemaker and arbitrator, the Quartermaster. He was usually well educated, or could at least read and write, and he was also elected. William Snelgrave, captured by Thomas Cocklyn in 1719, wrote about his ordeal, describing the quartermaster as overseeing all affairs and controlling the captain's orders. He it was who was first to board a ship they attacked. The quartermaster saw to the accounts, the sharing of everything gained, decided who was to board in an attack, and was responsible for the victuals, drink and punishments. Calico Jack Rackham enjoyed the life of a quartermaster before he became a captain of his own ship and met up with Anne Bonny.

Life in the 18th century, indeed most periods prior to modern living in the Western World, was harsh. There was no health service, no state schools, no minimum wage or trade unions. Laws, governments, masters and officers, whether in the army or navy, were more often than not uncompassionate and frequently outrageously cruel. This was a time when a court of law could sentence a man, or even a child, to be hanged for stealing a loaf of bread or poaching a rabbit. Aboard navy and merchant ships, food was insufficient and usually rancid, wages were low, discipline harsh, and desertion common. The men who opted for piracy opted for a shorter life but a better one, not least because they had an agreed set of 'rules', a Code of Conduct, or Articles of Agreement, which included such clauses as:

1 Every man has a vote in affairs and equal right to provisions and liquors.
2 Every man to be granted an agreed share of plunder.
3 No game of cards or dice to be played for money.
4 All lights and candles to be extinguished after eight at night. After this hour any drinking or gaming to be done on the open deck.
5 Pistols and cutlass to be kept clean and fit for service.
6 No boys or woman to be allowed aboard. (Obviously this one was not included on Jack Rackham's ship as he had two women aboard.)
7 To desert a ship or quarters in battle is to be punished by death or marooning.
8 No fighting on board. Quarrels to be ended on shore by sword or pistol.
9 Injuries, crippling or mutilation during the course of battle to be compensated.
10 Musicians to have their rest on Sunday evenings.

The quartermaster held the authority to rebuke men for minor misdemeanours, but greater punishments were jointly decided by the crew. Offences did not go unpunished. The quartermaster was empowered to flog a man, but a fine or the more unpleasant jobs aboard ship were usually given such as hauling in the anchor cable, which involved manhandling the entire length of the heavy cable which was wet, slimy and stank – and all in the confines of the lowest part of the ship, the bilge. Not many pirates bothered hauling the cable in and ensuring it was laid out properly to dry though, they just left it in a heap; what did it matter if it rotted or spoiled? They would simply replace it the next time they took a Prize.

Burning candles without the protection of a lanthorn (literally a lantern made out of horn) smoking below deck, and not caring for weapons were serious offences punished by having the nose or ears slit. Fire was always a great terror, for the obvious reason that ships were made of wood, but they also carried a vast amount of gunpowder. One spark and ... BANG. Faulty weapons could not only endanger your own life, but that of your brethren as well.

The Articles had their origin with the buccaneers in the form of the *Charte-Partie*, a contract, a legal document or the lease of a ship, from which the phrase 'to charter' a ship or boat comes. Such charters were used in Jamaican courts to settle disagreements, although the significance of such documents lessened as government-approved legal buccaneering turned to illegal piracy. Few of these documents survive, and I personally wonder whether all pirates had the articles written up, let alone observed them. Are we basing our entire assumption about piracy on the few documents we possess that were used by a few well-known thieves of the sea? Just a thought.

There was often a first and a second mate, although these were not the important officer positions embraced by the Royal Navy. Their function was to assume command if the captain was killed. Someone had to be ready and prepared to take over quickly in an emergency.

The Master Gunners were prized for their skills. Handling those guns accurately and safely, from small carronades to a big eighteen-pounder (or larger), took experience and knowledge. The ordnance needed special handling. Knowing how to clean, load, run-out and fire the guns was not just a matter of ramming in a cannon ball or sluicing a bucket of water over the gun. Gun practice was essential – the more capable the gunners, the more likely they would take a Prize. The Master Gunner took command of the guns during battle. He had to know his job and do it well.

If a crew were lucky, they might have a Sailing Master who specialised in navigation and the efficient setting of sails; if not, they relied on their elected captain. The cook, the carpenter, and the surgeon were all respected positions, often held by men forced into service from merchant shipping taken as a Prize.

It may be surprising but musicians were also highly valued members of the crew. They sang shanties to keep step and time while stamping around and around the capstan hauling in the anchor cable, or hauling on yards to manoeuvre the sails. They inspired and encouraged during the drudgery of routine duties, entertained of an evening or while carousing ashore and played during battle. Aboard ship, the steady rat-a-tat beating of the drums, the eerie wail of the bagpipes, the tune of the fiddle were as essential for pirates as for any army or navy – boosting morale for the crew, but demoralising the intended prey.

# 8

# A Prince of Pirates: Captain Samuel Bellamy

Possibly the wealthiest pirate, with a reputation for mercy, and gentlemanly, generous behaviour, was 'Black Sam' Bellamy. Like many another who followed the same nautical lifestyle, he had a short career of little more than a year.

Born in Devon in late January or early February 1689, he drowned at the age of twenty-eight off the coast of Cape Cod in a violent storm.

He was the youngest of several children. Sam's mother, Elizabeth, died soon after his birth and was buried in the parish churchyard at Hittisleigh, a village on the edge of Dartmoor. He joined the

Royal Navy in his late teens and reputedly took part in several sea battles, but a different life had its attraction for he sailed to Florida, lured by the call of treasure and a possible fortune from the stricken Spanish fleet. Love, however, interrupted his intentions, for while in Eastham Harbour, Massachusetts, he met fifteen-year-old Maria Hallett – although she might have been older, and her name might have been Mary or even something else because 'Goody Hallett' has also been suggested as her name. (There are lots of 'might have been' alternatives where pirates are concerned.)

Presumably the infatuation was returned as Maria gave birth to a child, who sadly died in infancy. Maria's parents, however, did not think a mere sailor good enough for their daughter, so promising to return a rich man Sam set out with his good friend, Paulsgrave Williams, to prove his worth. (The friend is also recorded as Palsgrave, Paulgrave, Paulgraves or simply, Paul. Take your pick.)

I suppose this was before the young lady realised her scandalous condition, for unmarried mothers were shunned, and Maria spent a while in jail as punishment for her shame – although other sources claim she was accused of murdering the child, hence the sentence. Either way, the poor girl had an unpleasant time of it.

Now we get to a few of the verified facts about Black Sam.

Willing to risk all to make his fortune, Sam joined Benjamin Hornigold's pirate crew aboard the *Mary Anne*, but in June 1716, after a revolt, Sam was elected captain with his friend Williams becoming quartermaster. One of the crew was another famous name – Edward Teach, who was to go eventually by the name Blackbeard.

Pirate crews were a mixed bunch: ordinary (either voluntary or press-ganged) seamen, free black men and escaped slaves, ex-indentured servants, political dissidents, men who wanted to make easy money, or to avoid jail or being forced into marriage because of an 'indiscretion'.

In one year, Bellamy and his companions successfully plundered fifty-three ships. For a short while, he joined with Henry Jennings, Charles Vane and French pirate, Olivier La Buse (Olivier the Vulture), between them taking several ships as Prizes in the vicinity of the Virgin Islands. One was the *Sultana* that was soon transformed into a galley – a ship with oars, which made her more manoeuvrable and not so reliant on wind power.

After a serious disagreement with their comrades, Bellamy and Williams branched out on their own. Paulsgrave Williams was elected as captain of the *Sultana* while Sam Bellamy took charge of the *Mary Anne*. It appears to have been a good move because their successes mounted.

Bellamy was an experienced strategist. Using the two ships together, the *Mary Anne* formidably armed with many cannons, and *Sultana*, smaller, lighter and faster, he co-ordinated attacks in a pincer movement, thus avoiding damage to his own vessels and often without firing more than one or two warning shots. All that was needed was to hoist the colours. Bellamy's personal emblem was a black flag adorned by a leering skull and crossed bones. In the spring of 1717, Black Sam captured a galley sailing through the Windward Passage between Hispaniola and Cuba. She was the *Whydah Galley* (pronounced *Whid-uh*) and she was every pirate's dream.

The three-masted *Whydah* was built in London in 1715, and was the state-of-the-art for her period. With the addition of oars, and designed specifically as a slave ship, she was fast and easily manoeuvred to get her living cargo across the Atlantic as quickly as possible. Dead slaves had no value. She carried 367 slaves, with the 312 who survived the voyage sold for profit at her destination of Jamaica. For her return voyage to England, she had a different cargo: gold, silver, indigo and gems worth more than £20,000 sterling. A captain of this period would be lucky to earn £50 a year. She was a valuable Prize and was like a magnet to Bellamy and his crew. Black Sam wanted her, and was determined to get her.

The Chase to capture her lasted three days. When Bellamy was close enough to fire a single shot, the *Whydah*'s captain, Lawrence Prince, decided he'd had enough, and did not fancy a fight. He surrendered. As a reward for giving in peacefully, Bellamy generously exchanged the *Whydah* for the *Sultana*, but without any cargo or provisions in her hold for it was all transferred to his new ship.

Bellamy set about making some improvements to the *Whydah*: levelling off the upper deck by clearing away unnecessary cabins and upgrading to twenty-eight guns, which were positioned on the upper deck and below. The *Whydah Galley* was now a formidable pirate ship.

Called 'Black Sam' because of his black hair tied with a black ribbon – he refused to wear a fashionable powdered wig – or perhaps because of his black flag, or the long, black, deep-cuffed velvet coat he liked to wear, Bellamy cut a dashing figure. He would have made an ideal movie character to be played by Errol Flynn, Johnny Depp or Kevin Costner because he became known as the Prince of Pirates, the Robin Hood of the Sea. (Although he robbed the rich, I have not found any evidence he gave to the poor, unless we assume his crew were the poor who benefitted.) The chroniclers of the early 18th century praised him as a distinctive, tall and well-mannered gentleman who wore tailored, expensive clothes: breeches, silk stockings, silver-buckled shoes, and he favoured four duelling pistols, which he carried in a sash. Quite the dashing hero.

Charles Johnson in his book of pirates quotes Sam Bellamy as saying to Captain Beer of a captured Prize, 'Damn my blood, I am sorry they [the pirate crew] won't let you have your sloop again, for I scorn to do anyone a mischief when it is not to my advantage ... Tho' damn ye, you are a sneaking puppy, and so are all those who will submit to be governed by laws which rich men have made for their own security ... They rob the poor under the cover of law, forsooth and we plunder the rich under the protection of our own courage.'

The captain refused to join the pirates because of his belief in God and the morality of Christian law. Bellamy then scolded him with: 'There is no arguing with such snivelling puppies, who allow superiors to kick them about deck at pleasure and pin their faith upon a pimp of a parson, a squab who neither practices nor believes what he puts upon the chuckle-headed fools he preaches to.'

I have a feeling this is a somewhat cleaned-up version of what was said by Master Johnson. I cannot quite imagine a pirate, even if he is of a gentlemanly demeanour, talking quite so politely. The 'f' word was well in use by the early 17th century, coming from German *ficken* or Dutch *fokken*, both meaning 'to breed'. The oldest known use of the word in English as an adjective was found in the margin of a copy of Cicero's *De Officiis* dated to 1528. A monk had scrawled his displeasure in the margin: '*f***in Abbot*'. Obviously the chap was not having a good day, although whether he meant the accusation literally and was questioning various ungodly morals, or the abbot had cheesed him off, we do not know. It does make you wonder though: if monks uttered the word, I suspect pirates made prolific use of it.

Heading north towards the rich shipping lanes, the two ships separated. Williams, possibly to take the *Mary Anne* to Rhode Island where he had family, while Bellamy supposedly announced, 'Lads, we have gained enough, it is time to go home!' Presumably, having made his fortune, Black Sam was intending to return to his sweetheart and make an honest woman of her. Alas, it was not to be.

On April 26th 1717, a violent nor'-easter storm with drenching rain and howling wind blew in off the coast of Cape Cod. The *Whydah* was driven on to shoals in sixteen feet of water, about 500 feet from what is now Wellfleet, Massachusetts. At a quarter-past midnight she was drawn into thirty feet of water, her masts snapped, she capsized and sank, taking Black Sam Bellamy and the crew with her. Only two men survived, 103 bodies were found and buried, leaving forty-one unaccounted for.

Further along the coast, the *Mary Anne* also ran into trouble and was wrecked leaving nine survivors. All were arrested and tried for piracy in Boston. Six were hanged, two were set free after claiming they had been forced into piracy, and one, a Miskito Indian from Central America, was sold into slavery. Nearly all we know about Black Sam came from these survivors.

The story does not end there. In 1984 wreckage was found by underwater archaeological explorer Barry Clifford beneath fourteen feet of water and five feet of sand. He was certain he had discovered the remains of the *Whydah*. Under US admiralty law, the Massachusetts Supreme Court ruled that the find, in its entirety, belonged to Clifford. In 1985, he came across the ship's bell, which had engraved upon it 'The Whydah Gally 1716', firm evidence that he had indeed uncovered Bellamy's pirate flagship. Rather than selling any of the discovered artefacts, he has ensured everything will be kept together so it can go on display in the newly refurbished Whydah Pirate Museum near West Yarmouth, Massachusetts. On view are iron bars, branding needles, shackles, canons and guns, as well as a treasure room with the gold and silver that was recovered from the wreck. Interactive displays depicting what life was like for Captain Bellamy and his pirate crew complete a worthwhile visit if you happen to be near Cape Cod. Just beware of storms if you go there by ship.

Human remains were also recovered, and research has identified an eleven-inch fibula with a shoe and silk stocking.

John King is believed to have become the youngest known pirate, between the age of eight and eleven years old. Born sometime between 1706 and 1709, he joined Bellamy's crew aboard the *Mary Anne* after the pirates had attacked the sloop *Bonetta*, that was voyaging from Antigua to Jamaica, and on which he was a passenger with his parents. While the pirates ransacked their Prize, taking more than two weeks to do so, young John made up his mind to become a pirate, the dream of many a boy – even now. He threatened his mother and father and eventually got his own way. Dare I say his parents were well rid of him? Apparently he kicked his mother, and Father did not like him much. Maybe he had good reason not to?

Boys of around twelve years old were common aboard ships, be they merchant, navy or pirate. Boys were useful as cabin boys or 'powder monkeys'; quick and agile young lads who carried the gunpowder from the magazine to the gunners. Many a Royal Navy captain started his career as a teenage midshipman.

John King was not the only ship's boy associated with pirates and the sea, although most of the names and ages that have been recorded are because a crew was captured and tried in a court of law for piracy. Eleven-year-old Phillip Middleton joined the crew of the *Charles II* with Henry Every in 1694. The crew mutinied, took over the ship and renamed her *Fancy*. With Thomas Tew and some other pirates, they preyed on the Muslim ships, taking the grand prize of the *Ganj-i-sawai*, often colloquially called the *Gunsway*. Her name means 'Exceeding Treasure'. When some of the crew were arrested in Ireland, in 1696, for Robbery on the High Seas, Philip turned King's Evidence, claiming he had been forced into piracy, and testified against his shipmates. (Give him his due, maybe he was telling the truth.) His evidence confirmed that not only was treasure taken from these ships travelling peacefully in the Red Sea, he testified that many of the Indian men were brutally murdered after being horrifically tortured and that the women, some of whom were the mothers, wives and daughters of important Muslims, were raped. Many of these women killed themselves because of the shame of their treatment. Philips' story was believed; he was found not guilty, and became a ship's purser aboard the *Halifax*, an East Indiaman merchant trading ship.

Samuel Perkins also had no choice. In 1695, he happened to be aboard his uncle Captain Robert Glover's ship when the dastardly relative decided to turn to piracy and forced his young nephew into serving as a cabin boy. Glover headed for the Indian Ocean. After some successful pillaging and plundering, they dropped anchor at Madagascar's St Mary's Island. Tribesmen attacked the village where the men were sleeping and killed the pirates, but took Sam prisoner. He was eventually ransomed but had endured being a kidnap victim for five years.

At least three boys sailed with William Kidd aboard the *Adventure Galley*: Richard Barleycorne, from Carolina, as well as William Jenkins, and Robert Lamely, who is believed to have been the son of a Southwark prostitute. Robert was about twelve years old; the other two were fourteen. They were arrested with Captain Kidd in Boston and, during his London trial in 1701, it was proven that the boys were merely following orders as servants. They were acquitted, and Kidd was hanged, but more of that in a later chapter.

Ten-year-old Tom Simpson signed aboard a merchant ship sailing to trade in the East Indies in 1698. The same old story: some of the crew mutinied, commandeered the ship and her cargo, and headed for New England. They reached Long Island Sound in the spring of 1699 and scuppered the ship. Once ashore, they were arrested and shipped to London for trial on the same vessel as Kidd and his crew. Unlike the boys with Captain Kidd, however, there is no further mention of poor Tom, so his eventual fate is unrecorded, although if he had been hanged, that would probably have been recorded; more likely, he died in jail or relatives paid to have him set free, no questions asked.

Thirteen-year-old Jean-Baptiste was not so fortunate. He and his father were arrested with several other pirates and stood trial in Boston. Baptiste Snr. swore they had been privateering against the French but his claims were disbelieved and, despite the fact that boys below the age of fourteen were usually regarded as being outside the age of discretion, both father and son hanged.

As for John King, Bellamy allowed the boy to join his crew but alas, the fate of the *Whydah* that storm-raked night had no mercy for grown men or a young boy.

9

# Harbours and Safe Havens

*Tortuga*

Fans of the first *Pirates of the Caribbean* movie, *The Curse of the Black Pearl*, will recall a scene where Jack Sparrow (sorry, *Captain* Jack Sparrow) has Will Turner dangling over the side of the ship while explaining that he cannot take a ship into harbour 'all on me ownsy'. The harbour was Tortuga.

*Isla Tortuga* is Spanish for Turtle Island. Situated off the northwest coast of Hispaniola, it forms a part of Haiti. Mountainous and rocky to the northern side, Tortuga covers an area of sixty-nine square miles and the natural harbour on the south side was a major haven for piracy in the closing years of the 17th century.

During Christopher Columbus's voyage of 'sailing the ocean blue, in fourteen-hundred and ninety-two' to the New World, he sailed into the Windward Passage that separates Cuba from Haiti on December 6th of that year. The island emerged from a dense covering of early morning mist and to Señor Columbus's mind, resembled the shape of a turtle shell, hence the duly dubbed name.

Skip forward a century or two. By 1625, the French and English had settled on the island as well as a few Spanish people and, at the end of the 1620s, they were joined by the Dutch who, having weakened the Spanish navy, took advantage of their new superior – if temporary – position in the Colonies. Although it was not to last. In 1629, the Spaniards took a dislike to their Tortuga neighbours and attacked them. In early 1631, more Spanish troops invaded – but the established settlers took to the heavily wooded hills where there was an abundance of water and wild game. They 'camped out' and waited for the Spanish to go away again.

Don Fadrique de Toledo was a little more successful with taking over the island. He managed to drive out the undesirable settlers then fortified the harbour against reprisal. He did not think ahead, though, for when the majority of his army left to assist in helping to expel the French from nearby Hispaniola in 1630, the treacherous French merely climbed into their little boats, rowed across the narrow stretch between the two islands and nipped back to Tortuga via the back door.

The first slaves were imported, in 1633, to work in the new-established tobacco plantations. With poor soil, made poorer by successive crops of tobacco, which poisoned the land, sugarcane was attempted but that also failed as a viable financial venture. For shipping, however, Tortuga offered a convenient harbour for routes to Cuba, Central America and Mexico.

The next phase was for the Providence Company to hold control of the island, under the governorship of Anthony Hilton. His main objective was to provide a safe harbour for his buccaneering comrades, for Tortuga had proven to be an ideal base to refit ships and trade a variety of supplies. He died in 1634, owing a lot of money to the company because he had not paid for any of the cannon or small arms with which it had provided him. The Providence Company withdrew and more neighbourhood disputes erupted with the French falling out with the English, the plantations becoming neglected and the slaves going their own way. In 1635, the Spanish marched back in and kicked the English out – was there much point? They left again because the island was of no major use to them. So the English and French returned, except not as settlers, but as pirates wanting to take advantage of the safety and seclusion of this ideal haven. Somewhat like children squabbling over a toy, the Spanish realised their error, swept back in and chucked everyone out again.

Around 1640 Jean le Vasseur, an engineer by trade, was sent to Tortuga by the governor of Saint Christopher Island (now St Kitts). Le Vasseur arrived with 100 or so men and built a stone fortress overlooking the harbour on the relatively flat top of thirty feet or so of steep rock. Defended by formidable guns, supplied by water from a natural spring, the fortress was almost impenetrable except by climbing up the rock. Le Vasseur ensconced himself there and reigned supreme as if he were buccaneer royalty. He took a percentage of all the plundered loot brought into harbour and taxed everything else, amassing a substantial fortune. The buccaneers, an eclectic mixture of French, English and Dutch, were now calling themselves a grander title: Brethren of the Coast. Whatever they decided to call themselves, the Spanish were not happy with these rogues who pillaged the sea-routes. Tortuga was a threat to Spain's security and its profitable shipping. The Spanish sent ships with about 500 men to destroy the new fortress, but Le Vasseur had known what he was doing. His guns sank one of the attacking ships and the rest scattered in panic. Most of the Spanish army had come ashore, away from the protected harbour, but were caught in an ambush. They fled back to Hispaniola. Le Vasseur's growing reputation was enhanced by the apparently easy victory and Tortuga flourished as a safe haven for pirates. Le Vasseur's prestige was to be short-lived, however, because absolute power does indeed corrupt absolutely. Minor things sparked his temper and he became suspicious of everyone. He began to rule like a tyrant and adopted a regime of abominable cruelty. His own men began to turn against him and, in 1653, he was murdered for raping one of his lieutenant's women.

For a short while after this, the Spanish regained control, taking possession of the island, a considerable amount of the looted plunder and the substantially equipped armoury. They ensconced 100 men in the garrison. But, when an English fleet invaded the area, the Spanish retreated in order to defend Santo Domingo. By 1656, Tortuga was firmly English and French again, under the control of Elias Watts who acted as an unofficial governor. Taking advantage of his protection, the pirates returned. By 1660, a Frenchman, Jeremie Deschamps, had replaced Watts. He hoisted a French flag over the fortress, declared for his king, and defeated several English attempts to reclaim the island.

With various wars and skirmishes between France, England and Spain, and occasionally the Netherlands, the Caribbean was frequently left to its own devices. The cotton, sugar and tobacco plantations had not, yet, become the highly valuable export industry that would soon be so cherished by the rich merchants 'back home'. In the Caribbean, there was little worth defending so the buccaneering Brethren were more or less permitted to do as they pleased. With each country concentrating on events in Europe, governments cared little for other nation's shipping being plundered, especially as much of that plunder gained by privateers went to finance their nation's wartime expenses.

By 1680, when the wars diminished slightly, and trade – and therefore pockets – were starting to be affected, the law was changed; sailing under the pretence of a foreign flag became illegal for English privateers. No longer could an English ship fly Spanish colours to surreptitiously get close to a Chase. Governments always have to spoil the fun, don't they? Although I do have to wonder, considering piracy, theft and pillaging was illegal anyway, and men by the shipload ignored the law, why government ministers thought any committed pirate would take note of this small change in the law.

Peace was established between the countries, for a while at least, and the adventurous buccaneering life fell into decline. Many of the men were turning to a more settled and profitable living of logging and wood trading, but then a Welsh privateer sailed into view and invited some of the Tortuga pirates to join him.

His name was Henry Morgan.

Perhaps the island is more famous in fiction and movies than it was in historical reality. *Captain Blood, Pirates of Tortuga, The Black Swan* and *The Curse of the Black Pearl* along with the novels *Caribbean* by James Michener and, published posthumously, *Pirate Latitudes* by Michael Crichton, all feature Tortuga as a den of pirate iniquity, where rum, gambling and a surfeit of buxom wenches abound. Maybe for the real buccaneers the rum ran out, the gambling taverns closed and the wenches lost their sex appeal, because by 1684 most of the sea-faring chaps had gone off elsewhere. Spain relinquished the island to the French in 1697, obviously coming to the conclusion that Tortuga was not worth the effort of fighting over after all.

*Port Royal*

The Wickedest City in the world: At the height of its wealth, and as the most important trading post in the West Indies, Port Royal, Jamaica, lived up to its notoriety as probably every pirate worth his (or her) salt would have been there at least once. These included such famous names as Henry Morgan, Blackbeard (Edward Teach) and Calico Jack Rackham, although his last visit was not exactly pleasant – he was executed there.

Port Royal was intriguing, beguiling and turbulent, there was a mass of riches and piratical depravity in taverns and brothels. Then, on June 7th 1692, Port Royal met a devastating fate by something more omnipotent than any seafaring pirate captain could ever hope to be. An earthquake struck and the sea, as if it were emulating a huge, gape-mouthed sea-monster, swallowed two-thirds of the town in one gulp. Geologically speaking, the earthquake must have lowered the level of the sea floor, one tectonic plate slipping under another, for the area to remain underwater because a tsunami eventually recedes again, leaving behind the destruction and acres of mud. Old Port Royal is an underwater town, and is in effect, a piratical Atlantis. There are some excellent documentaries, including images of what Port Royal would have looked like, on the National Geographic website at www.nationalgeographic.com. au/tv/wicked-pirate-city

Fires, and a series of hurricanes followed the earthquake, and the port's glory was gone from view forever. Today, what is left of Port Royal is nothing more than a small fishing village and a tourist attraction.

The United Nations Educational Scientific and Cultural Organisation (UNESCO) and the World Heritage Centre regard the archaeological remains of a mere thirty-seven years of bustling existence as highly important. Like the Italian town of Pompeii, preserved by layers of ash and molten lava, Port Royal sank in a matter of minutes with everything now as well preserved as it was on that day of mass destruction.

The first tremor was felt at eleven-forty in the morning, rapidly followed by two more undulating ripples of movement that caused buildings to collapse. Eye witness John Pike wrote to his brother two weeks later: 'The ground opened with a shake and swallowed whole houses, nay, the street I dwell in was in less than three hours after, four fathoms under water, and nothing of my house to be seen nor any other, only one timber house which George Philips lived in. The shake opened the earth, the water flew up and carried the people in quick. I lost my wife, my son, a 'prentice, a white maid and six slaves and all that ever I had in the world'. He mentions his house, his neighbour, the buildings and other people before, almost as an afterthought, mentioning the loss of his wife and son.

As many as 4,000 people were to lose their lives, half of them killed by the earthquake and tidal wave that followed, the rest by untended injuries and the onset of disease – cholera, caused by contaminated water, being the usual suspect. For the shame of Port Royal, regarded as the Sodom and Gomorrah of the Caribbean, it was declared that the devastation was a result of the Wrath of God.

The area has a tropical climate, including a short, dry season from January to April, followed by a wet season from May to October. The temperature usually remains steady between 25°C (78°F) and 27°C (82°F). Situated at the end of an eighteen-mile cay or sand spit called The Palisadoes, Port Royal is fifteen miles from Kingston, the capital of Jamaica. Its history goes back much further than the days of piracy, and even further than the invasion of white Westerners. Taino pottery, dated to about 1000 AD, has been found in various excavations. It is unlikely these artefacts were used by settlers; it is more probable people were periodically using the coastal area for fishing. By the 1500s, the same promontory was used by the Spanish as an ideal place to careen their wooden boats. With nothing except a few shacks and timber warehouses, they called the spot Cayo de Carena, although its original name was Caguay or Caguaya. Permanent settlement spread; Juan de Esquevil arrived in 1509 with the hope of finding gold and silver. He found none, but enslaved the Taino natives to farm sugarcane instead.

For more than 146 years, Spain dominated the island. However, realising its strategic importance for defence, its flatness and deep-water anchorage, the British took Jamaica in 1655. The Spanish of the 17th and 18th centuries were very slow to understand the importance of hanging on to these strategic sites; Gibraltar, at the gateway to the Mediterranean, was another example. The Brits set about building Fort Cromwell, which within a couple of years was tactfully renamed Fort Charles; such are the necessary consequences of political upheaval.

Once fortified, the town grew rapidly. By 1662, it boasted 740 citizens and by 1692, somewhere between 6,500 to 10,000 people occupied fifty-one acres with 2,000 buildings. A quarter of the population would have been slaves, with another quarter – at least – a fluctuating population of sailors, pirates and merchant traders.

In 1657, Governor Edward D'Oley invited the buccaneer privateers – those Brethren of the Coast who were finding Tortuga to be not so hospitable because of the Spanish – to use Port Royal as their main base. The idea was twofold: defence against the Spanish, plus the benefit of trading the plunder taken from their ships. Treasure as taken legally, because England was at war with Spain (again). The governor liberally issued Letters of Marque, an official licence to steal. Port Royal flourished. Merchants arranged to trade with the Spanish, knowing full well the sea-faring privateers would loot the ships en-route. The scam came to be known as Forced Trade. When Henry Morgan raided Portobello with over 300 men in 1668, it was believed each man had £60 in his coin-pouch to spend when they returned to Port Royal. Forced Trade, swindling the Spanish or stealing from them, was big business, especially for the inhabitants of Port Royal. With Forced Trade proving more profitable than sugarcane, bringing in something like seven times the annual value of legitimate exports, it was no wonder the majority of Jamaican plantations were abandoned.

Thomas Hickman-Windsor, First Earl of Plymouth, was removed as governor in 1663, having only served two short years because, when a tentative peace treaty with Spain was signed, he refused to stop the buccaneers from attacking Spanish shipping. He was replaced by Sir Thomas Modyford, who had been Governor of Barbados but was sacked from office and moved to Jamaica instead. Apparently he had more loyalty to the Crown's wishes. However, Modyford was more adept than his predecessor at issuing Letters of Marque – mostly for expeditions led by Captain Henry Morgan, and he excelled at turning a convenient blind eye to English despatches. Maybe, though, that was why he was given the post? Most governments of the day apparently had poor eyesight.

Privateering in the 1660s was so welcomed at Port Royal that returning ships were saluted firing a cannon, which was also the signal to hurry to the docks to see what was being brought ashore. Officials would board a ship as soon as it dropped anchor to remove 1/5th of the plunder for the King, 1/10th for the Admiralty and 1/12th for the Governor. (Even pirates paid taxes.) That still left a lot for the captain and crew. I can't help wondering if perhaps the king's share had been higher, maybe various governors would not have been removed for disobeying orders about plundering Spanish shipping?

The artefacts found in the underwater excavations have revealed it was not only the wealthy citizens of Port Royal who had valuable goods to their name. Items such as spices, silver, jewellery, porcelain and cloth abounded from Big House to Tavern alike. Port Royal was a thriving boomtown and everyone living in it during those few years of decadence enjoyed the consumer-goods luxury to the hilt. Between the 1680s to '90s, people of low social standing rarely possessed trinkets and non-essential items – Port Royal was different; even those of moderate means could afford to purchase quality household or personal possessions. The slave trade was also an important commodity, and Port Royal became a centre for off-loading the human misery of live cargo shipped across the Atlantic from Africa. From merchants, tradesmen, shipwrights, artisans, builders, brewers, smiths of every variety, to ships' captains, whores and pirates, the network for trade was vast. Port Royal had become the most important and lucrative town not only in the Caribbean, but in all the English-held territory of the Americas. It appears that only the slaves were poor in Port Royal.

Captain John Taylor described the town in his journal of 1688, as 'well built, strongly fortified.' The majority of better-class buildings, he proclaimed, were brick houses mainly four storeys high with tiled roofs and sash windows and with cellars below. There was a governor's house, a court, four churches, a cathedral and forty-four taverns. Chandlers, brothels and butchers, bakers and candlestick-makers ... Wig-makers, pie-makers, blacksmiths, four goldsmiths ... Jamaica was rich enough to use coin for currency instead of barter (often tobacco or sugarcane.) And did

I mention the taverns and brothels? Liquor and wenches drained the pockets of legitimate sailor and illegal pirate alike. The taverns had a reputation for excessiveness, both in alcohol consumption and debauchery. Dutch explorer Jan van Riebeeck reported that even the island's parrots drank from the stocks of ale with as much pleasure as the tavern drunkards. At the height of its fame, Port Royal had one tavern for every ten residents. Forty licences were granted in July 1661.

In 1688, 213 ships were registered as anchored in the harbour. Pirates congregated at Port Royal attracted by the deep water; it was easy to drop anchor, even easier to make a quick-getaway. The opportunity to trade their gained loot for supplies was a bonus; in addition to food, ammunition and equipment, supplies included liquor and prostitutes – and probably the various diseases connected with the two.

Port Royal was a multi-cultural city in terms of colour and creed. English people and the Anglican Church were dominant, but this was balanced by Jewish merchants, the Dutch, Brazilians, Mexicans, and West African slaves. Irish, Spanish and French Catholics mixed with Quakers, Muslims and the indigenous native survivors.

Captain Henry Morgan is the most famous name connected with Port Royal. Technically, he was a privateer, not a pirate, as he attacked Spanish ships and raided their towns with the endorsement of a Letter of Marque, although the issuing of such remains questionable. Did he have a vendetta against Spain, or was his aim to amass great wealth? Whatever fuelled his ambition, he became highly successful at achieving his goal. Morgan spent his last days in retirement drinking heavily and, no doubt, recounting his adventures to anyone who would listen. He died in 1688 and was buried on the spit of land that the earthquake swallowed.

Rather than re-build Port Royal, the survivors moved across the bay to Kingston. Prior to 1692, the area was mainly agricultural, ideal for setting up temporary camps, but the town itself did not start to emerge until a fire in 1703 finally destroyed what was left of Port Royal. By 1716, Kingston had become the centre of trade for Jamaica, for slaves in particular. By 1780, the population had reached more than 10,000.

After Morgan's death, and the subsequent earthquake, attitudes towards piracy were starting to change. Wars with Spain were less frequent and trade was becoming more important with the expansion of tobacco, sugar and cotton plantations in Virginia and Carolina. Buccaneering had ceased, and piracy had taken its place, but when thievery at sea started hitting the profits of wealthy merchants back in England, it had to be stopped. There had been a Royal Navy presence at Port Royal from the early days. A Navy hospital was eventually built next to the docks and wharves. When pirates and buccaneers were no longer required to defend the town, they were discouraged from visiting Jamaica and an anti-piracy law was passed in 1687. Pirates were possibly not taken very seriously by successive governors until around 1716, when Henry Jennings, after acquiring a shipload of wealth from the wrecked Spanish fleet off the coast of Florida, was turned away. And in the following years, far from welcoming pirates, Jamaica came to be their nemesis. Female pirates Mary Read and Anne Bonny were imprisoned there, and Gallows Point saw the hangings of Charles Vane and Calico Jack Rackham in 1720, with forty-one other pirates dancing a hempen jig during one month alone in 1722.

Jamaica and Port Royal had lost its charm for the men who went 'On The Account'.

### Nassau

In the early 1700s Charlestown, as it was originally known before being renamed Nassau, was to become a rival to Port Royal as a pirate haven. New Providence Island is located in the Bahamas with a moderately consistent climate and, being relatively flat, Nassau expanded outward from the original European shacks built along the beach and harbour. The pirate interest started in 1696, when the *Fancy* dropped anchor in the bay, loaded with plunder and under the command of Henry Every. He sweet-talked Governor Trott into letting the port become a secure base for pirate trade. Turning a blind eye was relatively easy when the price was right – in this instance, ivory, gold, silver and gunpowder.

Established in 1670 as a suitable port for commercial goods, the embryonic town was wiped out in 1695 – the Spanish burnt it down. Governor Nicholas Trott renamed the rebuilt settlement in honour of William III's Dutch-German connection to the House of Orange-Nassau, that Nassau referring to a town in Germany. But in 1703, in retaliation against buccaneering attacks on their shipping, the Spanish joined with the French and destroyed it again. Giving up on the place, the English government abandoned Nassau and in consequence, New Providence had no officially appointed governor; presumably, there was nothing worth governing except rowdy, unruly pirates, and no one in the first decade of the 1700s was going to be bothered with *them*.

When Captain Henry Jennings arrived in 1715, after being turned away from Jamaica, Nassau was not an expanding boomtown like Port Royal had been, but a squalid shantytown of shacks and hovels with the only advantages being a good harbour close to the busy mercantile shipping lanes and easily accessible fresh water. With Port Royal and Tortuga closed to those 'On The Account', Nassau shone like a Bahamas beacon, and the scattered shacks grew into a town, with the building programme funded by pirate loot. Nassau was run by pirate captains Thomas Barrow, Henry Jennings and Benjamin Hornigold, with up to 1,000 pirates settled there, or coming and going. They proclaimed their haven a Pirate Republic with all the usual suspects heading the roll call: Charles Vane, Jack Rackham and one of his two female sidekicks, Anne Bonny – plus Blackbeard, of course. Jennings became an unofficial mayor and all was pirate paradise until Woodes Rogers sailed over the horizon, broom in hand, to sweep out the dregs of pirate society and clean up the place. Jennings took the King's offer of amnesty and retired a wealthy man. Governor Rogers succeeded with his intentions despite opposition from the pirates and the Spanish attempting to claim the place back in 1720 – he had obviously made it attractive to Spain again.

The TV drama series *Black Sails* depicts Nassau as being run by pirates, for pirates. That is probably not far from the truth. The safety of Nassau's shallow waters and beaches were ideal for careening – stripping a ship down to clean the hull. Vessels at this time were made of wood, which, especially in warmer waters, was susceptible to Teredo Worm, which could bore into the timber. Barnacles needed scraping off, and rotten patches needed to be replaced. Ships that were not regularly cleaned became slow in the water, making them targets for good pirating. The Royal Navy were permitted to careen and provision at only a few dedicated English ports, which gave them, when they started to hunt pirates, a distinct disadvantage.

Piracy in the waters near New Providence increased to such an extent that trade in the area almost reached extinction. With profits affected, a crackdown had to happen, hence Woodes Rogers' government appointment. His aim was to expel the pirates and restore commerce, which he achieved but mostly at his own expense. Several pirates led by Charles Vane were disdainful of his interference and made a last attempt at regaining their freedom, an attempt that, in the end, failed, as Rogers employed the strategy of using pirates to fight pirates. Hornigold was one pirate to turn pirate-hunter. With a safe haven denied them and the Royal Navy increasing in number and efficiency, the Golden Age of piracy went into decline and was almost finished in the Caribbean by the end of the 1720s.

## Antigua

Although not a pirate haven, Antigua's strategic location on the south side of the island and at the gateway to the Caribbean, allowed control over the major sailing route to and from the island colonies, and it became an important asset for the Royal Navy. Now known as Nelson's Dockyard – before the Admiral's days it was called English Harbour – it formed a natural protection from hurricanes, as well as from attack. The first ship on record to visit was the *Dover Castle* in 1671, as it conveyed the governor of the Leeward Islands on his trip around the islands to see what was what. Fort Berkeley was mentioned in 1704 as one of twenty forts on Antigua. The Royal Navy was regularly using the harbour by 1707, although it was not provisioned with facilities to maintain or repair ships. In 1723, thirty-five ships anchored in other bays around Antigua suffered severe storm damage, while the two in English Harbour were unharmed. A petition to the British Government followed, pleading for facilities to be built and, in 1728, on the east side of the harbour, St Helena, the first dockyard, was established. It had a capstan house for careening, and storehouses. These meagre buildings soon became inadequate so wharves and new extended construction, built by slave labour, began in the 1740s. Quarters for officers were added, with more storerooms, kitchens and such, in 1765. Throughout the rest of the century, expansion and improvement continued, with the Naval Officer's and Clerk's House being among of the last to appear in 1855. Abandoned in 1889, the dockyard began to decay but the Society of the Friends of English Harbour started restoration work in 1951. In the 1960s it was opened to the public as a site of historic interest and, in July 2016, the United Nations cultural agency UNESCO, awarded it the accolade of World Heritage Site status. In his day, however, Nelson called it a 'vile hole.'

*St. Mary's Island*

The more well-known pirates undertook their illegal exploits in the azure blue waters of the Caribbean but many of them also operated in the Indian Ocean, preying on the rich-laden ships sailing towards Mecca, or the East India Trade merchant ships. From the late 17th century, buccaneers used the African island of Madagascar as a suitable base. They had a colony where they could repair and careen, sell their plunder and enjoy the merry life with the native women. St Mary's, on the north-east coast, was the most widely used port, although there were other strongholds. St Mary's boasted about 1,500 inhabitants in the 1690s, serving men such as Captain Kidd, Thomas Tew and Henry Every. Some of the plundered goods, sold on to shipping heading for London or the Americas, netted enormous sums for the traders – according to some reports, up to $2,000,000.

10

# Fictional Nassau

Fiction can bring the reality of the past alive. The trick of a skilled writer is to blend fact into make-believe to such a degree that the reader is unaware of which is which. I took my young pirate, Jesamiah Acorne, to Nassau in *Sea Witch*, the first voyage of my nautical series of adventures. I researched and imagined. What would this ragged, slum of an almost derelict port be like? I altered a few facts – Nassau was without a governor in 1716, but sometimes it is not always convenient to stick to the facts, not in a part-fantasy adventure anyway, so I put a governor *in situ*. Albeit not a very good one.

In this scene Jesamiah is not yet the captain of his own vessel, but he is taking part in a raid to steal some gold from Nassau's fortress. Would pirates steal from other pirates? Some would, some would not, but either way, it makes a good story.

Excerpt: *Sea Witch* by Helen Hollick:

*Pretending to be a merchant, Jesamiah (calling himself Oake, not Acorne) is heading for the governor's house with a companion, another pirate, Monsieur de Cabo. It is the early hours of the morning ...*

Nassau. The same as any other port. Ships at anchor, others heeled on their side, partially careened. Near the jetties a tramp of warehouses, chandlers' bothies, rope-makers, sail menders. Water barrels, hogsheads for flour, fruit, vegetables and salted meat. Kegs of gunpowder, piles of hemp. Pots of paint ... none of it tidy. This was a pirate haven, where all that mattered were the taverns and the brothels. There was one church, which, judging by the smell as Jesamiah walked past up the hill, housed pigs.

The rush of the wind rustled through the trees scattering the moonlight into dancing shadows. A dog barked somewhere, was abruptly silenced after a high-pitched yelp. A cat slunk from behind a heap of sacking, a dead rat clamped between its jaws, the head drooping, tail dragging in the dust. Jesamiah grimaced. He had no liking for rats.

At the main gate to the governor's house, a solitary guard, asleep. Jesamiah stepped across the inner courtyard and hammered on the worn and scratched oak door. After a long while, a bleary-eyed servant, in need of a shave and a wash, shambled up from the kitchens to see who was making all the noise.

'I must see the Governor. I need immediate interview with him!' Jesamiah thrust past the sleep-muddled footman, striding into the gloom of what could have been an attractive hallway had it been cleaned occasionally of dust and cobwebs. One corner of the ceiling was mildewed, in another the plaster was cracked and peeling, everything looked and smelt shabby and neglected.

Fifteen minutes. Twenty, twenty-five. A man lumbered, yawning, down the stairs, Jesamiah noticing his stockings were silk and the buttons of his waistcoat were silver with a diamond inlay. Very pretty.

'M'dear fellow!' Jesamiah boomed heartily, affecting an upper class accent and bowing in extravagant formality. 'Apologies for tipping ye from y'bed, I am in some grave dilemma and require urgent advice from someone of y'wisdom.'

The governor, suspicious, peered at him through sleep-tainted eyes. 'And you are, sir?'

'Oake, Captain Jesamiah Oake of the vessel *Salvation*,' Jesamiah lied, sweeping a second bow for all the world as if he were some dandy come straight from the coffee houses of London. 'This,' he indicated de Cabo, 'is m'first officer; the fellow is French, but of the Huguenot persuasion so has as much antipathy towards the Frogs as do we.' He glanced around the hall, at the several official rooms leading from it. Lowering his voice he coughed and said, 'Me enquiry don't warrant being imparted in the draught of a doorway.'

From somewhere in the house a clock was chiming three. Made aware of his lack of manners the governor reddened, ushered his guests up the stairs to his private quarters and shouted for breakfast to be brought.

'It is a little early, but once roused my stomach growls for sustenance. You will join me, gentlemen?'

A free breakfast too? How delightful!

Seating himself at a scratched cherry-wood table Jesamiah explained his need. 'As ye are aware, we sadly lost our dear Queen Anne some while ago, God rest her.'

Gravely, the governor shook his head. 'A sorry thing indeed. She was a good woman. I was at Court twice, don't y'know?'

'Sixteen children she bore,' Jesamiah continued, ignoring the boasting. 'Or was it seventeen? And not one of them surviving longer than their dear lady mother. No direct line of succession to call upon, o'course, leaving one hell of an Anne's Fan between the Scots Stuarts who want their James as King, and the English Government who are in favour of George of Hanover. A man wholly devoid of charm and speaks only German I b'lieve. A King of England, who cannot utter a word in English, eh?' Jesamiah paused, allowing his inference to sink in. 'When I sailed from Plymouth the Jacobites were about to rise in protest. I therefore need to know, Governor, whether their determination for civil war succeeded? Is King George overthrown?'

Spluttering indignation the governor pushed his chair aside as he leapt to his feet. 'If you are counselling I support rebellion, then you must think again. I am a loyal supporter of the Crown, and I beg you not to think otherwise!'

Placating him, Jesamiah patted the air with his hands. 'Nay, nay sir, be seated, I merely ask because I have a gang of scrofulous Scotsmen on board who have been plaguing m'patience to drink the health of his Majesty King James, third of that name. Before I hang them for treason, I need to know if they *are* treasonous. I'd look the fool were I t'set them decorating the yardarm only to discover Hanover had been plucked by the royal balls and sent back to Germany, would I not?' He chuckled, his fingers idly toying with the blue ribbon laced into his hair, his eyes lighting as the door opened. 'Ah. Breakfast!'

How – if – Jesamiah gets the loot is another part of the story.

11

# Captain Morgan:
# The Pirate, Not the Rum
# (That Comes Next)

I wonder how many adults enjoying their rum and coke in the light breeze of a cool summer's evening realise they are in the company of a real pirate? Although technically, Sir Henry Morgan, as he became, was a privateer.

Or was he?

Born in Wales in 1635, at Llanrhymny, Monmouthshire, Henry was the eldest son of a farmer. It seems various Morgan family members fought on opposing sides during the English Civil War. Henry's reputation began after 1655, of his early education he supposedly said; 'I am more used to the pike than the book'.

He became famous as a privateer, even more esteemed for fighting the Spanish in the Caribbean than his predecessor, Sir Francis Drake. Morgan planned his strategies well; he was a formidable and fearless commander and, by 1668, had become the leader of the Brethren of the Coast. He commanded huge fleets, attacked major targets and amassed a vast amount of wealth. In 1668, he sacked Portobello; in 1669, raided Maracaibo; and in 1671, destroyed Panama. He had no previous experience of sailing but reputedly joined the English Navy to take part in Oliver Cromwell's attempt to oust the Catholic Spanish from Hispaniola. That proved to be an unsuccessful mission, but the English force managed to acquire Jamaica instead – as it turned out, a far more lucrative gain.

The Dutch writer, Exquemelin, tells us that Morgan arrived in the Caribbean in the mid-1600s serving under General Venables and Admiral Penn. He had married his cousin, Mary, but does not seem to have spent much time with her because he was always off taking part in various nautical expeditions. He seems to have been a rough, tough, man; perhaps she was relieved to see so little of him? You can almost hear her sighing with relief as he sailed out of harbour and her life returned to quiet domesticity for a few blissful months.

He came to be admired by ordinary English folk, who loved tales of derring-do and loathed the Catholic Spanish, but he was the proverbial pain-in-the-backside to English and Spanish governments because his attacks made nonsense of various strenuously negotiated treaties aimed at stopping the successive wars. However, perhaps it could be argued the fear the Spanish had for him was what enabled those treaties to be agreed to in the first place.

Since the days of Columbus, Spain had ruled a vast empire. 'New Spain' – the Spanish Main – consisted of the Gulf of Mexico, what is now Florida, all the way across to California, Mexico and Central America. Add in Cuba, Puerto Rico, Hispaniola and South America, bar Portuguese-held Brazil. Spain's wealth had expanded from the days of the Conquistadors who had destroyed the Aztecs and Incas, the territories they had possessed all being rich in gold, silver and trade commodities. Since 1492, Spain had shipped treasure home in fleets of heavily laden galleons. War between Spain and England – between Catholic and Protestant – had fluctuated during the Tudor reigns and continued through Cromwell and the Stuarts. Morgan was undoubtedly Protestant. Was it this, his lust for fighting, or the lure of easy-come gold that drove his own, personal, vendetta against the Spanish?

Captaining his first vessel in 1663, Henry Morgan played a leading role in a raid on Campeche, a wealthy and important city on the Gulf of Mexico, and went on to plunder much of the Mexican coast over the next few years. He made good use of various Letters of Marque awarded by Jamaica's governor, Sir Thomas Modyford, who was later to claim that he did not receive despatches in time to stop the raids. A likely story.

Joining with Edward Mansfield's fleet in late 1665, Morgan took the islands of Providencia and Santa Catalina Island, Colombia. During the raid, Mansfield was captured and executed. In consequence, Morgan found himself elected as Admiral of the Fleet.

In 1667, ignoring government orders, Modyford issued yet another Letter of Marque to Morgan, who went to various ports in person. Dressed in finery and bedecked in jewels, he gave the impression of having a justified reputation for success. It worked. His planned enterprise was joined by 500 of the best fighters in the Caribbean. With ten ships, they attacked Puerto Principe on Cuba – but the town had been forewarned and the occupants had already fled, taking their valuables with them. Torturing the few remaining unfortunates for information proved of no benefit either, all the raiders went away with was 50,000 pieces-of-eight, not nearly enough to provide the dividend to share with Modyford, the Admiralty and the King, in addition to paying 500 men the handsome profit they all expected. Rather than return to Port Royal, they chose to attack the third most important Spanish city in the Americas, Portobello in modern Panama.

The privateers faced an intimidating sequence of fortresses. Morgan gave a rousing speech, promising gold and treasure in abundance and added that they had the advantage of surprise on their side. They certainly did for at the first fort they attacked, everyone inside was asleep, unaware of the approaching danger. At the second fortress, Morgan's force scaled the walls, sustaining heavy losses. But by the time they reached the third fort, the Spanish were not prepared to fight such an indomitable foe and surrendered, leaving the city itself wide open.

Morgan remained in Portobello for two months, his men collecting as much plunder as they could and ransoming the wealthier citizens. This alone brought in 100,000 pieces-of-eight, doubling their looted profit. It is perhaps best not to dwell on what the people of Portobello must have endured.

Back in Jamaica, Governor Modyford denounced Morgan's attacks – claiming he had only been ordered to harass shipping. The English Government was not impressed. Modyford was in trouble so he devised a cunning plan. Rumours spread like wildfire that Jamaica was in immediate danger of reprisals, which gave Modyford the perfect excuse to issue a further Letter of Marque to Morgan. He vociferously claimed that he was only protecting Sovereign Land – but it does make you wonder who started the rumours in the first place, doesn't it?

Yet again Morgan put a fleet together, attracting 900 men in eleven ships. Rendezvousing at Isla Vaca, Cow Island, they agreed to target Cartagena de Indias on the coast of Colombia. However, it turned out that it was not a good idea to celebrate their intention by consuming vast amounts of rum. Inebriated sailors lit a fuse that ignited explosives and Morgan's flagship, *Oxford*, blew up, killing many men. Many more then deserted, superstitiously assuming the incident to be a bad omen. Morgan, however, was determined and continued with his raid in March 1669.

Big problems awaited. His original 900 men had dwindled to half that force, nowhere near enough to try for Cartagena. So, instead, they headed for Maracaibo. That was not an easy option either, because to reach the town they would have had to sail through a narrow channel, which they would be unable to navigate while avoiding the heavy artillery fire from the fort dominating the passage. Using his initiative, Morgan landed his men on the beach and, come nightfall, penetrated the fortress. That bit was easy – too easy. The fortress turned out to be deserted. Instead of soldiers, it was packed with explosives. Morgan snatched up the slow-match fuse and thereby saved many lives, including his own. He and his men retreated, taking all the fort's supplies of food and ammunition.

Changing tack, Morgan's army paddled light canoes up the narrow channel, but forewarned, Maracaibo was also deserted. Morgan spent three weeks sacking the town then set off to try his luck on the nearby town of Gibraltar, which added to the plunder.

Deciding to return to Jamaica, he and his crew hit another snag; three Spanish ships now blockaded their escape route. Morgan's men had two choices; surrender or be arrested. They made a third. Fight. Outnumbered, they had scant hope of survival, let alone victory, but Morgan used one of his vessels as a fire ship, which gave a sudden, distinct advantage.

Fire and storms are the main hazards for wooden ships. By using hollowed-out logs to look like men, and with twelve actual men remaining aboard to steer the vessel into one of the barricading ships before the sailors leapt overboard, his plan worked perfectly. Morgan captured the second ship, and the third was scuppered by its own crew. Morgan still had to run the gauntlet of the fort protecting the channel, but he faked a land attack, which drew cannon fire, and he managed to escape. It does not come as much of a surprise that Spain now threatened to retaliate against Jamaica.

In 1670, Morgan captured the island of Santa Catalina and, a few days later, took the fortress of San Lorenzo on the Panama coast, killing 300 men. With 1,400 men in his army, he headed for Panama City, which was to become one of his most enterprising campaigns. In January 1671, he marched overland through the jungle. Terrified of Morgan's reputation, the Spanish initially abandoned their defensive position but met him in battle outside the city, on 28th January. They did not stand a chance of victory. Morgan and his men were seasoned fighters, armed to the teeth. The Spanish forces not butchered, fled. The people in the city were cut down without mercy, or were tortured and raped; the buildings were reduced to nothing but ash and rubble.

Morgan has, ever since, been lauded for his achievement – except by the Spanish who were, and are, justified in protesting that the attack on Panama and the subsequent violation of its residents went against the 1670 peace treaty between Spain and England. Morgan, for all his hero status in the eyes of the English, could be said to be little better than the pirates who were to follow him a decade later. He had no regard for peace treaties or settlements, all he wanted was to kill the Spanish and relieve them of their gold. His audacity and cunning remain admired, though, making him the ideal emblem for a brand of rum.

On Morgan's return to Jamaica, he and Governor Modyford were recalled to England to face charges of disobeying the king's command – both men protesting that the order not to attack any Spanish town had not been received before Morgan had set out on his final raid. Quite likely, this was all political show to appease the irate Spanish government.

Modyford was reprimanded but Morgan simply proved that he was unaware of a declaration of peace, so he was duly acquitted. He spent a few years as a popular celebrity, invited to most of the estates and homes of politicians and wealthy merchants alike. When war broke out again in 1674, Morgan received the honour of a knighthood and returned in glory to Jamaica in 1675, as Lieutenant Governor.

But his popularity did not last. In 1681, he fell out of favour with King Charles II and was replaced by a political rival, Thomas Lynch. Morgan remained on in Jamaica, in retirement, with drink and gluttony as constant companions.

His exploits were featured in Exquemelin's book *About The Buccaneers of America*. Morgan was outraged at being called a pirate – to his mind he had always acted under the legal code of a Letter of Marque – and he sued the publisher for libel. He secured a retraction, the offensive wording was removed and the book republished. He was also awarded damages to his reputation of more than £200.

By 1688, Morgan's health had declined considerably; he was diagnosed with dropsy, an accumulation of fluid beneath the skin and in the cavities of the body that can cause severe pain. He died on 25th August 1688, leaving no children. (He was probably not at home long enough to beget them.) His widow, Mary, passed away in 1696.

After his coffin was displayed in state at the King's House in Port Royal, his funeral cortege was honoured by every ship in the harbour firing a cannon in salute. He was buried at St Peter's Church – which was later to sink beneath the sea in the 1692 earthquake.

In his will, Morgan left all his Jamaican property to two godsons, Charles Byndloss and Henry Archbold, on condition they changed their surname to Morgan. Fair exchange I should think.

He has been a great favourite with moviemakers and novelists alike, popping up as various goody versus baddy characters, although nothing has portrayed him anywhere near accurately. *Captain Blood* was based on his exploits; the 1961 movie *Morgan, the Pirate*, starring Steve Reeves, recounts his life. Ian Fleming's *James Bond* spy thriller, *Live And Let Die,* involved events unfolding after Morgan's hidden treasure being found (not that he actually had any of it buried), and one of Isaac Asimov's tales, *Robots In Time,* depicted time travellers going back to meet him.

Captain Morgan is immortalised as a dashing hero and the conqueror of the Spanish Main by his flamboyant image appearing on bottles of a certain brand-named rum. I guess, even if his exploits were slightly suspect, having a best-selling rum named after you is no bad thing.

12

# A Rumbullion Rumbustion
# of Rum

Tradition has it that rum came from the island of Barbados, although it is just as likely to have originated in Brazil. There are white rums, light rums, dark rums, golden rums and spiced rums. And they could be premium rums, good rums or grog.

*Captain Morgan Rum* (other brands are available) is produced by the alcohol distillers Diageo, and has been in production since 1944 under the Seagram Company, with the slogan 'To Life, Love and Loot' being used since 2011.

Samuel Bronfman of Seagrams originally purchased the Long Pond distillery from the Jamaican Government, also buying the rights to the Levy Brothers recipe for adding herbs and spices to the raw rum. Tax laws changed in the 1950s and both Seagrams and the Bacardi family extended their production plants, which were situated near San Juan. Seagrams sold the Captain Morgan brand to Diageo in 2001, with the new company building a new rum distillery on St Croix in the Virgin Islands. In the UK, the spiced rum was rebranded as Captain Morgan Spiced in 2011.

All well and good but what *is* rum? Where does it come from, and how is it made?

Most rum comes from molasses, which is a by-product that comes from turning the juice from sugarcane into refined sugar. Various combinations of added yeasts, plus a fermentation period, and what it is aged in, make the various blends, tastes and brands. At first, rum is a clear liquid; once distilled, it is aged in oak casks for anything up to an entire year, achieving its golden colour from the wood, before the addition of any spices or herbs. Unlike whisky or brandy, there is no set production method: each area and distillery has its own formula. The slower the yeast fermentation, the more full-tasting the rum, and the longer the rum is aged, the better the taste.

Browse any UK off-licence or supermarket's liquor section and you will find *Captain Morgan* along with *Jamaica Rum, Lambs Navy Rum, Bacardi* and many others carrying exotic names such as *Sunset Reef* and *Kraken Black Spiced*.

The alcoholic residue of sugarcane was at first called *rumbullion, rumbustian, bombo* or *bumbo*. Mixed with water it became 'grog' in the navy, with sailors expecting their daily ration to be delivered, without fail. Tough pirates, such as Blackbeard, even added a pinch or two of gunpowder. *Rumfustian* was a slightly different drink: rum, port, brandy, wine or ale blended with raw eggs, extra sugar and spices.

Rumbullion and Rumbustion appeared in the English language in the mid-1600s, around the time rum initially appeared. In Spanish, the word *ron* appeared in 1770, all these words are slang terms for a tumult, rowdiness or an uproar – quite fitting for the after-effects of consuming too much rum. The large glass Dutch drinking vessels were called *rummers*, which could be yet another explanation for the derivative of the word rum.

The colonial sugarcane plantations came into being in the Caribbean during the 17th century. The slaves discovered that the by-product of refining the sugar could, when fermented, turn into a potent alcoholic beverage. Once impurities were removed by distillation, the drink emerged as a favourite.

In 1654 and 1657, the General Courts of Connecticut and Massachusetts banned the selling of, '*Barbados liquors, commonly called rum, kill devil and the like*'. But it was cheap to produce, '*hot and hellish*' to drink, so more distilleries began to appear, the earliest known being built on present-day Staten Island in 1604, with Boston producing a distillery a few years later. Rum rapidly became the largest and most lucrative Colonial industry. Before the Colonies broke away from British rule, it has been estimated that every man, woman and child in colonial America consumed three gallons each per annum.

The slave trade came into being because of the plantations – initially to produce the increasing demand for the stuff we are now realising, here in the West, is the main cause of obesity and rotten teeth: sugar. Rum was an unexpected and highly lucrative bonus, to merchant and pirate alike.

Rum's link with pirates came about, apart from the enjoyable taste of it, because the liquor was a valuable commodity that had to be shipped from the Colonies and the Caribbean to Europe. Anything worth stealing aboard a ship was fair game for the buccaneers and pirates. It does make you wonder, given that pirates had a thirst for the stuff, how much they actually had left to sell for profit. Probably very little, I suspect. The image of rum-drinking drunken pirates has been exaggerated by the influence of *Treasure Island*, which is often the presumed basis of all pirate behaviour – whether true or not. Captain Jack Sparrow's rum drinking ('why's the rum gone?') and the dashing figure of Captain Morgan as a brand's logo have added to the assumption that pirates only consumed rum but brandy, wine and other 'merry making' inducements featured just as heavily on the drinks menu.

The Royal Navy 'tot' had been a long-established tradition but the rum ration started in 1655, after a British fleet had captured Jamaica and made the island one of its main Caribbean bases. The rum produced there was more easily obtainable than the previous tot of French brandy, and so the change was made. Originally the daily tot was given neat, but watering it down was introduced around 1740 by Admiral Edward Vernon, which is when it began to be called 'grog'.

So where does the term 'grog' come from? All the important European navies had established the wearing of blue uniforms, with a red trim for officers and warrant officers, by 1740, but British Royal Navy officers were determined to stick to their tradition of wearing whatever they wanted. Admiral Vernon, however, realised the importance of a standard uniform so officers could be quickly and easily recognised. He had his tailor make him a blue coat from gros-grain (a shiny ribbon material). The English mispronounced this French word as 'grogran' and Vernon soon acquired the nickname 'Old Grog'. While cruising the Caribbean, a lot of men were killed after falling from the rigging because they were drunk on neat rum. Vernon experimented, establishing how much water needed to be added to stop the excessive inebriation while still allowing the rum to mask the horrible taste of sour drinking water. The solution was found to be a ratio of between two and four parts water to one part rum.

The watered rum very soon became to be known as 'grog'.

Later, in 1753, a Navy surgeon, James Lind, discovered that scurvy could be prevented by Vitamin C, So lime juice was added to the grog, giving rise to the word 'Limey', the slang term for an Englishman.

Sailors in the Royal Navy enjoyed their daily tot of rum until 31st July 1970, when the practice was abolished – apart from special occasions such as the monarch's birthday, when the order is given to 'splice the main brace'. This term also refers to a difficult and hazardous task aboard ship. Braces are the lines (ropes) that control the yards, the spar from which the sails are set. The main brace aboard a tall ship, man o'war or any similar sailing vessel, is the largest and heaviest of the running rigging, the lines used for controlling the sails. 'Standing rigging' is fixed in place to support the masts and other spars, and it is coated in many layers of tar to protect it from the weather and salt-spray erosion. Because it is not tar-coated, 'running rigging' is much lighter and more flexible. The main brace could be anything up to five inches in diameter – that's thick. The quickest way to disable a ship in a fight was for the gunners to sever the rigging, the main brace to the mainmast being the preferred target. Once damaged it meant the ship could not tack or manoeuver until repairs were made and this involved doing so *in situ*. The main brace ran through heavy blocks and required a long length of hemp to be spliced in, difficult to do even in good conditions but when the enemy was continuing to fire various missiles such as cannonballs, grape shot or langrage at you ... well, it was a real challenge. The reward for splicing the main brace was a double ration of rum, no doubt very gratefully received.

There appears to be a slight downside to rum drinking in the 18th century. Apart from the damage to the liver, a dependency on alcohol and the obvious side effects, lead poisoning caused many fatalities. Excavations at the Royal Naval hospital cemeteries in Antigua revealed, after examination of various exhumed skeletons, that several had high levels of lead in their bones. Food was not stored in lead cans until the 19th century, later than the deaths of these men, but the condensation coils and other parts of the stills used to produce rum were made of malleable lead. In addition, rainwater was often collected in lead-lined cisterns, which meant drinking water also had a high lead content. Maybe a quick death by pistol shot, or cannon fire or even the hangman's noose had its compensations? Lead poisoning is not a pleasant way to die.

Some modern-day liqueurs (lead free!) are enhanced by rum, as are a variety of marinades and cakes – fruitcake, especially. My favourite desert is rum and raisin ice cream. I am also fond of damson rum, made from damsons picked from the trees in my orchard and soused in rum and sugar for several months.

Damson rum is ideal in a hip flask on a cold winter's morning or as an after-dinner tipple. The longer you leave it to age, the better the taste. It takes willpower to leave it, mind you. (Talking of which, I think I have a bottle left over from last year. You get on with reading the recipe below and I'll go and look for it …)

Based on Sloe Gin, here is the recipe:

You will need:

1 ½ lb damsons (preferably post frost)
1 ¾ pints dark rum
10 ½ oz demerara sugar
3 ½ oz white sugar

Prick each damson with a pin, needle or a fork and place in a large bowl. Add the rum and sugar to the bowl and stir to dissolve the sugar.

Use a big, clean jar with a well-fitting lid (a demi john, or Kilner jar – doesn't matter as long as it is water and airtight.) Evenly decant the rum, fruit and sugar mix into your container/s.

Then you have to wait. For up to three months. Store the containers in a cool, dark cupboard, allowing time for the flavour of the fruit to seep into the rum. Turn the containers every other day and give a gentle shake to mix the contents up a little. If you forget, no worries, just try to be regular with your twisting and shaking.

After three months … Using a double thickness of clean muslin strain the mixture (don't squeeze it!) into a clean bowl. Repeat as necessary until the liquid runs clear.

Decant into clean bottles and you can drink it straight away but if you leave it for a year, it will be even better.

Provided the bottle isn't opened, it will last for years. Each autumn I make a batch for the following year.

You can use any hedgerow fruit, and almost any liquor, it doesn't have to be damsons and rum. Try dry, ripe blackberries in brandy, or damson gin.

Your only difficulty?

Picking the fruit before some darn pirate gets there first!

13

# The Dandy of the Caribbean – Jack Rackham aka Calico Jack

Jack Rackham – even the name has an intriguing, evocative ring to it, especially when you add the nickname 'Calico' and make mention of his two sidekicks, Anne Bonny and Mary Read. 'Jack' is a derivative of John, and the 'calico' refers to the material of his favourite clothing. He was something of a dandy, the eye-candy Jack Sparrow of his day. Although Disney has never specifically said so, Captain Sparrow was undoubtedly modelled on Calico Jack – even the pirate flag in the movie was similar to Rackham's skull and crossed-cutlass design. But there the similarity ends.

Born John Rackham (sometimes spelt Rackam or Rackum) on 26th December 1682 (possibly: there is doubt about the exact date) there is no information about his childhood and youth; all we know is that he was English. He first came to public attention as quartermaster (second-in-command) to Charles Vane aboard the *Ranger*, based in Nassau in 1718.

In October that year, Vane and Rackham were among a party of men who met at Ocracoke Island, off the coast of North Carolina. Their host was Edward Teach, Blackbeard himself, and one can only assume the gathering was to make merry and to discuss piratical matters. Blackbeard was soon to meet his fate, but towards the end of November, Vane urged caution and refused to pursue a French man-o'-war, counselling that it was too big to Chase.

Jack Rackham took the opportunity to contest the decision and deposed Vane as the captain. From then onwards, his career as a pirate took off.

Vane and his fifteen supporters – the rest of the ninety or so crew had backed Rackham – were sent off in a sloop leaving Rackham to plunder several small vessels in and around Jamaica. He improved his status when he managed to capture a merchant ship, *Kingston*, near Port Royal.

He had miscalculated, though, for his raid was within sight of the shore and several merchants funded bounty hunters to go after him. He was almost caught in February 1719, while his ship was anchored at Isla de los Pinos, off Cuba. Fortunately for Rackham and his men, they were all ashore so they escaped into the dense woodland. But they lost both the ship and her rich cargo.

Charles Johnson's *A General History of Robberies and Murders of Notorious Pyrates,* written circa 1723, recounts how Rackham and his crew commandeered a Spanish Prize. The account is a daring tale of masterly quick thinking while careening their own ship. The Spanish ship, patrolling the seas around Cuba, came into harbour with a captured English ship. Low tide was the pirates' only salvation – the inbound Spanish could not reach them, but they could drop anchor in the harbour entrance effectively blockading Rackham in it. All they had to do was wait for the tide to come in …
Jack and his men waited for nightfall and, slipping into the rowing boats, stealthily crossed the harbour and boarded the English vessel, which was undoubtedly undermanned being a Spanish Prize, and captured it. Come daylight, Rackham and his men sailed away while the Spanish opened fire on the pirates' now abandoned old ship.

Maybe their days of plunder had not been successful enough to tempt them to keep at it, because in 1719 Rackham and his crew headed for Nassau and Governor Woodes Rogers' offer of amnesty. A life of honest living, however, did not last long.

Taverns, drinking and whoring had their limitations, particularly when Jack met the wife of sailor James Bonny – Anne. They became lovers and rather than face public humiliation on the charge of adultery, in August 1719, Anne absconded with Jack and a new crew, stealing a boat – *William* – into the bargain, thereby breaking the granted amnesty.

They cruised the Caribbean, taking mostly smaller ships and modest Prizes. When Anne became pregnant, she stayed in Cuba for a while to give birth, but was soon back aboard enjoying her life of freedom. It is not known what became of the child.

Sometime during 1719, Mary Read joined the crew.

Then sometime in the autumn of 1720, Governor Woodes Rogers issued a warrant for the arrest of Rackham and his crew. Pirate hunter Jonathan Barnet picked up the challenge.

While Jack, his lover Anne, Mary and the rest of the crew were plundering fishing boats and small fry off the coast of Jamaica, they were unaware that their idyllic life was about to come to an end. While they were anchored at Bry Harbour Bay, Jamaica, Barnet took advantage of the darkness and surprised them by attacking during the night in early November 1720.

Rackham and his men were below deck, drinking heavily and almost certainly drunk. Although Anne and Mary put up a fight, they were overwhelmed. The entire crew was taken to Jamaica, where they were charged with piracy.

Rackham and the men were tried, convicted, and hanged at Port Royal on 18th November 1720, with Jack's corpse left on display on a small islet at the entrance to the harbour – a place now known as Rackham's Cay. Executed alongside him were George Fetherstone, Richard Corner, John Davis and John Howell.

The next day, Patrick Carty, Thomas Earl, James Dobbin and Noah Harwood were also hanged. Former crew, Fenwick and Bourn were tried and convicted of a mutiny they took part in during June 1720, while a further nine men who had been drinking below deck were convicted on 24th January 1721.

Another three were hanged at Gallows Point, Port Royal on 17th February, with the final three executed at Kingston. A sad end to a somewhat sorry crew.

In the realm of fiction, Calico Jack, as quartermaster to Charles Vane, was played by actor Toby Schmitz in the TV series *Black Sails*, created by Jonathan E. Steinberg and Robert Levine for Starz. This was an intriguing interpretation of the real man, although the character's Public School 'plummy' accent seemed inappropriate.

Rackham features in the Ubisoft game *Assassin's Creed IV* and is the protagonist in George McDonald Fraser's *Captain In Calico*.

14

# An Encounter with Blackbeard

Excerpt: *Bring It Close* by Helen Hollick
Late October 1718

Jack Rackham appeared in a cameo role in the third *Sea Witch Voyage*, *Bring It Close*; he will appear again in a further adventure, not written at the time of this publication.

*Captain Jesamiah Acorne is temporarily without his beloved ship,* Sea Witch. *Coerced against his will, he has been set the task of helping to destroy Blackbeard. Working 'under cover' he has joined with other pirates on Ocracoke Island, North Carolina:*

Beyond an initial scowl, Charles Vane had ignored Jesamiah since stepping ashore several hours ago. He ignored also his own quartermaster, seated next to Jesamiah and sharing a bottle of rum, John Rackham, known as Calico Jack, the fancy dandy of the pirate brethren. Rackham detested Vane.

'You want to sail with me, Jack?' Jesamiah asked, returning the bottle to him. 'I can offer you a better life than the one you have with Vane.'

'Will you make me a captain?'

'No. *Sea Witch* – when I get her back – is mine.'

'Then I thank you for the offer, but I have an idea to get my own vessel and my own captaincy.'

'Jack, that will lead only to the noose. Take amnesty and life. A long, quiet life.'

Jack Rackham drank a few gulps, handed the rum back. 'So why are you here, eh? Amnesty means a long quiet life of tedious boredom. Nay, give me the short but merry one, Jesamiah.' Jack winked and nudged him with his elbow. 'The ladies prefer a pirate in their beds, you know. They enjoy the added excitement.'

Jesamiah's thoughts did not exactly tally with Rackham's theory. He did not need the added excitement of saying he was a pirate to pleasure a woman. Aside, so far, since signing Governor Roger's book of amnesty he had been flogged, threatened with torture, sent spying in Hispaniola, and was now charged with spying on Edward Teach, Blackbeard. Amnesty? It was not proving restful or pleasurable, and was certainly not tedious or boring. He drank, swallowed; said grimly, 'Aye, I've heard that a man as he swings on the noose and evacuates his bowels and piece can be pretty excitin' for those watching.'

'You're turning into an old maid, Jesamiah Acorne.'

Jesamiah grinned. 'Nay, just a married one.'

Rackham raised his eyebrows in surprise. That Acorne had a wife was news to him, though there had been rumour of him being with a handsome, black-haired lass.

'Wife?' He asked. 'When did this happen?'

'Not long ago. Before I got myself too deeply into this damned mess.' Jesamiah tossed more wood on to the fire, eyed Teach and Vane roaring at some jest one of them had made. 'I tell you Jack, this ain't no life. Not once you find a good woman to love and to keep you warm at night.'

Rackham shook his head in disbelief and upended the bottle, disappointed to find it empty. 'I like bedding the lasses too much to have just the one. A wife ain't for me.'

For answer, Jesamiah just smiled. He liked Jack Rackham, an honest man – as far as a pirate could be honest. They had shared a few adventures in the past, and a few bottles – and more than a few women.

Getting to his feet, Rackham went to relieve himself, returned with another two bottles, one each.

'I thought Stede Bonnet was to have come?' he said to Israel Hands, seated on his other side. 'Why is he not here, I wonder?'

Overhearing this, Vane growled contempt. 'You're soft, you are, Rackham. As soft as a spent pizzle. It don't matter about Bonnet. If he ain't interested in joining us then he can go kiss his backside, and be damned. I never trusted the drunken sot anyway.'

'Thee's never trusted anyone,' Teach observed dryly. 'Not even thy own quartermaster over yonder.' He pointed at Rackham.

'That's because he's a traitorous little runt.'

Rackham was on his feet, pistol in hand waving it unsteadily. 'You take that back, Vane! It ain't my fault the men want me as Captain instead of you! You've been useless these past months. I'd make a better job of it than ever you will.' Worse the wear for drink, he waved the pistol again.

'Gentlemen, gentlemen!' Jesamiah stood and with a placating smile removed the weapon from Rackham's hand before he shot himself, or someone else, in the foot. 'We are here to discuss business, not kill each other.' He was also concerned that Stede Bonnet had not arrived, but was glad of it. Another vicious brute he would rather not renew acquaintance with.

'We all know Bonnet is not especially good at navigation. I expect he's got lost further down the coast.' Jesamiah did not add that for the same reason, he was surprised Vane had got here. But then Vane relied on Jack Rackham to navigate.

'We as don't need Bonnet,' Blackbeard announced, 'Us'n can doos what I have in min' without him.'

Rackham sat down again, Jesamiah also. This was it then, the Grand Plan. The reason they were all gathered here.

'I have a plan,' Vane announced, cutting in. 'We need to unite, work in consort.'

Teach growled, did not look too pleased at being verbally pushed aside, but like it or not, Vane was the most prominent pirate in the

Spanish Main. He had a good ship, an adequate crew. Teach's glory had peaked at his successful siege of Charlestown back in the spring. And then he had lost his ship. The *Queen Anne's Revenge* had been his great pride, he had done very little of note since losing her. What could he do with a sloop that was falling to bits?

Vane announced his proposal. 'I intend to reinstate Nassau as a place fit for pirates. Show this Governor Rogers he's bitten off more'n he can chew.'

Jesamiah roared with laughter. Perhaps not the best reaction; Vane was not amused.

'You think I am jesting, Acorne? You see something funny?'

Sobering, Jesamiah attempted to collect himself. He had been alarmed when first learning of a meeting of pirates here on the Ocracoke – Teach had obviously had this planned for some while, and was exactly the sort of thing Governor Spotswood, back in Virginia, needed to know about. It occurred to him, sitting here trying not to laugh any louder than he already was, that perhaps Virginia's Governor had already got wind of this grand parlez? If he had, that would explain his anxiety and the need to employ a reliable spy. Were these men sitting here not such greed-bound, drunken fools, both Spotswood and Rogers would have had justified cause for concern.

He said, quelling his merriment, 'It would have been a good plan, Vane, if you had not flapped your tongue.'

'Don't know what you are talking about,' Vane countered.

'Don't you? You mean you have completely forgotten that you personally sent a message to Rogers telling him of your intention? That you and Teach here, and one other pirate – I assume you meant Bonnet – were going to kick his arse? Told him to prepare for war?'

Silence.

'Well?' Teach asked, glowering at Vane. 'Did thee blab?'

Vane got to his feet, started waving his arms about. 'I might have done. I might have let a few things slip. What of it? I have got Rogers worried. He is no match for us. We sail in there, claim Nassau harbour as ours.'

Jesamiah crowed again. 'Oh aye, you got him worried! So worried he sent for Navy re-enforcements and has ensured every cannon on the fortress walls is in prime working order. You expect to attack an armed fortress with one brigantine and a leaking sloop? Rogers has Nassau battened down as if there's a hurricane coming.'

'Aside,' Blackbeard interrupted, 'I bain't interested in Nassau. I hunts these waters. I has deals made, and tha whole o' tha Ocracoke and Pamlico Sound here as mine. No skulking Navy frigate be goin' t'get me here.'

Jesamiah chewed his lip. He was right there. If Spotswood wanted to attack Teach, he would have to be drawn out from these shallows into open water.

'I propose,' Blackbeard spoke deliberately slowly, his cold gaze going from one man to the next. 'I propose we blockade Hampton Roads. Get Spotswood t'capitulate t'us. We cut off his shipping supply – his precious town'll be dead within tha month.'

Yet again Jesamiah roared with laughter. 'You are both barking mad! Your sloop will probably disintegrate in the next gale to hit her, and the Chesapeake is not exactly Charlestown Harbour, is it? You did a good job there with a blockade, I'll grant you – but Spotswood is no blustering housemartin. And he happens to have two well-armed fully crewed Navy frigates at his disposal. How are you going to fight them with your handful of men?'

'I have seventy in my crew when they are all mustered!' Blackbeard roared back. 'Good men.'

'Rubbish. You are left with twenty and six with merely six cannon. Against frigates? Against an army commander who distinguished himself at Marlborough?'

'The rest o'me men are at Bathtown. They'll join us when I sends fer 'em. We canst do it, Acorne. Despite your scorn, *Adventure* be a fast lit'le boat. Vane has tha most vicious crew on all tha high seas, and Bonnet has brawn if no much brain. We wait, we pick off them frigates one at a time, then sweep in. It'll work, I'm tellin' thee. It will work.'

'But Bonnet is not here is he? And we'll need quality vessels for what you have in mind.'

'Then quality sloops we will has.' Teach nodded once, curt, and poked a finger in the air towards Jesamiah. 'Thee will get 'em fer us.'

'And just how am I going to do that?'

Teach leered, his version of an amused grin. 'If thee be wantin' to stay alive, Acorne, thee'll think o'summat. All I want is'n excuse t'kill thee, an' I be right eager fer thee t'oblige me.'

Jesamiah made a pretence at scowling and huffed, puffed and tutted for the next half hour. Inside he was chuckling with delight. Teach had no intention of attempting to do away with him while there was a possibility of getting his hands on *Sea Witch*. And going off to fetch two seaworthy sloops was just the excuse he needed to be gone from here without rousing suspicion. It could not have worked out better if he had planned it himself.

15

# Here Come the Girls: Anne Bonny and Mary Read

Jack Rackham has been explored, but what of the ladies, what of Anne and Mary?

The early 18th century was not a good place to be if you were poor, black, or a woman. For women there were no human rights, they were regarded as little more than possessions. No right to freely decide who to marry, no right to equal justice – and one in four died in childbirth. Most women were ignored by those who wrote the history of the times, mainly because those who wielded the pen were all men. The women who were mentioned were associated with strong or notorious men, or because of their charitable works. A few, however, defied society, and the law, and gained notoriety in their own right. Mention pirates to anyone and Anne Bonny and Mary Read will probably be part of the conversation. Anne was Jack Rackham's lover, Mary Read was a member of his crew, although we do not know if she was initially disguised as a man or not. As with Calico Jack, we know of them because they were captured and tried in Jamaica. Rackham hanged but the two women did not.

As with every other pirate of this period, little is known as definite fact. As usual, even the spelling of Anne and Mary's names differ with Ann Bonney and Mary Reed as variations. Apart from the trial transcripts, most of what we 'know' comes from Charles Johnson's *A General History of the Pyrates* – which is not always reliable or accurate.

### Anne Bonny

Did Anne know what she was doing when she went aboard a boat with Jack Rackham and a few men, intent on stealing it and sailing away for a (short) life of piracy? Or was she merely after an end to the boredom of a miserable marriage and an even more miserable husband? There was nothing for her in Nassau, and meeting the flamboyant Calico Jack Rackham must have been a breath of fresh air for this adventurous young woman. Did she always jump before she thought? Was her heart ruling, not her head? Did she, a few days out to sea, regret her choice and want to go home to the comfortable life with her rich father? Or maybe she liked the thought of knowing where her lover, Jack, kept the strongbox, liked looking at the glittering treasure stowed within: the gold and silver, the sparkling jewels? As the Captain's 'lady' did she enjoy the prestigious place of authority, the opportunity to order men about? Perhaps, more intriguing but unanswerable, did she like Mary Read, her fellow female crewmate? It is always assumed that the pair were friends – but there is no evidence to show it. As far as we know, they could have been bitter rivals. Anne was 'queen bee' aboard the ship, Mary was crew. Did Anne look down upon Mary, I wonder? Did Mary consider Anne to be a spoilt, rich bitch?

Anne was born around 1700 in County Cork, Ireland, to a serving woman, Mary Brennan, who was in the employ of a lawyer, Master William Cormac (or McCormac; he dropped the Irish 'Mc' soon after arriving in the Colonies.) There are some tales that Mr McCormac dressed Anne as a boy and called her Andy. To what purpose is unclear, and given that information about Anne's early life is scarce, this little snippet is unlikely to be true; it seems more of a reason to explain why she was of a 'tomboy' type and, later in life, occasionally dressed in male apparel – although even that might be fabrication.

When she was about twelve years old, the family emigrated to the American Colonies, settling in Charlestown, South Carolina. The town had been founded in 1670 in honour of King Charles II of England, but became Charleston, its present name, in 1783. Anne's mother died soon afterwards and her father looked to re-establishing himself as a man of law. He did not do very well (which makes you wonder if this was the reason why he left Ireland?) Instead, he pursued a career in a profitable merchant business and managed to amass a sizable fortune.

According to subsequent reports, Anne had red hair, a fiery temper and was 'a good catch'. Whether this meant she was attractive, or referred to her father's fortune is unclear.

Aged thirteen she allegedly stabbed a servant with a kitchen knife, which, while only supposition, does seem likely given her later life aboard ship. Presumably the servant was not killed – or the childhood misdemeanour was not brought before the courts. With her father being an ex-lawyer, that is entirely feasible.

She married against the wishes of her father, taking a poor sailor, James Bonny, as her husband. He probably had hopes of eventually owning his father-in-law's estate. He was to be disappointed, however, as Master Cormac disowned both of them and, at some point between 1715 and 1718, the young couple moved to Nassau. Although the date 1715 would have made Anne only fifteen years of age, it is not implausible.

James does not seem to have been much of a 'good sort'. Lazy, slovenly, probably a drunkard, he spent most of his time in the bars and taverns, and was employed surreptitiously by Governor Woodes Rogers as an informer. The pirates of Nassau had signed the Articles of Agreement, which meant they were given amnesty after committing earlier crimes – providing they did not return to piracy. Informers like James Bonny were spies keeping a watchful eye on who broke the agreement.

What Anne was doing is open to conjecture, but the likelihood is that she too spent her time in the taverns. (Doing what, I will leave to your own imagination.) She met Calico Jack Rackham and became his lover. Her husband was unhappy about this – which is understandable, and had Anne arrested for adultery. This was a serious charge because the punishment was for the woman to be stripped bare to the waist, and publicly flogged.

At the last moment, James Bonny and Jack Rackham came to an agreement. Bonny sold Anne to him.

Tired of the boredom of straight life, Rackham and Anne stole a ship, which they renamed *Revenge*, from the harbour, they put to sea and became pirates, menacing merchant shipping across the Caribbean waters, although never hitting the 'big time' with their plundered loot. Anne gave birth to a son. What happened to him, beyond the rumour that he eventually changed his name to Cunningham, is unknown. Whether he was abandoned, or taken in by Anne's father, is mere speculation.

While not achieving a fortune from their ill-gotten gains, they were a moderately successful pair, capturing many small vessels. Anne's name and gender was widely known, she openly fought among the crew. Many accounts portray her as competent and efficient with weaponry, so I would wager that although not disguised as a man, she did prefer to wear male apparel; it would not be easy to fight wearing a pretty gown and lacy petticoats.

The character of Anne Bonny in the TV drama *Black Sails* is not at all accurately based on history – she did not sail with Charles Vane, as the series depicts, but that's fiction for you.

### Mary Read

A small woman with brown curly hair, who loved the freedom of the sea, Mary was unafraid of hard work, and enjoyed the pleasure of watching dolphins skim past the hull.

Mary was the daughter of a sea captain. She was born illegitimately in England at some time in the late 17th century. Johnson refers to her birth during the 'Peace of Ryswick', the treaty signed on 20th September 1697 that settled the Nine Years War, a conflict against France by the Grand Alliance of England, Spain and the Holy Roman Empire. Although, as usual, Johnson cannot be relied upon.

Mrs Read received an allowance for her eldest (legitimate) son, Mark, from his paternal grandmother. When he died, to retain the financial support, Mary was disguised as a boy and took his place. Mother and daughter relied on this aid until Mary's teenage years. Presumably the money dried up (did the grandmother find out? Did she pass away?) Continuing to dress as a boy, Mary/Mark found work as a footboy – a servant or pageboy – and then served as crew aboard a ship.

When the British military allied with the Dutch against the French, very likely during the Spanish War of Succession 1701-1714, she joined the army, still dressed as a young man (with another assumption that this must have been towards the end of the war when she was about seventeen.) In male disguise, she fought in battles and proved herself as capable as any man.

Her army career halted when she fell in love with a Flemish soldier. They married and using his military commission, they purchased a tavern, the Three Horseshoes, near Breda in the Netherlands. Sadly, her husband died not long afterwards and Mary returned to the Dutch army in male uniform. Peace came, however, and with nowhere else to go, she joined a ship's crew bound for the Caribbean.

Pirates captured the ship and she was forced to join them. It is assumed she maintained her male role and it is also to be assumed that she was skinny, with not much 'chest-wise' to give her away.

She accepted the King's Pardon in 1718 or 1719 at Nassau. Then, after meeting Anne Bonny and Jack Rackham, she joined their crew and returned to piracy.

A different account states that she came aboard Rackham's vessel, when he captured a Prize, and was enticed by the crew into piracy. The big question: was Anne, or Jack, or were both, aware of Mary's gender identity?

### The End of the Adventure

*The Boston Newsletter* published in October 1720 reported that Jack Rackham, his crew, and two women, had been apprehended by Captain Jonathan Barnet, a pirate hunter. Drunk and carousing below deck, the male crew had made no attempt to defend themselves, while Bonny and Read, swearing at their comrades to come on deck to help, fought hard to resist capture. Outnumbered, and despite their ability with weaponry, the two women had little chance of success. The entire crew was taken to Jamaica to face trial, and the noose.

The trial was a sensation and the interest was in Anne and Mary. During the trial, several witnesses confirmed that the two women fought alongside the men and Anne, in particular, encouraged excessive bloodshed and violence. They were not destined to hang, however, for both 'pleaded their belly' – both were pregnant, so execution was postponed until the birth of the babies. Mary died in jail a few months later of fever. There is no record of Anne's labour or delivery, release or execution.

It may be fact, legend, or pure fiction, but Bonny's last words to Jack Rackham as he was led out to the gallows were, apparently, full of contempt: 'Had you fought like a man, you need not hang like a dog.'

The most likely outcome for Anne was that her wealthy father ransomed her and married her off. The most popular rumour about such a marriage being to a Virginian with whom she had at least eight children and lived to the ripe old age of eighty. If this was her fate, I wonder if she ever told her children of what she had once been and done in her youth? Did she ever lust after the sea and the excitement, or was she relieved to lead a quiet life that was preferable to no life? Or is it possible this end to the adventure could have been fabricated, the women's roles glamorised and sensationalised, to amuse the newspaper readers of the day?

There is no record, beyond Johnson's book, of Anne and Mary fighting to survive while the men caroused below deck. It is just as possible that Anne was abed with Jack in their Great Cabin, while Mary played cards or dice with her crewmates gathered around a charcoal brazier beneath the star-studded night sky. They were taken by surprise, that seems a genuine account, but perhaps the end was far more mundane and less exciting?

Maybe Anne was relieved to be rid of it all. Maybe she settled quietly into the role of wife and mother, firmly on land with not a single glimpse of the sea to stir memories of days that, beyond the excitement of adventure, were not quite what she had been expecting that day when she stole a ship from Nassau harbour with Captain Jack Rackham?

Or maybe, for the rest of her life, she grieved over that last fight when the man who had been her lover had let her down, and failed to fight for their life of freedom together?

16

# Their Last Fight

In my opinion *The Only Life That Mattered* by former sailor and rigger – now author – James L. Nelson is the best novel about Jack, Anne and Mary. (Warning it has explicit adult scenes.)

Excerpt: *The Only Life That Mattered* by James L. Nelson

Mary released Anne's hand, jerked a pistol from her belt. The sloop, this enemy, hit their ship with an impact that jarred the *Pretty Anne* and made the women stagger.

'Bastards!' Mary screamed, and she fired the gun into the mass of men as they broke over the rail and crashed down onto the deck. She flung the gun away, snatched up two more that hung from ribbons; Anne did the same and they fired, four guns at once, but it did not slow the rush for an instant.

They dropped the guns and pulled their swords, in perfect synchronization. Pistols went off, lead balls plucked at Mary's clothes, she felt the burn of a grazing wound on her leg. Then, together, Mary Read and Anne Bonny charged headlong into the press of men, screaming like demons, sweeping great arcs with their blades, striking their tormentors down as they came; Anne and Mary plunged into the fight.

It was the maddest thing that Mary had ever seen, and she had seen some madness in her day. Faces loomed up around them, men shouting, weapons flashing as she and Anne hacked away, slashing at whatever was before them. Mary could feel the warm, wet blood running under her clothes from a dozen wounds, but the wounds themselves did not hurt and she fought on. Already her throat ached with screaming.

'Watch the scuttles! Watch for the others!' she heard someone shout, and in another circumstance she might have smiled. How could these men guess that she and Anne were all there was, all who were willing to stand the deck and fight?

Arms enveloped her and she put her shoulder into the man's chest and heaved him back, half turned. Anne was surrounded; hands reached up behind her, swords flashed like a school of fish.

'Anne!'

But before Anne could react, before Mary could move to protect her, an arm wrapped around her neck, choking her, hands grabbed on her arms, and suddenly she could not work her sword. More hands snatched at her, and then more, like devils grabbing her up and dragging her down into hell. She felt the weight of the men on her, hands holding her like she was bound with rope. She could not see Anne through the press of men who were falling on her. Fleeting images of faces and hands and shirts and feet, the smell of stale sweat and rum on breath.

'Stand to the scuttles and hatches! Keep a look!' There was that voice again, still convinced that this was a trap, still sure that it could not be only these two women standing in defence of their vessel.

Down, down to the deck, Mary was pressed, first to her knees, then on her side, hands grabbing her everywhere, and she could not move. She had meant to die fighting, but now she realized that she might not.

She cursed, kicked, and twisted, but she could not break free of the hands. She struggled until she had no strength left and then she just stopped and closed her eyes.

'Down below! You lot, down the forward hatch. The rest follow me! Have a care!'

Mary listened with eyes still closed as the boarders prepared to search the vessel for the others. She listened to the sound of the scuttle doors thrown open, of footsteps rushing below. She could hear shouts of surprise, roaring, drunken curses from her own shipmates, harsh orders, the sounds of submission. She heard not one gunshot or clash of steel, not one note of even token resistance.

Up from below, feet on the ladder and on the deck, and someone said, 'They was all bloody below, and drunk as lords. Not a one but these bloody sluts would stand and fight!'

The hands that held her pinned now rolled Mary over on her stomach and pulled her arms behind her. A thin rope cut into her wrists as she was bound and she thought, *Please, oh please, kill me now*, but she knew that it would not be that simple, not that clean and quick.

## 17

# Were Women There in the Golden Age of Piracy?

The answer to that question is, we don't know for sure how many there were. We have only heard of a handful – Anne and Mary being the two most famous because they were captured and had their story made public. A few who eventually turned away from a life at sea made their past known. But how many women remained in secret is unanswerable. One clue that there were more women serving aboard Royal Navy ships can be found in the sea-songs that the men sang. There are surprisingly quite a few about women disguised as men who get found out – see the chapter about shanties.

With men away serving in various wars (or hanged, or jailed, or plain cleared off with someone else), life and trade back at home had to continue. Women took over earning a living by managing shops and businesses, keeping the accounts, trading in mercantile goods, running estates, or inns and alehouses. Keeping commerce going was more important than the male (sometimes female as well) prejudices against the 'fairer sex'.

The same happened during both World Wars in the 20th century. In Britain, it was the women who kept things going, the women who worked in munitions, as mechanics, doing engineering and farming. Even our Queen, Elizabeth II, or Princess Elizabeth as she was then, served during World War II in the Women's Auxiliary Territorial Service, and was known as Second Subaltern Elizabeth Windsor – she trained as a mechanic and military truck driver.

As far as the pirates were concerned, the businesswomen ashore served as brothel-keepers, taverners, pawnbrokers, they bought and sold plundered loot and boarded, fed (and bedded) the men. They even hid them when necessary or acted as doctors, surgeons, and undertakers. The TV series *Black Sails* portrays Eleanor Guthrie (Hannah New) as running a trade post at Nassau, exchanging pirate loot for cash, although the business did not always run smoothly; of course, this is a drama series. But the concept of women in charge of businesses during past centuries is not as far-fetched as it at first may seem.

So what of women serving in the army and Royal Navy? Officially, women were not permitted on Royal Navy ships. But they were there all the same, and not just the wives tagging along with their captain husbands. Few people are aware that there were women below decks aboard Nelson's various ships, as wives, sweethearts and whores. Most captains of non-passenger carrying ships, however, refused to have women aboard, not because of the disruption of 'intimate relations' but because they made a nuisance of themselves – imagine a woman wanting to hang laundry to dry from the rigging and how well that would go down with a salty sea dog.

The reason given, particularly for pirate vessels, not to permit women aboard was that they supposedly brought bad luck. What a shrewd move that was by whatever man dreamt it up. Sailors, whether pirate, privateer or King's or Queen's Man, were a highly superstitious lot. One whiff of anything unlucky – the colour green, whistling on deck – or having a woman aboard – was anathema. It has been suggested the majority of pirates were homosexual and this was why they did not want women aboard, but the number of brothels in proportion to taverns in harbour towns such as Port Royal and Nassau disproves this. The same nonsensical argument has been suggested about why men want to join the army, navy, or keep the local golf club women-free.

There is quite a bit of evidence to show that women did go to sea as pirates, sailors or commanders. Disguise was simple. Few sailors washed, so clothes were rarely removed, breeches and shirts were loose and baggy, easy to conceal female curves, particularly if the woman bound her breasts or had little to conceal in the first place. Fresh-faced youths did not shave, many a lad aboard ship was a few years shy of puberty. Some women fashioned pipes to conceal how they urinated, bleeding was not a setback as many sailors carried venereal diseases and bled in the nether regions. Menstruation would have been irregular – if at all – because of poor nourishment. Hair was worn long anyway, often plaited and tarred. The hard part would have been to adopt male mannerisms such as swearing, the way a man walked, chewed tobacco or smoked a pipe, drank, belched and farted!

Why would a woman wish to play the part of a man and go to sea is even less answerable than how many sea-going women were there. Maybe, for some, it was a choice between the sea or destitution, a way of escaping a violent or unwanted marriage, or to evade punishment – women were hanged for minor crimes just as readily as men were.

It is believed there were possibly about forty women pirates during the Golden Age but that could be a misleading figure. It could have been much higher.

*Some Notable Women in a Man's World at Sea*
Æthelflæd, The Lady of the Mercians, was the eldest daughter of Alfred the Great. After her husband's death in battle against the Danes in 911, she became the military leader of the Mercian Anglo-Saxons and took command of the Mercian fleet against Viking raiders.

Jeanne de Clisson, circa 1300–1359, was a Breton called the Lioness of Brittany. She turned to piracy to avenge the execution of her husband. She attacked only French vessels.

Elise Eskilsdotter, who died circa 1483, was a Norwegian noblewoman. She also became a pirate to avenge the execution of her husband. She menaced the seas outside the city of Bergen.

Lady Mary Killigrew, 1530-1570, was the wife of Sir Henry Killigrew, a former privateer and a Vice-Admiral to Queen Elizabeth I. When Sir Henry was at sea, Mary engaged in piracy, using the servants from her castle in Cornwall as crew, and very probably with the queen's private blessing. Off the coast at Falmouth, she captured a German merchant ship in 1570, and her crew sailed it to Ireland to sell it. Unfortunately, the ship's owner was a close friend of the queen's. Queen Elizabeth ordered Lady Mary's arrest and trial at Launceston assizes. Either the members of court were bribed, or the queen pardoned Lady Mary, because she was set free. Although she abandoned piracy, she continued to receive and sell plunder. There is no record of what percentage of the profits the Queen received – but you can bet she received some.

Lady Elizabeth Killigrew, circa 1570-1582, and her husband, Sir John Killigrew, lived in Pendennis Castle, Falmouth. A Spanish ship, the *Marie*, was blown off course in 1581 and damaged so it took refuge in Falmouth harbour. Lady Elizabeth plundered the ship and sold the loot for profit. She was arrested for piracy and sentenced to death, but Queen Elizabeth I pardoned her. Again, for what percentage of the profit I wonder?

Jacquotte Delahaye, circa 1650-1660, was a Caribbean pirate commonly known as 'Back from the Dead Red' because of her red hair, faking her death and hiding dressed as a man for several years. What a novel or movie that story would make.

Anne Dieu-le-Veut or Marie-Anne / Marianne, circa 1650-1704, was a French pirate based in Mississippi after Tortuga denied access to the Caribbean-based pirates. 'Dieu-Le-Veut' is a nickname meaning

'God wills it', bestowed upon her because she usually got anything she wanted. The pirate Laurens de Graaf killed her husband in 1683 and Anne challenged him to a duel. He refused to fight a woman. She became his common-law wife instead, fighting by his side and sharing command of his ship. Obviously, she was not *that* bothered by her husband's death. Thinking as a novelist about an Agatha Christie-type murder mystery storyline, I wonder if the whole plot was a pre-arranged idea? If they were lovers before the husband's death, she was the real murderess, he protests innocence, no one suspects their collusion or already-established relationship ...

Jeanne Baret, c1740-1807 was a French botanist and possibly the first woman to circumnavigate the world; she was disguised as a man at the time. With a passion for botany, and to accompany her lover, Philibert Commerson, she sailed on *L'Étoile*, commanded by Louis Antoine de Bougainville.

Rachel Wall, was an American. She was born in 1760, in Pennsylvania, to devout Presbyterian parents. She eloped with a fisherman, George Wall. In Boston, Wall deserted her and Rachel turned to domestic service to earn a living. Her husband returned some while later with a substantial amount of plundered treasure, and she joined him in his life of piracy. Their technique was to anchor near a shipping route in a storm. When it had passed, they waited for another ship to appear and cut the boat adrift. Rachel would scream for help and, when rescuers came aboard, they would all be murdered, the saviour's ship ransacked and sunk. Anyone who found remains of the wreck would put it down to the storm. Rachel and her husband took twelve vessels in this manner, killing more than twenty-four sailors and making about $6,000 profit. In 1782, a storm really did take its toll. George and several other pirates were drowned. Rachel was rescued and taken to Boston where, a few years later, after serving as a maid, she was accused of robbing a woman, tried, and found guilty. She confessed to piracy but denied the theft. All the same, she was hanged. What goes around, comes around, as they say.

Hannah Snell, joined the army in 1745, disguised as James Gray, then, as a cook's assistant, joined the navy before becoming a foremast jack. During her nine years at sea, she fought in battles and served with great courage. In 1750, tiring of the sea, she revealed her true identity but, shunned by men and women because of her deception, she had difficulty in finding alternative work. Coming up with a good idea, she produced a pamphlet relating her story and started lecturing on a grand tour, which became an enormous success. She retired on an army pension and was buried at the Chelsea Hospital, an English retirement home for accomplished soldiers.

Mary Lacy, dressed as a man, took the name of William Chandler, and joined the crew of HMS *Sandwich* in 1759. She served as assistant to the ship's carpenter and, in 1763, became a shipwright's apprentice at Portsmouth's dockyard. When her secret identity was suspected, Lacy revealed herself to two male friends who supported her as 'a man-and-a-half to a great many.' After seventeen years of posing as a man, Lacy applied for a pension under her true name and was granted £20 per annum.

Grace O' Malley, (or Gráinne in Irish), circa 1530-1603, is known as The Sea Queen of Connacht, or sometimes even The Pirate Queen. She was Queen of Umaill and chieftain of the O'Malley clan in Western Ireland. On her father's death, she inherited his entire shipping and trading business, the income from which brought her considerable wealth. When her sons and half-brother were captured by Sir Richard Bingham, the English Governor of Connacht, Grace sailed to England to petition Queen Elizabeth I for their release, presenting her request to Elizabeth at Greenwich Palace in 1593. With Irish pride in her own status as an equal, she refused to curtsey to the Queen who, it seemed, was impressed by Grace's confidence because she agreed to the release of the captives in return for Grace's agreement to keep the Spanish out of English waters. Now, why hasn't that story been made into a movie or a novel? All these wonderful plots not yet explored.

## 'To Wives and Sweethearts: May They Never Meet'

Did pirates marry? Jack Rackham and Anne Bonny were partners and lovers, but they were not husband and wife. It is thought that of about 521 recorded pirates only twenty-three had wives; most men sentenced to hang for the crime of piracy requested that their parents be informed and their forgiveness begged, but few wives or children were cited. William Dampier (technically a privateer) married, but he scarcely mentioned his wife in his otherwise prolific journals. Stede Bonnet turned to piracy to escape a nagging wife (maybe a bit extreme?). Henry Morgan and William Kidd were both married. Blackbeard reputedly had several wives at the same time, his last being a sixteen-year old from a well-to-do North Carolina family. It is alleged that on his wedding night, he took her aboard his ship and forced her to prostitute herself with his crew. Nice man. Not.

In England before the Marriage Act of 1753, the Church of England required that Banns had to be read over three consecutive weeks, or a licence obtained. The marriage vows had to be sworn in the parish where one, at least, of the couple legally resided. The requirements were not mandatory, however, and were suitable when most people were born, lived and died within the confines of one village, town or rural area. Once travel, be it for merchant or military reasons, became widespread there was little, legally, to stop a man, especially a sailor or soldier, having several wives in several places with the women none the wiser. The marriage was not regarded as void even if the Banns had not been read, if a licence had not been obtained, or if the ceremony did not take place within the sanctity of a church; the only legal requirement was that the ceremony had to be presided over by an Anglican clergyman. A simple exchange of consent did not suffice; it only served as a legal agreement to marry.

The Act strengthened the legal requirements of Banns, a service within the Church, etc. Anyone under the age of twenty-one required parental or a guardian's permission if a licence was required, but when the Banns were called, the marriage was valid – providing no one forbade it.

The Act did not validate marriages between Jewish or Quaker couples; these faiths were exempt from the law. It also had no jurisdiction over marriages made overseas, or in Scotland, resulting in the famous Gretna Green elopements after the toll road was built in 1770.

Pre-1753, there was nothing, outside the Church, to legitimise a marriage. There was no protection for a 'common-law', or handfasting, marriage – although between the 12th and 17th centuries, the latter was legally binding as an intention to marry. Church courts dealt with marital issues, divorce was rare and difficult to obtain, as Henry VIII discovered. Marriage was mainly about the acquisition of property or wealth, and access to consent for sex. Many a young maid must have thought herself wedded before she was bedded, only to find, nine months later, that she had been well and truly duped by a man who she would never see again because he had sailed away to sea. All of which meant that many a sailor would marry whenever, and as many times, as he wanted without any fear of reprisal – as long as he kept away from certain ports and changed ship regularly.

The myth that a ship's captain could perform a marriage ceremony is just that, a myth. Unless he is also an ordained priest, he cannot legally do so.

Sexual pleasure was another matter entirely. Prostitution was the most common liaison for sailors, 'Wine and women drained their wealth' (Charles Leslie, 1740). The pirates spent most of their money gained from the plunder, they collected in the harbourside brothels and taverns. One man paid a harbour-side doxy 500 pieces of eight just to see her naked. I wonder if he felt he got his money's worth or if he got something extra as a reward?

Several of the 'girls' were convicts escaping a jail sentence. One of the most infamous was Mary Carleton, of Port Royal. She turned up in Jamaica in 1671 convicted of theft and bigamy. Her services proved to be most popular for the two years she was there.

She had initially married a shoemaker, Thomas Stedman, and had two children who did not survive infancy. Moving to Dover, she married a surgeon and, soon after, was arrested for bigamy. Presumably there was no evidence against her as she next turns up in Cologne, where a nobleman was expecting to marry her – but she disappeared with all the gifts and money he had presented her with. Returning to London in 1663, she pretended to be the orphan German Princess Van Wolway, using this alias to marry John Carleton, the brother-in-law of a tavern landlord. An anonymous letter exposed her fraud soon after the wedding.

Again she was arrested and tried in that same year, charged with masquerading as royalty and marrying under a false name. She, in turn, claimed her husband had also pretended to be a lord in an effort to secure liberty from an unwanted marriage and thus avoid scandal. Mary was acquitted.

She wrote her own account of the affair, *The Case of Madam Mary Carleton*, and acting in a play about the same subject, gained many admirers, one of whom she married. Needless to say, she soon disappeared with the gifts he had lavished upon her. She then claimed to be a rich heiress running away from an unwanted suitor, going so far as to arrange letters to be sent to prove the validity of her claim. When one of the letters was intercepted and read by her landlady, it claimed Mary's brother had died and she was now entitled to his entire fortune.

Through the next ten years, she extracted money by similar methods, using false identities and claims. After she was arrested for stealing a silver tankard, she was sentenced to penal transportation and found herself in Jamaica, where prostitution was her only means of survival.

Two years later, she returned to London, pretending to be a wealthy plantation heiress. She married again and, yes, you've guessed it, she stole all her new husband's money and disappeared.

In 1672, she was arrested again when someone recognised her and she was tried on 16th January 1673, at the Old Bailey, where due to her return to England from a sentence of penal servitude without permission or completing her sentence, she was hanged on 22nd January 1673. She led a life of crime that did not pay; she should have stayed with the pirates in Jamaica.

18

# Governing the Ungovernable: Woodes Rogers and Alexander Spotswood

*Woodes Rogers*

Although not a pirate, Woodes Rogers was acclaimed as a successful privateer. He served as a merchant sailor, circumnavigated the world, went on to amass a fortune in treasure for the British Crown and Government, became Governor of the Bahamas and, almost single-handedly, put an end to piracy in the Caribbean. For doing all that, he received very little official reward and, as with many a hero, his achievement was not especially noted or appreciated at the time.

Born circa 1679, his childhood was spent in Poole, in Dorset. The eldest son of a successful shipping family, with his father holding shares in the ownership of several ships connected to the Newfoundland fishing fleet, Rogers would have been familiar with the sea, ships and everything nautical.

The family moved to Bristol sometime after 1690, with Rogers finding himself apprenticed to John Yeamans, a Bristol mariner, completing his apprenticeship in 1704. Taking such an apprenticeship would have been a route for him to become a freeman, and therefore a citizen with full voting rights for the city and a member of the Bristol Maritime Society. Soon after, he married Sarah Whetstone, the daughter of Rear Admiral Whetstone, and in 1706, during his mid-twenties, when his father died, Rogers took over the family business. Between then and 1708, Sarah gave birth to a son and two daughters with Rogers' nautical career taking off also in 1708, when he led an expedition to the Pacific, privateering against the French and Spanish. With the births of three children so close together, I wonder if Mrs Rogers was quite pleased to see the back of her husband for a while?

It is possible that his desire to 'have at' the French and Spanish was purely personal. Early in 1708, his slave-trade ship *Whetstone Galley* was captured by the French, which caused him heavy financial loss and damaged his pride. The resulting expedition consisted of two ships, *Duke* and *Duchess*, both heavily armed and capable of taking on the Spanish. He was to return to England in 1711 with both ships intact. On board one of them was Andrew Selkirk, who had been marooned on an island off the coast of Chile.

With a circumnavigation of the world under his belt, most of his men alive and enough profit to double the investment of his sponsors, even after the Crown had taken its share, Rogers should have been satisfied. That said, he had lost a brother in one of the sea battles, he himself was badly wounded and disfigured when a bullet tore into his jaw and another entered his heel. The profit was not of much benefit because the rest of the crew demanded their share, which they had not received, so they successfully sued him, as did the East India Company with whom he'd had a disagreement. Within a year of his return, Sarah gave birth to another son. Regrettably, the infant died, the marriage disintegrated and he became bankrupt. The book he wrote, however, *A Cruising Voyage Round the World*, recounting his experience and the rescue of Selkirk, sold well.

The expedition had not all been plain sailing. He spent an entire month in Ireland before they had properly set out, recruiting a new crew after forty or so of the original one had deserted. He had to put down a mutiny after some of the crew rebelled against his orders not to attack a Swedish vessel. The ringleader was flogged and sent home, clapped in irons, aboard another ship.

The voyage itself encountered many of the hazards sailors at this time faced, notably bad weather and extreme cold in the southern latitudes near Cape Horn. Despite the unusual step of provisioning with limes to ward off scurvy, seven men had died of the disease by the time they reached the Pacific. His navigator, William Dampier, had sailed in the area before and knew some of the islands – hence their arrival at Juan Fernandez Island and the goatskin-clad Selkirk's rescue. Soon after, they captured a number of vessels, plundering them of all they carried. Then they attacked the town of Guayaquil, in Ecuador, without much success. Six men died of disease. With disillusionment setting in, fortune turned when they captured the Spanish ship *Nuestra Señora de la Encarnación y Desengaño*.

They sailed to Dutch-held Batavia, in modern Indonesia, where surgery was undertaken to remove a musket ball from the roof of Rogers' mouth. He returned to England as a hero, not that his fame paid off the debts his family had accrued in his absence.

To recoup his financial losses, another expedition seemed the ideal choice, this time against a rising menace that was hitting the mercantile sea trade hard. He decided to do something about the rising nuisance of pirates. (This is somewhat ironic given that although, technically a privateer, to the French and Spanish he was little more than a pirate himself!)

He set off in 1713 with the intention of purchasing slaves from Africa, but his other aim was to see for himself the pirate haven on Madagascar where looted plunder was freely traded and pirates could take their ease in safety. His aim was to either reform the scoundrels or destroy them.

He achieved the success of persuading many of the Madagascar pirates to sign a plea to Queen Anne to grant them amnesty – quite a few had 'gone native' and given up piracy for the good life ashore, anyway. All well and good, but by the time he got back to London in 1715, the queen was dead, George of Hanover had taken her place on the throne, and the East India Company was unwilling to accept his petition from the ex-pirates.

Rogers abandoned his attempt to reform Madagascar and turned his attention to the ungoverned New Providence Island in the Bahamas instead. Nassau had become a safe haven for anything up to 2,000 pirates and escapees from Spanish-held colonies, all of whom disrupted trade profits. He offered to clean up the town, make it a healthy place to trade and rid the seas of marauding pirates, while taking a hefty share of the profits for himself as a reward.

A Royal proclamation was issued in January 1718, offering a pardon for all pirate-related offences. Those who accepted the King's Pardon by September 1718 would receive clemency. Rogers was appointed Captain General and Governor in Chief of the Bahamas by George I on 6th January 1718. But Rogers did not set sail immediately. Spending several months to prepare a fleet of seven ships to hold 100 soldiers and 130 colonists, he added supplies which, as well as ammunition and food, included religious pamphlets that he intended to distribute, believing the fear of God would help his reformation of the ungodly. (One wonders if he took into account that most pirates could not read?) He finally weighed anchor on 22nd April 1718, accompanied by three Royal Navy ships as his official escort.

His fleet arrived at Nassau on 22nd July that year and immediately engaged with the notorious pirate, Charles Vane, who attempted to ram the navy vessels with a fireship. Although he didn't succeed, Vane and his crew escaped unharmed to sea.

After offering amnesty to all who remained on the island, Rogers set about rebuilding and repairing the fortifications. Within a month, Vane had threatened to join with Edward Teach, also known as Blackbeard, with the intention of retaking Nassau. The Spanish were also eyeing Nassau. Disease was rife and it took the lives of more than 100 of Rogers' followers, and two of the three Royal Navy ships left for New York, with the third one setting sail in September. With Vane and Teach on the rampage, and no Royal Navy backup, Rogers declared martial law, redoubled efforts to complete Nassau's defences and sent ex-pirate Benjamin Hornigold out to deal with the troublemakers. Hornigold failed in his main mission but returned with a captured ship, ten pirates and several dead criminals. Nine of the prisoners were convicted; eight were hanged three days later, the ninth being reprieved for being of good birth. In late December, some of the Nassau residents attempted a coup but failed. Rogers had the dissenters flogged then released.

With Rogers successfully curbing piracy, many of the more notorious Sea Wolves, such as Howell Davies, soon avoided Nassau; others, such as Jack Rackham, tired of the amnesty and went back to sea.

In 1719, war broke out again between England and Spain, Rogers learnt about it in mid-March. Knowing that Spain would attack, he frantically attempted to finish the repairs to the defences, purchasing supplies in hope of being repaid by the expedition's investors.

He was right, the Spanish sent an invasion fleet in May, but at the last moment redirected their attention to Pensacola, which had been captured by the French (on this occasion, Britain's ally). Rogers now had breathing space to finish his fortification of New Providence.

The Spanish tried again in February 1720, landing troops on Paradise Island (known then as Hog Island), which gave shelter to Nassau's harbour. They had left it too late, however, Rogers was now fully organised and his troops successfully drove off the invaders. Soon afterwards, the war was over and peace settled, at least for a short while. Teach was dead, and Vane never returned. It was not the end of Roger's problems though.

He was in debt again because he had overstretched his finances to complete the defences and with no repayments forthcoming from his backers, or the British Government, he fell into poor health. He went to Charlestown, South Carolina; presumably because there were good physicians there. However, his time there was not as he had planned it would be because he fell into a squabble, resulting in a duel in which he was wounded. Hoping to sort out his financial worries, he returned to London. When he arrived in June 1721, he discovered a new governor of the Bahamas had been appointed and his company had been liquidated. As a consequence, he ended up in a debtors' prison. His backers eventually played fair, however, and paid up what they owed him, although not before Rogers became 'perplexed with the melancholy prospect of affairs'.

Things were to get better again in 1723 with the publication of Johnson's *A General History of the Robberies and Murders of the Most Notorious Pyrates*. Rogers had provided the author, whose identity to this day remains unknown, with vast amounts of information. As soon as the book was published, it became an almost overnight bestseller in Britain and the Colonies, bringing Rogers back into public attention. The sudden new status as a national hero gave him the opportunity to petition the King, in 1726, for financial compensation, which was granted, with a pension, and in 1728, the new King, George II, reappointed Rogers as governor of Nassau.

His second term of office saw no threats of invasion. But there was another problem to solve: tax. The Bahamas Assembly, put in place during Rogers' absence, objected to a proposed tax to raise money to continue to ensure the standard of New Providence's defences. Rogers dissolved the Assembly, but the political arguing exhausted him physically and mentally.

Once again, in the spring of 1731, he went to South Carolina for the benefit of his health, returning to Nassau that July. He died there, aged about fifty-three, on 15th July 1732. He was a man who should have received far more credit for his achievements – both then and now. But his phrase of 'Piracy expelled, commerce restored' remained as the Bahamas motto until independence in 1973.

## Alexander Spotswood

Across the sea in Williamsburg, Virginia, another governor, Alexander Spotswood, was also attempting to deal with the problem of Pirates. He had a slightly different approach to Woodes Rogers: hang 'em or shoot 'em.

Born in Tangier, Morocco, in 1676, Spotswood was one of the first British governors to explore and understand the significance and value of the Western Frontier of what would, in the next century, become the United States of America. He served as an ensign in the Earl of Bath's Foot Regiment and was promoted to lieutenant colonel in 1703. Later that year, he became quartermaster-general in the Duke of Marlborough's army. Spotswood was wounded at the Battle of Blenheim in 1704, served during the War of the Spanish Succession and then was appointed Lieutenant Governor of Virginia in 1710. Once *in situ* he sent a troop of Royal Marines to North Carolina to assist with putting down a rebellion, and passed a Tobacco Act in 1713 to ensure a certain standard for export, thus eliminating the poorer quality 'trash' tobacco, which was bringing the trade into disrepute. He established the Virginia Company to promote trade with the American Indians and advised on the building of forts and stockades along the frontier.

In 1716, he organised and took part in an expedition along the Rappahannock River, going over the Blue Ridge Mountains into the Shenandoah Valley. This was the furthest west that an Englishman had been at that date. He called the expedition The Knights of the Golden Horseshoe. He founded several colonies and established various industries, including a pig-iron works and was responsible for initiating what was probably the first purpose-built foundry in the Colonies. Added to all that, he oversaw a treaty between the settlers and the Iroquois and Catawba peoples who agreed to remain to the west of the Blue Ridge Mountains and north of the Potomac.

A previous Governor, Edward Nott, had initiated the construction of the Governor's Palace in Williamsburg, the new capital of Virginia, with building started in 1706. (Edward Nott, incidentally, was the ancestor of Sir John Nott, the Conservative Secretary of State during the Falklands War.)

The lavish brick-built building was to be of a splendid grand design consisting of two storeys with sash windows, a cellar, vault, kitchens and stables. When Spotswood arrived, the grand house was still incomplete because money to fund the considerable expenses had run out. He pushed for the work to be finished, and added outbuildings and a four-foot wall around the gardens. The impressive octagonal entrance hall, finished in 1711, had a black-and-white tiled floor and a formidable display of weaponry adorning the beautiful timbered walls. The house was not fully completed, however, until 1718. Governor Spotswood took up residence in 1716. The term 'Palace' had been applied in 1714 – but not as a compliment. Several of the hierarchy of Williamsburg disapproved of Spotswood, his ideas, and the huge financial cost of building that was deemed an unnecessary luxury. 'Palace', was intended as an insult, which obviously backfired as this beautiful Georgian house has lived up to its regal name ever since.

When his term of office ended, Spotswood returned to London in 1724 or 1725. He married Anne Butler Brayne on 11th March at St Marylebone Parish Church. They were to produce four children, John (1725 – 6th May 1756), Anne Catherine (1728 – c.1802), Dorothea (c.1729–23rd September 1773) and Robert (c. 1732–1758).

Yearning for the Colonies, he took his wife to Virginia where, in 1730, he was offered a ten-year term as Deputy Postmaster General for North America. While serving in this capacity, in 1737, he employed a man called Benjamin Franklin as the postmaster for Philadelphia – as we now know, Franklin was destined to achieve greater things.

Next Spotswood was appointed as Brigadier General in the British Army, but he was not to see any military action because he became ill and died on 7th June 1740, at Annapolis, in Maryland. The location of his grave is unknown.

For the pirates, however, none of his achievements, or disagreements with the Williamsburg officials, meant a thing. To the pirates he was known as the man responsible for the demise of Edward Teach, Blackbeard.

In 1718, having had enough of these seafaring marauders disrupting valuable imports and exports along the Chesapeake, Spotswood decided to do something about it. In particular, he was outraged that Governor Eden of North Carolina was openly welcoming pirates' trade for his own benefit, and providing a safe haven for Edward Teach. Spotswood resolved to put an end to the blatant flouting of the law by sending two sloops to do something about the situation. They found Teach anchored in the shallows off Ocracoke Island, and set about completing their appointed mission ...

19

# Meeting the Fictional Woodes Rogers

Governor Woodes Rogers, as you would expect, bobs up in various fictional situations, including the TV drama series *Black Sails*. For the *Sea Witch Voyages* he appears several times in Jesamiah Acorne's adventures, but here is the first time the two characters meet. I had to imagine a voice behind what we know of the man, and how my protagonist would react when meeting him. For the continuity of story, I also tweaked history slightly by altering the date of when Woodes Rogers and William Dampier were in Africa.

Excerpt: *Sea Witch* by Helen Hollick

*The pirate ship, Mermaid, has dropped anchor in Cape Town harbour and Jesamiah has gone ashore. He rescues a young girl from an altercation with an irate horse rider and marches her back to her guardian, not realising that he has met her before – she was on the* Christina Giselle, *an East Indiaman that the Mermaid has recently attacked ...*

Cape Town, 1716

Jesamiah found Captain Woodes Rogers to be a stout man, full of self-importance and liking the sound of his own voice. Unsightly scarring marked what was left of the upper part of his left jaw.

'Pistol ball shot it away,' Rogers explained, offering his hand and seeing Jesamiah's gaze stray to the scarred damage. 'Can't go capturing the Dons' ships without expecting some form of retaliation, eh lad?' He slapped Jesamiah heartily on the shoulder, ushering him down an unlit corridor towards the private saloon of the tavern.

On behalf of the girl's guardian, Rogers thanked Jesamiah repeatedly. 'The dear lady has been frantic with worry about the lass these past two hours – ye'll join m'party for a glass of wine?'

Jesamiah preferred the taste of rum or brandy, but flattered at being invited, did not refuse.

'I thank you again sir, for your kindness with the young miss,' Rogers enthused as he waved Jesamiah ahead of him. He lowered his voice, although even then he had a tone that could carry a quarter of a mile. 'Child's been here five weeks, but has already caused no end of disruption. Needs a good thrashing if you ask me. Comes from Cornwall. Rough lot, those Cornish. Like the Welsh, untameable.' He shrugged. 'Her guardian is a wonderful woman, for all she is of the servile class.' Impatient, he gestured for his guest to open the door, go through. In the sudden light of a room full of sunshine, Jesamiah realised Rogers' foot was swathed in bandaging.

'Another misfortune,' the captain explained as he hobbled into the room. 'Shot through the heel. Blasted thing has played me up the entire voyage, these two years or so. The girl's guardian, Mistress Pendeen, bless her, knows a thing or two about poulticing, almost has it to rights now. Damned good woman.' He gestured a large bosom with his hands. 'Shame I have a wife, eh?' He laughed. 'Come, let me introduce ye. William, we have a saviour of errant young ladies among us! Sir, meet my friend and navigator, William Dampier.'

'Er, Acorne,' Jesamiah said, politely bowing, unexpectedly flustered. 'Jesamiah Acorne, with an 'e', at your service, sir.' He could not believe his fortune; here he was making the acquaintance of the great William Dampier himself!

A third man, tall and thin with a grey beard and a head of thick, white hair, was rising from a chair. Rogers introduced him also. 'Alexander Selkirk. Found him marooned some several hundred miles west of Chile. Been there over four years, had ye not, Selkirk?'

Jesamiah did not know whether to gape in admiration or guffaw out loud. Were these men serious? If it were not for the credentials he could merit to Dampier, the conversation would have seemed nothing more than a mother's telling of a fabulous bedtime tale. Marooned for four years? How had the man survived?

Seating himself, Rogers, oblivious to Jesamiah's amusement, forged on. 'My good friend, Defoe, back in England, so his prattling letters mention, cannot wait to meet Selkirk. He intends to write his experiences down as an adventure story. Says he'll call it *Robinson Crusoe* to protect the innocent involved in the tale. Absurd eh? Ha, ha!' He had a habit of laughing at his own poor jests.

Selkirk had the manners to blush. 'Nothing to tell. I had a falling out with the captain and demanded to be put ashore for m'own safety and sanity. Hadn't bargained on another ship not coming by the sooner.'

'Now my book,' Rogers interrupted, 'I shall call *A Cruising Voyage Round the World: first to the South Seas, thence to the East Indies and homeward by the Cape of Good Hope*. What think you of that? A title to stir the vitals, eh?'

Politely, Jesamiah agreed. What was it the harbourmaster had said? '*I wish to God he'd stay his mouth, and clear off back to England.*' With that, too, Jesamiah found himself agreeing. He so wanted to talk to the quiet and polite Dampier, but Rogers was not the sort to heave to in a following wind. Nothing was going to stop him from bending a new ear to his account of heroic privateering.

'It is interesting to hear you talk so freely of your commission,' Jesamiah said at one point, while Rogers was issuing a refill of wine. 'There are more than a few who insist privateering has much in common with piracy.'

Rogers spluttered indignation. 'Good God man, pirates are the dregs of this Earth! Rogues the lot of 'em. I took only ships at war with my country, and every last gold and silver piece shall go back to m'sponsors.' He cleared his throat and brushed at the stains he had splashed over his embroidered waistcoat. 'Of course, I shall receive my share of the profits. I carry about two million on board, ye know.'

'I would not let any self-respecting pirate hear you boast that fact too often,' Jesamiah said quietly, with a deceptively charming smile.

'They do not scare me, son. Let 'em come! Let 'em try at me! I'd wipe my arse with them, as easy as pissing.'

'Even so...'

'The difference between a pirate and a privateer, my boy, is that of a matter of honour. The former has no idea of the meaning of the word.'

Jesamiah was beginning to weary of Roger's arrogance. 'What is the British government to do with all these privateers who carry the excuse of a Letter of Marque, such as yourself, when this current skirmish with Spain is over? As it soon shall be. It is only a matter of time for a treaty of peace to be signed. What do the politicians expect the privateers to do then? Shuffle off home to sit with their feet in the hearth, smoking pipes of heavily taxed tobacco? Or go on The Account?'

'Pirates?' Rogers repeated. 'Swabs, the lot of them. Washed up, drunken swabs. I have no concern for pirates; they hold no threat for me.'

Jesamiah was tempted to prove this blustering idiot wrong by suggesting to the crew that they board one of those ships sitting idle in the harbour and strip it of everything of worth. Ah, Rogers was right, no pirate would think of attacking him. Pirates tended to pick on the weak, the stragglers, the undefended merchantmen. Those ships in the harbour? Too many guns and experienced gunners.

'Nevertheless,' William Dampier suggested after a silence, 'Pirates do roam these African waters, and they are a threat. The *Christina Giselle* was attacked, was she not?'

Rogers barked a derisive guffaw. 'Attacked, aye, but the cowards came off worse, no match for her superiority. That's it with pirates, y'see, no guts.'

To hide his expression, Jesamiah sipped at the wine, a nasty feeling sinking heavily into the pit of his stomach. He wished he had asked for rum now. He felt his throat run dry, the colour fade from his face. 'The *Christina Giselle*?' he asked, hoping they did not hear the unnatural croak that came out.

Rogers answered in his gruff, no-nonsense manner. 'Dutch East Indiaman put in here at Cape Town a few weeks past. Had a brush with a bunch of scoundrels. Soon sent them packing. That's where my good lady with her poultices and bandages came from. The Captain, good fellow, well mannered, can't remember his name, recommended her. Passenger on board, making her way here with her ward, bit of a rough child. Always up to something, little madam. You know her of course, you trudged her back to quarters did ye not? Has eyes that follow ye – gives me the shivers frankly. Let me at a pirate over a precocious young wench, any day eh? Ha, ha!'

Jesamiah's skin crawled. He *knew* he had seen her before! He swallowed down the wine, suddenly finding it unpalatably sweet and sickly. He thought perhaps it might be prudent to get back to the *Mermaid*. And wondered how practical it would be to round up the crew.

Hell's bits! If the little brat opened her mouth to sing …

The 'little brat' keeps quiet of course, and on their next meeting, some good while later, Jesamiah realises he has met the love of his life – but that is another part of the story.

20

# Pleasure and Leisure

Life aboard a pirate ship was not all daredevil chasing about after victims to plunder. Nor was it all drinking and wenching, although the latter possibly filled several hours when the opportunity arose. There must have been long hours – days, weeks, even months, at sea with little to do. The ships of the early 1700s were not large. Blackbeard's *Queen Anne's Revenge* was only about 103 feet in length, which is just a little more than the length of three London Routemaster red buses. The days of luxury cruise ships with en-suite cabins, bars, swimming pools, theatres, restaurants, shops and perambulatory promenade decks more than mile long from bow, round the ship and back to the bow, were far from envisioned.

The effort of sailing a ship took up a lot of time: sails had to be constantly tended, not just altered to meet the fancy of the wind but mended and patched using sailmaker's palms (which are leather patches for protecting the hands) needles, and pickers – a tool to make small holes in the tough canvas. Frayed rope and cordage had to be mended – spliced. Wooden ships had to be kept watertight using oakum, made out of old bits of rope mixed with rags and fibres, which were then coated in pitch and rammed between the timber joints or between the deck planks with a caulking iron. The decks needed daily scraping or 'holystoning', and the hull and keel needed regular careening to clear away barnacles and Teredo worm, which damaged the woodwork and slowed the ship down.

Ironically, unlike the pirates who could use any convenient flat beach and shallow water, the Royal Navy had to careen in regulation ports, Port Royal, for instance. This left the Navy at a distinct disadvantage and resulted in the pirates, who took care of their ships, being faster and more difficult to pursue.

In times of peace, the majority of sailors, whether merchant or navy seamen, were volunteers. When yet another war loomed, particularly at the end of the 18th century when war with Napoleon Bonaparte's France broke out, bigger and better ships were being built, often requiring more than 800 men aboard to sail them and man the guns. It was not easy to fill a crew to capacity. Convicts were given the choice of whether to go to gaol or accept the King's Shilling in either the army or navy, but still there were not enough men.

This is where the Pressed Men came in – men kidnapped by the press-gangs were unfortunates who were forced aboard ship, although fiction and movies make more of this than there was in practice. Men who did not know how to sail were not much use. British law decreed that press-gangs could only take seafarers or rivermen if they were between eighteen and fifty-five years old, but when ships were short-handed and Old Boney was thought to be on his way to England by sea, landsmen were also taken. There is no record of pirates being pressed into service, but then the Royal Navy ships were not large or men-hungry in the opening years of the 1700s.

Night was the best time to take men, either when they were asleep or drunk. Many a poor soul found himself groggy (yes the word comes from the watered rum that was known as grog) aboard a strange ship with naught to call his own, save what he stood up in.

As Roy and Lesley Adkins point out in their excellent book, *Jack Tar*: 'British freedom, much celebrated in songs like *Rule, Britannia,* was defended in times of war by a navy totally dependent on conscripting the lower classes into what many regarded as legalised slavery.' These pressed men might have to serve the King for many years, and in too many cases, were never to be seen again by loved ones or family.

The numbers of press-ganged men cannot be sufficiently established because once aboard, with their names entered in the ship's register, they were indistinguishable from volunteers. Many were exempt from pressing, but they had to prove they were foreign, an apprentice, or a debtor. Maybe it paid to be a bankrupt, after all?

Usually, these unfortunate men were pressed into work on Men O'War ships from harbour ports where sailors and seamen abounded.

Pirates also acquired forced labour – their victims. After a Prize had been plundered and stripped of everything of value, any surviving crew were invited to become a pirate or be killed. Surgeons, carpenters and navigators did not have a choice. They were hauled aboard and forced into service.

A sailor's life required stamina and strength. Rope and sails were heavy, especially when wet, and when the wind was blowing a gale. Pumps to keep the lower part of the ship free from water seepage, especially after a storm or a battle, often needed to be manned for hours on end – hard, backbreaking work, as was weighing anchor, even with the use of a capstan. Other jobs would be as the cook, surgeon, carpenter, master gunner, boatswain, quartermaster – all with their understudy mates: bosun's mate, surgeon's mate, carpenter's mate ... The names used for officers such as captain, lieutenant, admiral etc., derive from the Norman-French language, while the common sailor's status is Anglo-Saxon, a class distinction arising after 1066 and the Norman Conquest of England.

Once the essential tasks of actually sailing and caring for the ship were completed, what else was there for a pirate to do? It would not have been a life of luxury, nor even comfort. Below deck was a dark, damp, world. The prevailing stench would be of a musty dampness, of stagnant bilgewater, body odour, and human and animal waste if livestock was kept aboard. Men rarely washed – fresh water was a precious commodity, although the occasional dousing in seawater might have been the order of the week, or month. The living and working areas, both one and the same, were desperately cramped, especially aboard a pirate ship where anything from sixty to 160 men could be aboard, depending on the size of the vessel, and the nature of the captain's appetite for giving Chase. The food was rancid, mouldy, or full of maggots and weevils. Rats gnawed at everything. Literally everything, except metal.

So why volunteer for such a life? The lure of possibly making a fortune and male companionship, perhaps? Life ashore was no bed of roses. Unless you were rich, most of the same harsh and foul conditions existed for everyone.

Whatever was needed – food, clothing, weapons or replacement parts for the ship itself – was obtained because the pirates stole, without guilt, from their victims. Then there was always the rum. It is likely that most pirates, in fact most people, be they army, navy or lower class civilian, were rarely sober. Water was not safe to drink so ale was preferred, and a tot or two during the day of something stronger such as rum or gin, helped get through from sunrise to sunset. Glass bottles have been found at the site of shipwrecks from the Golden Age of Piracy that contained wine, sherry, gin, rum and brandy, as well as earthenware jugs of beer and ale. Leather tankards to hold the liquor were known as 'black jacks' because they were coated in tar to make them watertight.

Everyone, men and women, knew the rules of various gambling games. Board games, cards and dice were popular, although most Articles of Agreement – the Pirate Code, forbade gambling for money so stones or sticks were used, much as 'chips' are used in casinos today, and that could, when land was reached, be redeemed as coin once the men were paid.

Board games, such as draughts (the Americans call it checkers), chess, backgammon and goose were the favourites. Made of simply painted wood, the board would be stored as two or four sections in a canvas or linen drawstring bag, with the playing pieces, which were carved from wood, bone, walrus ivory or shell. Backgammon is one of the oldest board games, and was very similar to today's game, while goose was one of the first games to be made and sold in a printed format. Players would roll dice to move their playing pieces and chase each other around the board with the first to land on the last square being declared the winner. Chess was the same as today, often with elaborately carved chessmen; the better the quality the playing pieces and boards, the higher up the social ladder was the owner. The common foremast jacks would only possess very simple, crude sets.

Cards were easier to store and carry about, with various decks easy to obtain and printed at low cost, although the well off could afford hand-painted sets. There were fifty-two cards in a deck, but no jokers and no number or letter in the corners. Each card was also much narrower and longer than modern ones, and usually made of rag-paper with the images varying, especially on the better-produced, fancier decks. The Puritans, during and after the English Civil War in the 17th century banned cards, calling them 'the Devil's picture book', although they banned most games, dancing and entertainments as well, so cards were not singled out. The fact that the rules of all these games – and songs and dance steps – were not forgotten somewhat shows that the majority of people continued these entertainments in the privacy of their own homes.

The card game whist, which seems to be of English origin, was closely followed in popularity by cribbage with a five-card deal being used instead of today's six.

Games using dice, however, were the favourite pastime, especially aboard ship. Hazard was the most popular, a forerunner of the American game, craps. The dice themselves were traditionally made of bone and fairly small, about the size of the little fingernail, with numbered spots being arranged as they are now. Often, though, pistol balls were flattened into cubes and used as dice. You can imagine a man who had survived being shot cherishing his lucky die, a musket or pistol ball that had been removed from a wound to his body or limbs.

Ball games were out of the question on a ship; 'creckitt', billiards, English football (played with an inflated animal stomach or bladder) and early forms of tennis would have been impossible – forget retrieving the ball! Bowls using the smaller cannonballs was perhaps a possibility while at anchor in a calm-weather harbour.

Racing, however, was always a good entertainment. Sailor against sailor would be easy to organise with a set track around the deck, or fastest up and down the masts, but betting on anything from the fastest moving weevil to training the chickens, kept aboard for their eggs, all had their possibilities as races. If it moved it could run, if it could run it could race, and if it could race it could be wagered upon.

Clay pipes were smoked, but mostly tobacco was chewed because of the ever-present risk of fire. Smoking below deck was not permitted. Singing and dancing – the well-known shanties and sailor's hornpipe as example, were popular. Carving and whittling were often good ways to spend spare time, using wood or walrus ivory.

Another way to spend an enjoyable evening was to hold a mock trial with men taking the parts of jailer, lawyer, judge and juror – and hangman. With amusement and, no doubt, great gusto, the make-believe accused was arrested, tried and mock-hanged for his spurious fictional crime. I guess we do something similar today given our interest in murder-mystery TV dramas and the docu-dramas about real-life crime. I wonder if those mock-hangings ever went wrong?

Tattooing was as much in vogue then as it is now. The art has been around for many centuries stemming from various cultures, countries and religions. It is thought that the word comes from the Tahitian 'to mark', appearing in print in Captain Cook's account of his first lengthy voyage in 1769. The tattoos themselves could be mere decorative patterns, or designed to ward off evil or bring good luck, they could be keepsakes and memory-markers, or to show a religious faith or even carry a secret message. Several English Royals had tattoos, as did Sir Winston Churchill's mother, Lady Randolph Churchill – she had a snake on her wrist. During the Roman period early Christians often had a crucifix, the Chi Rho symbol, or a fish tattooed to show their faith. The 'Iceman', a 5,000 year-old body discovered in the mountains between Italy and Austria boasted sixty-one carbon-ink tattoos on his well-preserved frozen skin, which included groups of simple dots and lines on his back, straight lines a little above his kidneys and ankles, and a cross inside one knee. Maoris in New Zealand had a form of tattooing known as *Tā moko*, created by using chisels (ouch!). In the late 18th century many of the Maoris were murdered to supply a growing macabre European trade of collecting their tattooed heads.

In 1691, William Dampier brought a heavily tattooed man from New Guinea back to England from one of his several voyages around the globe. He made quite a bit of money displaying him to the public.

Sailors have decorated themselves with tattoos from as early as the 16th century – the claim that they only appeared after Captain Cook's voyages is fanciful, they were around long before then – it is only the word, *tattoo*, that dates from Cook's time. Sailors would tattoo each other, using gunpowder mixed with urine for ink and any needle that came to hand. It is not known how many seamen subsequently died from blood poisoning! Gunpowder, it was believed, had the power of ensuring a long life; stemming, maybe, from the notion that to shoot your opponent first, either with musket, pistol or cannon, meant you were more likely to stay alive. Men, navy, merchant and pirate, often had tattoos to remember loved ones back home; wives, sweethearts, mothers. The red heart with an arrow piercing it is nothing new.

To bring luck for voyages, to mark momentous occasions, or as the equivalent of 'war paint', sailors had lurid patterns on the face, forearms and chest that could look frightening to an opponent. Sailors were highly superstitious so their tattoos reflected their desire for a protective talisman. Pigs and roosters were favourite images as it was believed that because these animals could not swim the image would save a man from drowning, (although that is an old wives' tale: pigs can swim.)

Various images had different significance although these were not necessarily used as early as the 1700s. Dragon tattoos, for instance, denoted a sailor had sailed the China seas, but trade and commerce was not opened up to this part of the world until the latter half of the 18th century, so these tattoos would not have been found amongst the Caribbean pirates.

'*Hold*' and '*fast*' on the knuckles of both hands were believed to help the bearer keep a tighter grip on the rigging.

A *swallow* represented a certain distance sailed, usually 5,000 nautical miles, but also indicated a safe return home, which could either mean the home port, or safe to God because birds were thought to carry souls to Heaven. A dagger piercing a swallow was to commemorate a fallen comrade.

An *anchor* indicated a sailor had crossed the Atlantic. It could also indicate steadfast loyalty.

A *turtle* or *Neptune's trident* was to show the equator had been crossed.

A *harpoon* indicated the bearer was a member of a fishing or whaling fleet.

*Rope* tattooed around the wrist showed the man was, or had been, a deckhand.

*Crossed anchors* marked between the index finger and thumb indicated a boatswain or bosun's mate.

*The Compass Rose*, or Nautical Star represented the North Star used for navigation purposes and served to remind the wearer of the way back to his home port.

*A ship under full sail* showed the man had sailed around Cape Horn.

*Women*, often naked – well, they are self-explanatory.

*Mermaids*, half fish, half women (again usually naked,) were believed to lure men to a watery grave with their exquisite singing, so presumably the tattoos were to ward off the mermaids.

Singing was not for entertainment but served to help keep time during various tasks – hauling in the anchor for instance. These sea shanties, or chanties, helped maintain a steady rhythm for hand, eye and foot co-ordination, although the practice of shanty singing was not permitted aboard Royal Navy vessels. Dancing was limited because of the small deck space. The Hornpipe became the most popular and famous dance. Thought to have been associated with the sea around the early 16th century, it required a small area and no partner. Samuel Pepys mentions the Hornpipe in his diary, naming it the 'Jig of the Ship', while Captain Cook ordered his crew to dance the Hornpipe on a regular basis to remain in good health, although you would have thought that the hours of hard, strenuous work would have been enough to have seen to that.

Ashore, the entertainment was mainly drinking and having sex. For pirates their ill-gotten gain would be spent almost immediately in the taverns and brothels. According to *The Secret History of Georgian London*, by Dan Cruickshank, one out of every five women worked, in one form or another, as a prostitute. As early as 1751 there were laws banning the keeping of brothels, not that the law stopped the trade. Homosexuality was illegal; nevertheless, there were male sex-workers – mollies, or molly-boys, but there is very little written evidence about their lives beyond the many court records of the poor unfortunates who were hanged for being gay or having performed homosexual acts.

21

# The Chicken Race

Excerpt: *Sea Witch* by Helen Hollick:

The noise on deck was so loud it could have roused the dead, what with the cheering and shouting and the squawking of flustered chickens. Hen racing was a favoured pastime, although Finch, the galley-cook and Jesamiah's self-appointed personal steward, grumbled that making them run up and down the deck tainted the eggs and addled the yolks.

Jesamiah had his bet – five black pebbles – on the hen with one white feather in her tail. He did not permit gambling for money on board, it led too easily into vicious fights. Her opponent, the fat one with short legs, reminded him of Mistress Jenna Pendeen. Perhaps it was the way she stood, head cocked to one side her beady eyes staring at him disapprovingly, or the width of her broad backside? Aside, young Jasper had been diligently training White Flash these last few days. She had a good chance of winning.

Two lines of sand marked the start and finish on the deck, the track between covering five yards. This was the final race, the two best contenders left from a series of exciting heats. The loser faced the threat of becoming the prime ingredient in tomorrow's stew. Jesamiah stroked the soft feathers along White Flash's back, crooning to her as he held her beneath his arm.

'Now then, m'beauty, you know what you have to do. Look, there's our Jasper with your reward.' He held her up showing her the lad at the far end of the track, Jasper's tin mug held provocatively in his hand.

'You ready?' Rue asked. He lifted his hand, paused, chopped downward, and the two hens were set off with a hefty shove forwards. The crew, spread each side, roared encouragement.

Jasper rattled his mug, shouting. '*Chuck, chuck, chuck!*'

'Go girl!' Jesamiah yelled clapping his hands, itching to give her a prodding kick up her feathered arse.

As a race it was not exactly exhilarating. Both chickens strutted for about two feet then stopped to put their heads on one side and then peck at insects crawling on the wooden planking. White Flash's opposition even turning around to amble back towards the start – against the rules to touch the runners once they were released!

Then White Flash heard the rattle of Jasper's mug; she hitched her wings like a little fat lady lifting her skirts and scurried at a waddling comical run towards him, her bright black eyes fixed on the glint of the tin and the sound it made. She was across the line and Jasper tipped out the contents for her to gobble as a mixture of dismal groans from the losers and the exultant cheers of winners leapt towards the Caribbean sky. Some of the winners hurled their hats into the air and then cried out in dismay as an unexpected gust of wind took the lot of them overboard. The two sails on the fore and main mast, the one a-back with the wind full on its face, and the other counter-balancing to hold *Sea Witch* hove to, flapped, cracking, as the gust rippled through the canvas.

Jesamiah patted Jasper's shoulder well pleased. Grinned as the lad confessed his secret.

'I've been collectin' the weevils from the food barrels – trainin' her to recognise the sound they make rattlin' around in the mug 'ere!'

Addendum: There truly was a pirate crew who celebrated something by tossing their hats in the air, and the wind took them all overboard. It was later recorded by a captured Prize that the pirates gave Chase, boarded – and took nothing but the hats off the heads of the defeated crew.

22

# The Not So Private Privateer: William Dampier, and a College Founded on Pirate Loot

Williamsburg, Virginia. William and Mary College: a respectable place of learning, except – would you believe – it was built with money from pirates' plunder!

When privateering was still being funded by King and Government, a group of men – who were unsure whether Catholic James, brother of Protestant Charles II, was going to be a poor king (he was) – decided to go off and seek their fortune, although they knew next-to-nothing about sailing. They didn't bother getting an official Letter of Marque either, but these were minor details when you were young and up for a Grand Adventure.

They purchased the *Revenge*, hired its previous owner, Captain John Cooke, and sailed off to the Caribbean in search of fame, fortune and a ship's surgeon. They found Dr Lionel Wafer (also spelled Dela Wafer) in Panama. He had been with Cooke's pirate fleet in 1679, and with him, they found John Hingson, who was also welcomed aboard *Revenge*. These two knew of another potential colleague, William Dampier, who in April 1683 was keeping out of the way after some illicit pirate shenanigans in Elizabeth City, Virginia, (which in 1706, became known as Hampton).

Dampier was an experienced sailor, and a remarkable man: four years before this enterprise he had circumnavigated the world – a feat he was to achieve three times. He was the first Englishman to explore what later turned out to be Australia, and his drawings and notes that he made on the Galapagos Islands inspired another naturalist a century later: Charles Darwin.

William was born in Somerset sometime before 5th September 1651, recorded as the day he was baptised. He received a solid education at King's School, Bruton, then sailed as a merchant seaman to Newfoundland and Java before joining the Royal Navy in 1673. Falling ill, however, Dampier returned to England to recuperate. With his health restored, and in desperate need of money and employment, he hired himself out for indentured service managing a Jamaican plantation, and then logging in Mexico. That was not working out very well so he joined buccaneer Bartholomew Sharp, raiding in the Spanish Main, leading to his first circumnavigation voyage when the crew attacked Spanish ships in the Pacific and settlements in Peru before returning to the Caribbean, with William heading for Virginia.

The *Revenge* sailed on 23rd August, heading for Africa and an upgrade of the ship. They found a suitable Danish vessel at anchor in the Sierra Leone River, and with a certain amount of subterfuge involving a card game with the ship as the stake, they renamed their new prize *Bachelor's Delight* (sometimes spelt *Batchelor's Delight*) and set sail for the Pacific Ocean via Cape Horn. Spanish treasure mined from the South American interior beckoned – the only way to take it home to Spain was by merchant ship to Panama, and then by galleon to Spain. Few ships or crews were experienced enough to sail around the Horn, so the Spanish assumed their nice little earner was a safe gamble. They reckoned without Cooke, Dampier and the rest of the *Bachelor's Delight* crew. For several years, they happily plundered their way from Chile to California, hiding from the enraged Spanish between the numerous Pacific Islands – including the Galapagos. It was Dampier who drew the first charts of the islands and gave them their English names. The men were the first Europeans to see what became known as Easter Island – not rediscovered until 1772. They did not sail alone but collected buccaneers and ships as they went along, at one point of the adventure amassing a fleet of ten vessels.

Cooke died of illness in 1684, off the coast of Costa Rica, and was replaced by the elected captain, Edward Davis. The fleet was supposed to attack the Spanish, but their French allies failed to give the agreed support to *Bachelors Delight*. As a result, it suffered heavy damage with several of the crew being killed. There was to be no more trusting the French.

Thoroughly annoyed by the cheek of these Englishmen, the Spanish gave chase, and the *Bachelor's Delight* fled westward from

Chile. The Spanish, tiring of the game, gave up – but not knowing this, the English crew kept going. They were the first Westerners to see the east coast of New Zealand, although they named it Davis Island after their captain. Realising their pursuers had gone, they returned towards South America, taking a more southerly course as a precaution.

In March 1686, Dampier transferred to Captain Charles Swan's *Cygnet* as navigator. They sailed west across the Pacific on a voyage that became Damper's second circumnavigation. Swan was abandoned on a beach in the Philippines, and in 1688 Dampier and another crew member were marooned in the Nicobar Islands between India and Malaysia – although prior to this in January of that year Dampier'd had the chance to observe the fauna and flora and geographic terrain of Australia's north coast. Unperturbed by the prospect of being marooned, they made a dugout canoe and sailed, in great hardship, until rescued near Sumatra by a merchant ship heading for England.

I must make it clear at this point that this chapter is not fiction. It happened. (I did say that Dampier was a remarkable man.)

Returning to England in 1691, rounding the Cape of Good Hope, Dampier was deep in poverty but he had his precious journals intact, and his tattooed slave, Prince Jeoly, whom he exhibited for profit in London.

Meanwhile, the remaining men aboard *Bachelor's Delight* had also decided to call it a day. Catholic James Stuart was gone, in his place William and Mary, a far better option, or so the crew believed. They shared out a good bit of the accumulated treasure, but buried some of it, just in case, on the north coast of Cocos Island, 300 miles from Costa Rica, rounded the Horn in late 1687, and decided to split up because it would be a little suspicious if they all arrived home in England together. (Keep in mind they had not been carrying a Letter of Marque so were, most definitely, pirates.) Some went to Jamaica, some to the Bahamas, some to South Carolina. The remainder took the ship to sell her in Philadelphia. They were then to stay in the Colonies for a few years and return to England man by man.

Unfortunately, one of them, Davis, who had gone to Virginia with a few of the men, blabbed. He let on that between them, they had a combined fortune – the equivalent of several million pounds sterling in today's money. They were arrested and spent three years in Jamestown's gaol. Eventually they were sent to London for trial in 1690, their confiscated loot safe aboard a different vessel. Reaching London they were freed on bail, but still had to face trial, which eventually took place in 1692.

Dampier, while making money from displaying his tattooed slave, was having his book *A New Voyage Round the World* made ready for publication. That came about in 1697 and it became an immediate sensation, including at the Admiralty in Greenwich.

In 1699, Dampier was offered the command of the warship HMS *Roebuck* to explore the east coast of the Dutch-named New Holland – now known as Australia. The expedition was a partial success, with Dampier achieving his aim of making many notes and charting the currents and wind patterns of the southern oceans. But the ship was in poor condition and eventually foundered at Ascension Island, in February 1701. Many of Dampier's papers were lost in the wreck but as many were salvaged and although he and the crew were marooned for more than five weeks, they were rescued by an East Indiamen and returned to England in the summer of 1701. (The *Roebuck* was located in Clarence Bay, Ascension Island, by an Australian team of divers, in 2001.)

Dampier's records of the expedition were published as *A Voyage to New Holland* in 1703, but he was court-martialled on his return to London on a charge of cruelty. On the outward voyage, he had removed Lieutenant George Fisher from office and had him jailed in Brazil. Managing to get back to England, Fisher had complained to the Admiralty about his unacceptable treatment. Dampier was deemed guilty, dismissed from the Navy and had his pay for the voyage confiscated. You can't help but wonder if it was a put-up job to save making payment, can you?

Privateering had broken out again in 1701 with the War of the Spanish Succession. On 11th September 1703, Dampier sailed from Ireland as commander of the *St George*, with a 120 men as crew, and accompanied by the *Cinque Ports* crewed by sixty-three men. Rounding a stormy Cape Horn, and while refilling their water supply in February 1704 at the Juan Fernández Islands off the Chile coast, they spotted a French merchantman. The subsequent seven-hour battle failed. They had more success with capturing several Spanish ships near the Peruvian coast, although they did not relieve these Prizes of all their plunder as Dampier decided to attack the town of Santa Maria on the Gulf of Panama where, supposedly, a grand haul of Spanish treasure was stock-piled. They attacked, but the town was so heavily defended Dampier ordered a withdrawal. Consequently, in May 1704, the *Cinque Ports* and *St George* parted company.

One of the officers, Alexander Selkirk complained about the seaworthiness of the *Cinque Ports* and demanded to be set ashore. He was right about the ship: she sank. He was to be marooned for several years, however.

Dampier now decided to attack the main object of the voyage, the Manila treasure galleon, the *Nuestra Señora del Rosario*. Caught unprepared, she did not run out her guns. But Dampier and the officers wasted so much time in debating the most effective way to attack that the Spanish got their act together and inflicted such ferocious damage on the *St George* the whole idea had to be abandoned and that was the end of the expedition. Many of the crew transferred to other ships and Dampier had to abandon the cannon and the worm-damaged ship off the coast of Peru, where he and the remaining crew were thrown into prison, as pirates, by their supposed allies the Dutch. Later released, but without a ship, Dampier made his slow way back to England, reaching there at the end of 1707.

He was a brilliant navigator, naturalist and explorer but a lousy commander and even worse pirate.

Another chance to redeem himself came in 1708 when he went aboard a privateer, *Duke*, as Sailing Master. With *Duchess*, commanded by Woodes Rogers, he was part of a voyage once again to sail to the Pacific with the intention of harassing the Spanish. The trip was highly successful, amassing a total of just under £148,000 – something like a Lottery Rollover win today: nearly £21 million. Much of this was taken from the *Nuestra Señora de la Encarnación y Desengaño* in December 1709.

In January 1710, the *Duke* and *Duchess* crossed the Pacific, remaining at the Cape of Good Hope for more than three months awaiting a suitable convoy escort. The ships finally dropped anchor in the Thames on 14th October 1711.

Here the story ends. Dampier did not live long enough to receive any of his share of the wealth from Woodes Rogers' expedition. He died early in 1715 in poverty, leaving debts of £677 17s 1d, although the reason for his death and the exact date is unknown. He was buried in an unmarked pauper's grave, the whereabouts of which is also unknown.

A sad end to a most remarkable man.

But what about that crew from the *Bachelor's Delight*? At the end of the trial in 1692, the judge told the accused men that they were guilty of piracy. Fortunately for them, the prosecution had made a right mess of things so they were offered 'a plea bargain' – in other words, a hefty ransom. They would see their freedom if they accepted a deal, which amounted to a pardon in exchange for the loot. As the (alleged) pirates had been arrested in Virginia, and a delegation from there had recently petitioned the Crown for a college to be built, King William and Queen Mary decided the confiscated money was to partially fund it. William and Mary College was founded in 1693. It was built of brick, supposedly to a design by Sir Christopher Wren, at the village of Middle Plantation, situated six miles from Jamestown. It was the second permanent college built in English America. (The accolade of being the first is claimed by Harvard University, which was founded in 1636 as 'the oldest institution of higher education in the United States'.)

Middle Plantation was enlarged six years later to become the new capital of Virginia, and was renamed Williamsburg after King William. The college itself was redesigned by amateur architect, Governor Francis Nicholson after fire destroyed the original building in 1705. He also designed Williamsburg's street plan, the Capitol building and the Governor's Palace.

Without pirates – without Dampier – would Virginia have had such a prestigious building? Would Darwin have had the inspiration to travel to the Galapagos Islands and there explore his theory of evolution? James Cook would not have had Dampier's extensive contribution of charts for tides, current and winds across all the oceans. Jonathan Swift included Dampier in his novel *Gulliver's Travels*. Dampier's mention of breadfruits led to the ill-fated voyage of the *Bounty*. One of Dampier's crew,

Simon Hatley, reputedly shot an albatross off Cape Horn, an incident that inspired Samuel Taylor Coleridge to write his epic poem, *The Rime of the Ancient Mariner*. All that because of William Dampier.

Dampier published the following books:

*A New Voyage Round the World* (1697)
*Voyages and Descriptions* (1699)
*A Voyage to New Holland* (1703)
*A Supplement of the Voyage Round the World; A Discourse of Winds; The Campeachy Voyages* (1705)
*A Continuation of a Voyage to New Holland* (1709)

To Dampier falls the acolade of using various words in print for the first time: *barbecue, avocado, chopsticks* and *sub-species* to name but a few of the eighty or so words cited in the Oxford English Dictionary. Several places in Australia are named after him and in 2015, a minor planet was given his name, *14876 Dampier*.

I think he would be most pleased with that last one.

23

# A Matter of Medicine

If you fell through a time-warp connection between the present and the past and found yourself, as in many a good fiction tale, stuck a couple of centuries in the past the first thing you would notice would be the smell. Open sewers and unwashed bodies. The food, while the same sort of meat and vegetables, would taste very different to what we are used to – none of it carried sell-by or use-by dates, for a start! We would become accustomed to the fetid stench, the dirt, the debris. Most of all, we would miss the healthcare that we are used to, even for simple cuts and illnesses. No antiseptics or antibiotics. No over-the-counter painkilling tablets. No spotlessly clean hospitals. Wounds become septic very easily and in the years before penicillin, when gangrene set in and septicaemia followed, amputation of limbs was a first resort, not a last. A skilled surgeon could remove a limb in a matter of minutes, but keep in mind that apart from strong liquor or laudanum, if you were lucky, there was no anaesthetic. False limbs – the familiar pegleg of Long John Silver or the hooked hand for Captain Hook, were commonplace, but whether they were comfortable to wear and use was another matter.

The ship's surgeon was as important as the captain. When pirates attacked a Prize they would force a captured surgeon to join them. The Romans had surgeons aboard their warships, and physicians accompanied knights to Jerusalem. They trailed with the armies through the English Civil War and were as much a part of any Royal Navy crew as any high-ranking officer. There were eighty-five surgeons with the 1588 Spanish Armada. Disease, especially dysentery, typhus and cholera, spread in the close, cramped, dirty conditions below deck. That's not to mention the wounds received during a fight. Cannon fire is not very compatible with flesh and bone. Without a surgeon, the only option was to drink a bottle of rum and wait to die.

Life ashore was not much better. Hospitals barely existed. The first clinic in Britain to dispense medicines to the poor opened in London in 1696, with other dispensaries not appearing until the 1770s. A hospital was opened in 1752 in Philadelphia, with New York following suit in 1771. Guys Hospital, London, opened its doors in 1721 – funded by businessman, Thomas Guy.

The majority of surgeons, doctors and physicians had little to no training, while many of the cures, remedies, pills and potions did as much harm as good. Bloodletting, thought to assist a patient to recover from various ills, could result in as much as half-a-pint of blood being taken. William Harvey published his theory of blood circulation in 1628, but it was to be many years before his thesis gained credence, let alone widespread acceptance.

Diseases and injuries caused by accident, or sustained while fighting, were not the only problems. Lice, fleas and worms all took their toll. Poisoning was common, both from tainted supplies and trying new foods gathered from tropical islands and unfamiliar places. Then there were Acts of God to contend with: the lightning conductor had not yet been invented (Benjamin Franklin came up with the idea for shipping), it was dangerous enough to cling to rigging and yards atop the masts without the fear of being struck by lightning, yet more than a few men tragically died in this way.

Causes of illness were not understood, disease was thought to stem from noxious vapours from unclean rain or the stench of putrefying waste. Germs, bugs and viruses were unknown. So was the need for cleanliness. A surgeon rarely cleaned his knives and saws between amputations, let alone sterilised the blades, or washed his hands. His clothes would be blood-soaked, as would the operating table, which was often nothing more than a plank of wood stretched across two trestles. Sand would be scattered on the deck to soak up the blood and prevent him from slipping.

Sores, cuts and lacerations were not kept clean, there were no antiseptics beyond a thorough dousing with alcohol or scraping a wound until it bled then using saltwater, lemon or lime juice or vinegar to pour into the open wound. No wonder the poor patients (I am tempted to say victims) shrieked in agony.

Not all surgeons were useless at their job, although it is unlikely that the caring, compassionate experienced surgeons were aboard the pirate ships. In 1617 John Woodall published *The Surgeon's Mate*, which was a basic first-aid type manual for shipboard needs. It contained information on ailments and diseases, had lists of useful herbs, what should be in the medicine cabinet, useful instruments, what they were for and how to use them. It listed, as well, instructions for dealing with medical emergencies.

Some popular beliefs seem most odd to us now. Swallowing a spider apparently cured a fever; was that why the Old Woman in the nursery rhyme swallowed a spider to catch a fly? Toothache was caused by worms in the gum, cured by extraction or oil of cloves. Apart from eating spiders, herbal remedies were all that were available: horseradish, mint, rosemary, comfrey, sage, juniper, angelica, willow bark (interestingly, aspirin comes from willow). Absinthe and laudanum were additional extras, if you were lucky.

A surgeon's tools included razors, knives, probes, forceps, cauterising irons, syringes, scissors, needles splints, sponges. Tools for teeth extractions, equipment for drawing blood, saws with varying blades. The surgeon's skill included his ability to prepare the medicines he needed – there was no handy Boots the Chemist in the High Street, although there were apothecary shops where the surgeon would purchase his raw materials. Pills, potions, ointments, liniments and medications all had to be made from scratch. Ground in a mortar with a pestle, mixed together, boiled or steeped. Glycerine, lard or wax were binding agents for pills, ointments could include turpentine, mercury, hemlock or sulphur. It was usually believed that the worse the smell or taste, the stronger and more effective the medication. For medicine that had to be drunk, liquorice, sugar, mint or honey were common flavourings. Almonds, saffron, lemons and various aromatic plants were made into syrups, along with vinegar, sugar or honey. St John's Wort helped clear mucus from the lungs by being plastered over the skin. Lavender, chamomile, lead and quicksilver were useful, as was mustard, cinnamon and ginger. Bark from the cinchona tree was found to be effective against malaria; we now know the bark contains quinine.

Treatment consisted of procedures which horrify us today: bloodletting, blisters – caustic agents applied to the skin with cloths, or clysters which were given rectally. Leeches to draw blood, maggots to remove dead flesh, spiders' webs to heal wounds and remove poison.

In his diary, Samuel Pepys describes in detail the procedure he went through to remove stones from his bladder in 1662, which involved inserting a probe into the urethra. He was lucky to survive the procedure, which often left infection in the urinary tract and severe incontinence due to sphincter damage. Pepys was so proud of the successful operation that he celebrated the anniversary each year.

Medical practice in the 17th and 18th century was based on beliefs about the four humours: blood, phlegm, yellow bile and black bile. Illnesses were thought to arise from an excess of one humour outdoing the other, although these theories were starting to be questioned by the late 1700s.

At sea, accidents happened; falling from the mast, slipping on a wet deck, rope burns, heat exhaustion, sunburn, hypothermia, weeping sores, ulcers, bruises, broken or dislocated bones. How many men had backache and arthritis of the joints caused by the constant damp, and hard work? Hernias were the bane of many a sailor's life. Head injuries were commonplace. Until the importance of fresh citrus fruit was fully realised in the later 1700s, scurvy was the biggest curse apart from diseases such as yellow fever, typhus, and smallpox. Scurvy killed more seamen than any other disease, the number of deaths amounting to something like 2,000,000 between 1492, Columbus' first voyage, and the 1850s. The gums started to rot, the teeth fell out, breath stank, limbs became weak, blue or red marks spotted the skin. Death was inevitable.

For women, the risk of death during or shortly after childbirth was high, one in four died. Contraception was a case of 'pull back' (withdrawal) and as ineffective as it still is today. The few cundums (condoms) in use were made of soft leather, oiled cloth or animal intestines and used to avoid getting disease, not for ensuring unwanted pregnancies. Abortion methods were more likely to kill the mother. Babies born alive were often exposed, abandoned, or sent to baby farms, assuming they lived long enough. The infant mortality rate was also very high. But families were usually large. Sexually transmitted diseases were rampant, with the cures as dangerous as the disease; mercury was used to cure syphilis, for instance. The alternative, not to use such treatment, could mean teeth falling out, soft tissue eaten away, ulcers, abscesses, debility, incontinence, blindness and madness before death finally, mercifully, arrived. Untreated gonorrhoea could affect the blood and lead to death.

Alexandre Exquemelin, who wrote many a pirate tale, was by trade a ship's surgeon. He had an enquiring mind and studied the native population's cures and remedies whenever they made landfall on a distant shore.

But even for him, a bottle of rum was more often than not the best and most efficacious medicine.

24

# The Black Heart of Blackbeard

Blackbeard is one of the best known of all pirates because we have a full account of several of his more outrageous escapades, his somewhat grisly end and a record of the trial and hangings of what remained of his crew at Williamsburg, Virginia.

His real name was Edward Teach or Thatch, and he is believed to have been born around 1680 in or near Bristol, an important and busy port in England's West Country. Some sources state that his mother's name was thought to have been Mary Drummond, but there does not appear to be much evidence for this.

The names 'Thatch' and 'Teach,' are also noted as 'Tache' or 'Thach', the discrepancy caused by the frequent inconsistent spelling of the period. Few people outside the clergy or well-to-do families could read, let alone write, and the written word tended to follow the spoken word, so regional accents played an important part in how spelling was interpreted. If Edward Teach was born and raised in Bristol he would have had a broad Somerset accent, which could have resulted in him pronouncing his name as something like 'T ... aa ... tch'. Alas, there is no official tax or census records for any of his believed names to verify which one is more correct: but then it is highly unlikely that Blackbeard paid taxes or bothered to fill in his census form. He could almost certainly read and write, for he wrote to, and received letters from, the Chief Justice and Secretary of Carolina, Tobias Knight.

Coming from what was possibly a reasonably-placed, if not a well-to-do, family he had some sort of career as a mariner, either as a merchant seaman or serving in the Royal Navy prior to turning to a life of piracy, for he knew his job when it came to sailing a ship. He seems to have been a privateer during the War of Spanish Succession. When the war ended and peace settled, temporarily, between Spain and England (and variations of France, Holland and Portugal supporting one side or the other) Teach ended up at Nassau to take advantage of the New Providence benefits offered to those with a tendency towards piracy. He joined with the crew of Benjamin Hornigold between 1714 and 1716, meeting several of the men who also become notable pirate captains in their own right. Men such as Sam Bellamy, Charles Vane and Jack Rackham. Hornigold gave him command of a sloop in 1717 and together they captured Prizes coming out of Havana, Bermuda and another sailing from Madeira to Charlestown, the latter carrying a cargo of best quality Madeira wine. In September 1717, Teach's crew took the *Betty of Virginia* as a Prize, but all they stole was her cargo of Madeira then scuttled her, sending her to the depths with the rest of her cargo. Maybe the cargo was rotten, or of little mercantile value? Maybe they had developed a taste for Madeira.

Late in September 1717, he met with Stede Bonnet. Bonnet's crew were dissatisfied with his command so, in accordance with the Pirate Code, they voted for a new captain. Teach got the job and took command of *Revenge*. (Did these pirates not have a book of potential ship's names to hand? They had very little imagination for thinking up something different.) The fleet now comprised *Revenge*, Teach's previous sloop, and Hornigold's *Ranger*. In October they plundered *Robert* and *Good Intention*.

Hornigold was sticking to the rules of privateering by only attacking non-British ships but this loyalty was rapidly becoming unpopular with the crews who saw ship after ship sail by laden with rich pickings. So Hornigold was kicked out of office and he retired, taking *Ranger* and one of the sloops to Nassau – where he accepted Woodes Roger's King's Pardon the following year.

Teach was now in full command of the fleet and successfully attacked various ships, bringing terror to the Caribbean and Colonial waters off the coast of the Carolinas and along the Chesapeake Bay sea-lanes. He was not known to be a compassionate man, and his reputation was starting to put fear into anyone who heard the name 'Blackbeard'. It has been suggested his alleged violence towards his various victims may have been exaggerated, a deliberate ploy on his part to instil fear into the crew and passengers of any ship he encountered. There is very little evidence, beyond anecdotal, to confirm or deny his reputation. However, the stories that have been related are more than horrific and I personally believe, despite the speculations of those who regard him as something of a hero, that Edward Teach was not a very nice man.

His appearance alone was enough to make anyone opposing him to use common sense and surrender without a fight. Teach was a tall, stout man, broad shouldered, broad chested. He went into battle with several pistols suspended across his chest, hanging from coloured ribbons. Entwined in his hair and his great black beard (for which he was named) would be several of the fuses used to ignite gunpowder. These would burn slowly and let off a cloud of smoke about his face. With what appear to have been bulging eyes and a cruel grin his victims must have thought that Old Nick himself had come for them.

On 28th November 1717 he acquired his prestigious Prize of a French slaver, *La Concorde*, which he renamed *Queen Anne's Revenge*. The new name, honouring childless Anne of the Royal Stuart line, may have indicated his support of the Jacobite movement and the Stuart cause of attempting to put James Stuart on the throne of England instead of German George of Hanover.

The vessel boasted twenty-two guns and Teach proudly made her his flagship at the head a fleet that still included Stede Bonnet's *Revenge*. Somewhere in the area of the Grenadines Islands, they careened and converted their new vessel, making her sleeker and therefore faster, increasing her guns to a total of forty. It is not known what happened to the slaves aboard *La Concorde*, some may have joined his crew, but in all likelihood they were sold for a handsome profit. Later in the month, back at sea, Teach attacked the *Great Allen*. She was forced towards the shore where she was emptied of crew and cargo then burnt. By now, Teach was in command of more than 150 men divided as crew through three ships. They initiated a spree of seizing ships and looting them before destroying them.

Not only shipping suffered at his hands, he and his fleet attacked and burnt down the town of Guadeloupe. He destroyed most of the vessels harboured, assumed safely, at St Kitts. Following this latter successful raid, Teach and his men passed the winter of 1717-1718 in the Spanish Main, before sailing back to the Carolinas then on to Nassau for a temporary stint ashore, and possibly to trade their stolen goods for food, drink and essentials. Woodes Rogers was on his way with his offer of amnesty, but Teach was not to be lured by the prospect of retiring from piracy and figuratively gave Rogers' expected arrival a two-fingered salute. During that month of March, more crew were invited to join the pirates, one of them being Israel Hands.

By May 1718, Teach was calling himself Commodore and had a large fleet under his jurisdiction, which he used with great effect to blockade the harbour port of Charlestown, South Carolina. During a course of the next week, at least nine vessels either sailing past the harbour or trying to enter it were stripped of cargo.

During the blockade, the Governor's son was kidnapped and held for ransom, which was duly paid without quibble and the boy was returned, although whether he was harmed mentally or physically, or both, is not recorded. Maybe he enjoyed his time among the pirates? Surprisingly, it was not money that Teach demanded but expensive medical supplies, including mercury – the commonly used cure for syphilis. Contemporary records place the value of the medicines he demanded at between £300 and £400. Did Teach have this terrible sexually transmitted disease? It seems very likely that he did, for he was becoming an erratic and unpredictable man, common symptoms of this scourge spread by having sex with prostitutes.

From Charlestown, Teach's flotilla headed north along the Atlantic coast towards Beaufort Inlet, off the coast of North Carolina. Was there now a falling out between thieves? Was Teach's reputation being shown for what it was, or was what happened next nothing more than an accident and sheer bad luck? Was Bonnet perhaps lusting after taking command? Did he want the bigger and better ship, *Queen Anne's Revenge* for himself? Was Teach becoming too much of a lunatic to remain as commander?

We can only speculate why, but *Queen Anne's Revenge* ended up foundering on a sandbank in the shallows off Beaufort Inlet, her damage so great that she was irreparable. The wreck has since been found and many treasures and artefacts brought to the surface – including some of those medical supplies and instruments provided to Teach at Charlestown harbour. Was she deliberately scuppered or was it just bad sailing? Did, perhaps, Edward Teach decide that he would rather destroy her than see her in the hands of Stede Bonnet?

As a consequence of the wreck, Bonnet went off on his own. He was captured by a pirate hunter on 27th September 1718 and tried and hanged in Charlestown.

With his much-reduced fleet and a life of ease beckoning, Teach now decided on an alternative to what was on offer at Nassau. If he was ill, this prospect made sense. Governor Charles Eden of North Carolina had prepared a similar pardon to the one Woodes Rogers was promoting, but to his personal advantage. Eden's proposal had a lucrative twist to it. As with many a corrupt man (or woman) in a position of power, his intention was to make as much money as he could, as easily as possible, from his position of authority. Teach must have thought he could trust the man or manipulate him. The plan was to quietly fence the stolen cargoes through North Carolina, with all parties concerned making a handsome profit.

Teach made himself comfortable on an estate just outside North Carolina's capital, Bathtown. He resided in apparent legal luxury, wooing the townsfolk with stories of adventure and excitement (pirate tales are nothing new). His occasional sailing trips appeared to be quite legal but he was actually accruing plunder, which was secretively sold by Governor Eden and Tobias Knight. Those ships found crippled or destroyed had, so it was said, fallen foul of the weather – or pirates. Teach, on the surface, remained squeaky clean. So much so that he courted a local merchant's young daughter and married her – probably for her dowry and the higher social stratus, and probably without mentioning his several other wives or the possibility that he was infected with syphilis. The tales of his violent behaviour might have been exaggerated but I do not believe they are false. He had, a few months previously, (allegedly) courted another girl who refused him: her betrothed was later found dead, both his hands cut off. On one occasion Blackbeard shut himself with his crew below deck and made them endure the toxic fumes emitted from sulphur used to clear the hold of rats, threatening to shoot the first man who tried to escape. He did shoot Israel Hands, his second-in-command. And that young wife on their wedding night? Teach got bored with her and forced her to prostitute herself with his crew.

As I said, he was not a nice man. Governor Alexander Spotswood of Virginia thought so too.

Spotswood had no jurisdiction over North Carolina, but he did have the governorship of the Chesapeake Bay area. Incensed that pirates were affecting trade and shipping, and that Eden appeared to be every bit as much a pirate as the rest of them, the Governor of Virginia decided to take matters into his own hands. He organised a counter-attack against Blackbeard, under the command of naval Lieutenant Robert Maynard.

The Ocracoke Inlet, offshore of North Carolina, was an ideal place for Teach to lurk. The gusting wind and hidden shallows were suitable for luring ships to their graves, and then looting them and later saying their wrecks were all natural disasters. With no witnesses left alive, who was there to gainsay his statements? Ocracoke was also an ideal place to rendezvous with other like-minded captains. Bring a bottle or two, a few whores and let's party, party, party! Which is precisely what Teach, Vane and Jack Rackham did with their crews for several days in the autumn of 1718. The party eventually broke up (maybe they ran out of booze?) but Teach remained in the Ocracoke area. Big mistake.

Maynard had been given command of fifty-seven Royal Navy men with instructions to finish Blackbeard – one way or another. He sailed from Hampton Roads, Virginia on 11th November 1718, with the sloops *Jane* and *Ranger* (another one!) commissioned temporarily as Royal Navy ships. On the evening of 21st November, Maynard found his prey, Blackbeard's ship, *Adventure*, anchored in an inlet off Ocracoke Island. Maynard thought it best to remain out of sight and wait for the more favourable tide of the early morning. Come daylight, Blackbeard saw the danger, cut his anchor cable and attempted to make a run for it with his crew of nineteen men, 'thirteen white and six negroes' as Maynard's report later testified. Maynard gave chase, but ran aground. *Adventure* was also aground – the tide not yet high enough for any of the vessels to float free.

There followed a robust verbal exchange, most of which, it can be assumed, would today be highly censored for bad language. Teach reportedly damned Maynard to Hell and swore that he would give the insolent pup no quarter. As the tide rose, Maynard made headway but when they came in range, Blackbeard's crew hit the attackers with a tremendous broadside. Midshipman Hyde, in command of HMS *Jane*, died along with six men, with another ten men wounded. *Jane* was badly damaged. In *Ranger* alone, Maynard continued the pursuit, firing on *Adventure* whenever he could, causing damage to her rigging and partially disabling her.

With *Ranger* closing the gap Maynard sent the majority of his men below deck and as the two ships came together Teach fell for the trap and boarded, assuming most of the crew had been lost in that initial broadside. He very quickly realised his error and the fight that ensued was brief but bloody. Small arms were fired and Maynard and Teach grappled each other, their swords clashing, each drawing blood. Then Teach broke Maynard's blade; the Lieutenant drew his pistol and fired. Teach fought on but was now surrounded by Maynard's men and bleeding profusely – still he fought on. He was slashed across the neck and Maynard was preparing to fire another pistol; Teach was down, dead from blood loss. His remaining men abandoned their weapons and surrendered. The casualties of this fight vary in the various reports between eight of Maynard's men and twelve pirates, to eleven of Maynard's and ten pirates. Governor Spotswood tallied the dead as ten pirates and ten King's men.

On examination, Teach's body was found to have suffered five gunshot wounds and about twenty sword slashes. Maynard ordered Blackbeard to be decapitated, with the severed head to be displayed on the bowsprit and the body tossed overboard, where it proceeded to circle around the *Ranger* several times. (Not that fanciful, the tide was coming in, remember? The body would have been swept in and out with the current.)

The legend of Blackbeard's ghost is another matter, however. It is said his decapitated corpse haunts the Ocracoke, searching for his missing head. Sometimes the gruesome body is seen floating in the water, swimming around and around, sometimes a strange light, 'Teach's Light', is seen near the Ocracoke shore nearest to the Pamlico Sound. On such nights, if the wind blows inland, the sound of his feet can be heard, along with his bull's roar of, 'Where be my 'ead?'.

However, back to the facts. While searching the *Adventure*, where the remainder of the pirates were arrested, Maynard found damning evidence against Governor Eden's secretary, Tobias Knight, of receiving stolen goods and a hoard of loot, most of which Maynard dutifully handed over to Governor Spotswood – assuming he and his men would be rewarded with a suitable share, but which they did not get. Maynard retired from the Navy soon afterwards and disappeared. Was this with his own hefty portion of undeclared goods, which he had secretively stashed aside, one cannot help but wonder?

The captured pirates were incarcerated in Williamsburg gaol and tried on 12th March 1719 in the Capitol Building – the Courthouse had not, then, been built. Their time locked up had been uncomfortable and cramped, for winter in Virginia can be cold with deep snow. The gaol is small, cold, and miserable. Meals of watered-down corn mash would have been frugal. If they were lucky, they had mouldy straw to sleep on. I wonder if, when they finally went to the gallows they were relieved to see an end of it all?

Colonial Williamsburg today is a popular tourist attraction with most of its major buildings having been reconstructed as they would have been in the 18th century. A visit is most highly recommended.

Fourteen of the sixteen accused were found guilty and hanged. One of the remaining two was able to prove that he had only been a guest aboard Teach's ship and had been inadvertently caught up in the fighting. The other was Israel Hands, who had been found ashore with a gunshot wound to the knee inflicted by Teach.

Hands testified against Eden's secretary, Tobias Knight, confirming that he had met with Teach on several occasions. Governor Eden protested strongly against Governor Spotswood's action, which had been, technically, illegal. The battle of wits between the two men only ended when Eden died in 1722. Knight, was found to be innocent. I wonder who he bribed, and how much he had paid?

Blackbeard's legacy has survived with his name being synonymous with the evilness of pirates. As a character, he has appeared in films, comics, plays, songs, yet as an actual pirate he was not all that successful, nor was he the cruellest of the pirates. Others outdid him tenfold. So what? It is the stories that matter, and we have the stories of Blackbeard because he met an exciting end and his exploits were recorded in the Williamsburg trial records.

The third *Sea Witch Voyage*, *Bring It Close*, is based around Blackbeard. Ex-pirate Captain Jesamiah Acorne is blackmailed by Governor Spotswood into seeing to Teach's end but he makes it quite plain that he would have no mention of his assistance in Maynard's recorded log. That is why the name Acorne is not mentioned in any of those official documents.

Don't you just love plausible fiction?

25

# Captain Jesamiah Acorne

So who is Jesamiah Acorne? He is a fictional character, he does not, nor ever did exist, but once created in that alternative universe that is the world of story any character becomes alive and real, be he Long John Silver, Captain Hook, Jack Sparrow or Jesamiah Acorne.

Quick to laugh, formidable when angry. That's Jesamiah. Add to that, trouble follows him like a ship's wake.

He was born on December 4th 1693 on a beach in North Devon, England, to Charles Mereno's second wife, Dona Sofia Calderón, a Spanish beauty. Jesamiah had no recollection of his birthplace, grandfather, or even that the house of Tawford Barton at Instow existed. Disagreeing with his father over a small matter of legitimacy and inheritance, Charles sailed away with his wife and baby son, never to return. At least, not openly, and not to see his father or sisters, although along with companion Henry Jennings he regularly participate in a great deal of contraband smuggling during his long voyages away from the Virginia plantation where Jesamiah grew up.

Jesamiah's childhood was not a happy one due to the bullying of his jealous and vindictive elder half-brother, Phillipe. The rare occasions when his father took Jesamiah aboard his ship were bliss because Phillipe had no taste for the sea – Jesamiah was a natural sailor, however.

Charles Mereno and Jesamiah's mother, Dona, both died of fever within a week of each other a few months before Jesamiah's 15th birthday. Charles had given Jesamiah his own small boat, which he called *Acorn*, but now that his vicious actions could go completely unchecked, Phillipe set fire to it. Losing his bottled-up temper, Jesamiah turned on his half-brother, and then fled Virginia. Needing a new name in a hurry he chose Acorne – with an e.

It was now 1708, and the escalation of piracy in the Caribbean. Jesamiah blagged his way aboard a ship at Hampton Roads, Virginia, then jumped ship at their first port of call, Port Royal. He was in search of his father's friend, Captain Malachias Taylor.

Under Malachias's tutelage aboard *Mermaid*, Jesamiah learnt his trade as a sailor – and a pirate – working his way up to quartermaster, second-in-command. When the crew were eventually arrested, Jesamiah escaped gaol, but Taylor was hanged.

A short while prior to this, *Mermaid* had attacked an East Indiaman the *Christina Giselle*, off the coast of South Africa. Aboard, and watching the ensuing fight, which *Mermaid* lost, was a dark-haired girl. Jesamiah was to meet her a few months later in Cape Town, although until a moment of panic triggered his memory he'd had no recollection of her.

She was sixteen-year-old Tiola Oldstagh, who had fled with her companion, Jenna Pendeen, from Cornwall, England, when her mother had murdered Tiola's assumed father for attempting to assault her. Accused of witchcraft Tiola's mother hanged – the irony, Tiola was the one who was the white witch, not her mother.

Created millennia into the past, Tiola's soul had transposed from grandmother to granddaughter through successive generations, her physical identity always the same, her gift of Craft, healing and midwifery, always staying with her. Through the long centuries Jesamiah's male ancestors had occasionally crossed her path, but it was not until after *Mermaid* had attacked the *Christina Giselle* that Tiola and Jesamiah were finally to meet.

A few months later, injured while fleeing pirate hunters in Cape Town, Jesamiah was in trouble again. Tiola rescued him and nursed him back to health. He fell in love – but he had the opportunity of gaining a ship from one of Tiola's admirers. He had to choose; Tiola or the ship, which he was to call *Sea Witch*. What was more binding? Love, or the call of the sea?

Their paths were to separate, but true love always wins and Tiola had to rescue Jesamiah again from the clutch of his foul brother and her other suitor, both of whom had their reasons for seeing Jesamiah dead.

There are other supernatural elements in the tales that Jesamiah is unaware of – Tethys, the spirit of the sea wants his soul for herself; her daughter, Rain, is sent to watch him; he encounters the ghost of his father, and in the fifth Voyage a predatory Night Creature, the Nightm'n, appears on the scene: but no, he is not a vampire. Exactly what he is will not be revealed until a later Voyage.

The *Sea Witch Voyages* are tales of adventure, blending real characters such as Henry Jennings, Calico Jack, William Dampier and Woodes Rogers alongside the fictitious, the Doones of Exmoor's *Lorna Doone*, for instance. They are sailors' yarns, but with an adult content of some bad language and sexual scenes. Jesamiah himself is a blend of Hornblower, Jack Sparrow and Jack Aubrey, all mixed together with Richard Sharpe, James Bond and Indiana Jones.

Throughout the Voyages, the relationship between Jesamiah and Tiola, like all relationships of the heart, whether with real or imaginary peoples, has its ups and downs. Jesamiah finds himself caught in various situations, usually involving beautiful spies, ex-lovers and dastardly villains. He has to find a cargo of lost indigo, gets involved in rebellion on Hispaniola, and smuggling James Stuart – the Pretender Jacobite King – into England.

And he encounters Blackbeard:

Excerpt: *Bring It Close* by Helen Hollick:
1 October 1718

Jesamiah Acorne, four and twenty years old, Captain of the *Sea Witch*, sat with his hands cradled around an almost empty tankard of rum, staring blankly at the drips of candle-wax that had hardened into intricate patterns down the sides of a glass bottle. The candle itself was leaning to one side as if drunk. As drunk as Jesamiah.

For maybe ten seconds he did not notice the two shabby ruffians sit down on the bench opposite him. One of them reached forward and snuffed out the guttering flame, pushed the bottle aside. Jesamiah looked up, stared at him as vacantly as he had been staring at the congealed rivers of wax.

One of the men, the one wearing a battered three-corner felt hat, leant his arms on the table, linking his tar and gunpowder-grimed fingers together. The other, a red-haired man with a beard like a weatherworn, abandoned bird's nest, eased a dagger from the sheath on his belt and began cleaning his split and broken nails with its tip.

'We've been lookin' fer you, Acorne,' the man with the hat said.

'Found me then, ain't yer,' Jesamiah drawled. He dropped his usual educated accent and spoke in the clipped speech of a common foremast jack. He was a good mimic, had a natural talent to pick up languages and tonal cadences. Also knew when to play the simpleton or a gentleman.

He drained his tankard, held it high and whistled for Never-Say-No Nan, a wench built like a Spanish galleon and whose charms kept her as busy as a barber's chair.

She ambled over to Jesamiah, the top half of her partially exposed and extremely ample bosoms wobbling close to his face as she poured more rum.

'What about your friends?' she asked, nodding in their direction.

'Ain't no friends of mine,' Jesamiah answered lifting his tankard to sample the replenished liquor.

The man with the hat jerked his head, indicating she was to be gone. Nan sniffed haughtily and swept away, her laughter drifting behind as another man gained her attention by pinching her broad backside.

'Or to be more accurate, Acorne, Teach 'as been lookin' fer yer.'

Half shrugging, Jesamiah made a fair pretence at nonchalance. 'I ain't exactly been 'iding, Gibbens. I've been openly anchored 'ere in Nassau 'arbour for several weeks.'

Since August in fact, apart from a brief excursion to Hispaniola – which Jesamiah was attempting to set behind him and forget about. Hence the rum.

'Aye, we 'eard as 'ow thee've signed for amnesty and put yer piece into Governor Rogers' 'and,' Gibbens sneered, making an accompanying crude gesture near his crotch.

'Given up piracy?' Red Beard scoffed as he hoiked tobacco spittle on to the floor. 'Gone soft 'ave thee? Barrel run dry, 'as it?' Added with malice, 'Edward Teach weren't interested in fairy-tale government amnesties, nor 'ollow pardons.' He drove his dagger into the wooden table where it quivered as menacing as the man who owned it.

*That's not what I've heard*, Jesamiah thought but said nothing. He had no intention of going anywhere near Edward Teach, better known as Blackbeard, though Black Heart would be as appropriate. Even the scum and miscreants who roamed the seas of the Caribbean in search of easy loot and plunder avoided the brute of a pirate who was Blackbeard.

Aside, Jesamiah was no longer a pirate. As Gibbens had said, he had signed his name in Governor Rogers' leather-bound book and accepted His Majesty King George's royal pardon. Which was why he had nothing better to do than sit here in this tavern drinking rum. Piracy, plundering, pillaging, none of that was for him, not now. Now, Jesamiah Acorne, Captain of the *Sea Witch*, had a woman he was about to marry, a substantial fortune that he could start using if only he knew what to spend it on, and the dubious reputation of becoming a respectable man of leisure.

He was also bored.

26

# No Quarter: Weapons and Fighting Skills

My thanks to Phil Berry, swordsman and Man-at-Arms, for providing his expert guidance regarding fighting skills and the use of a cutlass – the weapon most commonly associated with pirates.

Pirates when boarding a Chase (or in a drunken brawl in a harbourside tavern) would not be following the etiquette rules of gentlemanly swordplay, instead, they would make use of every dirty trick they knew off. Designed for close-quarter fighting, the cutlass had great cutting power and was brutal for close fighting, with the user's hand protected by a basket-style metal hilt, which could also be useful for punching and bludgeoning. The heavy blade was used to great effect against other weapons, especially lighter military-style swords, knocking them aside then cutting and stabbing with the point.

Often with a slight curve, or occasionally straight, with a length of about two feet to twenty-eight inches, the 18th century cutlass proved to be so effective that many naval forces adopted it as a preferred weapon.

A Chase could last from as little as an hour to several days, depending on the skill, and determination, of each party. Most pirates planned to take the Prize with as little effort as possible. While the pirates were at a far range, warning shots from cannon and swivel guns would be used. At close quarters, and once alongside, the order was to make as much noise as possible – all scaremongering tactics. Anything to hand was banged against the gunwales and rail; there would be shouting and chanting, the firing of pistols. Hove to, grappling irons would be swung out, then in a flood of bodies, the rampaging pirate crew would be set loose.

Other weapons ranged from bare fists to eighteen-pound (the weight of the ball, not the gun) cannons. Bigger cannons came later, towards the end of the 1700s.

The shot used could be actual balls or:

Chain shot: two balls linked together, which could loop around a mast, stay or rigging.
Grape shot: small balls held together by a canvas bag that split open when fired, scattering like modern shotgun pellets
Langrage: case shot, which exploded when fired showering out pieces of jagged metal, nails etc, in a wide pattern inflicting maximum damage over a great area.

In addition to the shot itself, splinters flung out by the impact could impart fearful injuries. Pieces of jagged, sharp-ended wood of anything between half an inch to spear-length could do a lot of damage to the soft flesh of a man's body.

### Hand Weapons
Flintlock pistols and muskets: ideal for short range, but limited to just one shot and often not very accurate.

Boarding axe: thirty-five inches in length and with an eleven inch head. All ships carried axes, primarily as a tool, but also as effective weapons. The boarding axe was much lighter and smaller than a woodsman's tree-felling axe, and consisted of a wedge-shape axe head to one side of the haft with a spike on the other. The edge would need to be kept sharp enough to slice through any width of rope with one or a few blows – or through flesh and bone, and have superb cutting and concussive power. Its spike could be used against an opponent to hook down a shield, or to climb the side of a ship. It was not so useful as a defensive weapon, though.

Buckler: a small round shield of about twelve inches diameter. In addition to being a defensive weapon, it was also useful to punch into a face, or to use the edge to smash down onto a sword arm. In conjunction with a cutlass, a buckler could be most effective at warding off retaliatory blows. It was effective also for blocking stabs to vital and vulnerable body areas. When sword and buckler are held together, they can absorb a heavy blow from above – from a boarding axe, for instance. Modern police forces still use the same principal with a small shield and a truncheon.

Boarding Pike: eight feet long, with a ten-inch point. Commonly stored in buckets around the masts, these were deadly when used in a line with the men standing shoulder-to-shoulder. If the sailor you are fighting does not get you, the one at his side probably will. Pikes can be beaten, though. Once past the point, you can deal with the man. The Royal Navy trained sailors to use them, but with pirates lacking the discipline were they as effective in the confines of a crowded deck? Perhaps not. Great thrusting power. Very effective to keep an opponent busy, but vulnerable when an attacker has managed to get past the point.

Grenados: an early form of hand grenade.

Anything else that came to hand: belaying pins, marlin spikes and such.

Until the opposing crews met, all manner of incendiary devices would have been employed to clear the decks but about to go face-to-face and hand-to-hand, single shot flintlock pistols and muskets would be the last resort before the full fight commenced.

Apart from the conventional weapons, feet, knees, fists, heads, elbows came into play. A finger poked into an eye, a shoe scraped down a shin, an elbow jabbed into the stomach, or a knee rammed into the groin was mightily effective. In addition to twisting an ear, nose or genitals. Then, when things got really down and dirty, when a pirate was fighting with all his (or her) concentration, energy and the intention of staying alive, the biggest defensive weapon would be to trust the men fighting alongside, ahead and behind him or her.

27

# A Successful Pirate; Bartholomew Roberts

Bartholomew Roberts initially had no interest in becoming a pirate – but he ended up as the most successful of them all, amassing over 470 Prizes. He did not hang for his crimes but was killed in action against the Royal Navy. He earned the respect of his crew, and when he was elected as captain, he is recorded as declaring that if he had to be a pirate, he would prefer to be the one in charge. His first command was to avenge the murder of his former captain, Howell Davies.

He was the stereotypical sort of pirate captain we all think of: dressed in fine clothes and wearing 18th century 'bling' he would prowl the deck of his ship keeping a sharp eye for his next Prize, which he would take with ease. He had some non-piratical quirks, however. He preferred tea to rum and had a dislike for unruly drunkenness, although there is no evidence that he was a teetotaller. The typical qualities for a pirate were also in abundance; he was intelligent, articulate, competent at navigation, bold and brave. He was also ruthless. While he often did release captives who had surrendered without offering a fight, even presenting them with various riches, he did not take kindly to fools or those who opposed him. He hanged the governor of Martinique as an act of revenge, and burned a ship with eighty slaves aboard because he could not be bothered to waste time unshackling them.

Born as John Roberts in Pembrokeshire, Wales, on the 17th May 1682, his name 'Black Bart' – *Barti Ddu* in Welsh, was not used during his own life. Going to sea at the age of thirteen, there is a record of him in 1718 as mate on a sloop registered in Barbados. By 1719, he was third mate aboard a slaver, *Princess*. Anchored off the Gold Coast of Africa, she was captured by pirates led by Howell Davies – who was also a Welshman. As was often the case, Roberts and many of the *Princess*'s crew were forced to join the pirates. Robert's navigational skills were quickly recognised, and the ability for both men to talk in secret in Welsh soon became an additional advantage. It seems that while Roberts was reluctant to turn pirate, he very soon realised the potential for bettering his previous low wages of £3 per month.

Not long after Roberts had agreed to the idea of becoming a full-fledged pirate, Davies anchored in the harbour off the island of Principe and invited the Governor aboard for a meal. The gesture was accepted with a note to 'come for a drink first'. Davies sent boats to collect his guest, and made his way to the Governor's house to partake of a glass of wine, but his plan of kidnap for ransom had been rumbled. Davies was ambushed and killed. The pirates fled and within six weeks of being captured from the *Princess*, Roberts found himself elected as Captain, probably because of his navigational abilities and outspokenness. Reputedly his acceptance speech was, 'Since I have dipp'd my hands in muddy water, and must be a Pyrate, it is better to be a commander than a common man.'

His first orders were to take the crew of the *Rover* back to Principe to avenge Davies's murder. They landed at night, killing many of the male population and plundered as much of value as they could. Soon after, he took a Dutch ship. And then a British vessel. Then he headed back across the Atlantic, towards Brazil. His skill for planning and proven results sealed the crew's admiration for him and cemented their loyalty. Nine weeks of cruising the Brazilian coast brought no profit but, about to leave for the Caribbean, they came across a Portuguese fleet about to sail for Lisbon. Roberts captured one ship and forced the captain to reveal the richest-laden vessel in the fleet. This turned out to be the *Sagrada Familia*, with a crew of 170 men, forty guns and, after Roberts had captured it, it was revealed to have a fortune in her hold. They spent much of the plunder along the coast of Guiana, then sailed for the River Surinam and captured a sloop, which they commandeered to chase a brigantine, leaving the *Rover* in the care of Walter Kennedy, who they discovered, upon their return a few days later, had cleared off taking ship, crew and looted cargo with him. The stolen sloop was renamed *Fortune*, new Articles were agreed and in early 1720, they sailed back to the Caribbean and teamed up with the French pirate, Montigny la Palisse in command of the *Sea King*.

Fed up with the threat of pirates, the Barbados governor sent two sloops out on patrol. On seeing them, the *Sea King* fled and the *Fortune* was forced to cease engagement after suffering great damage. Roberts lost twenty of his crew. Furious, he had a new flag made depicting himself standing atop two skulls labelled ABH and AMH signifying A Barbadian's Head and A Martiniquian's Head, having vowed vengeance on the population of both places.

Newfoundland was to be the next destination for the *Fortune*, where it took a number of merchant ships as Prizes. On 21st June, Roberts attacked the harbour at Trepassey, where he found twenty-two merchant ships and 150 fishing vessels all abandoned by their panicked crews and leaving the harbour for him to take as his own without encountering any resistance whatsoever. Enraged by this blanket cowardice, Roberts summoned every captain to see him; anyone who failed to turn up would have his ship burnt. He commandeered a brig to replace *Fortune* and fitted her out with sixteen guns. Before he set sail again in June, he set fire to every ship in the harbour. He then took several more French Prizes during July, upgrading his own ship again by taking a captured one that was faster and more superior, fitting her with twenty-six guns and renaming her *Good Fortune*. With her, he and his crew took yet more lucrative Prizes.

They careened in September 1720 at Carriacou Island, and with repairs completed and the ship afloat again, he renamed her *Royal Fortune*, the first of many of his ships to be honoured with this name. They then headed for St. Christopher's Island and with pirate flags flying, beaten drums and trumpets blaring along with a general hullabaloo, they accepted the surrender of every ship at anchor in the harbour.

St Bartholomew Island was their next destination, where the French governor gave permission for them to stay for several weeks, no doubt realising that it was better to be agreeable and have a boatload of pirates spend money in the brothels and taverns than to have his town burnt to the ground. Sensible chap.

October found them off the coast of St Lucia where they took fifteen various ships within three days, (busy lot weren't they?) James Skrme, mate of one of the ships, *Greyhound*, joined Roberts' crew and became captain of a consort ship, *Ranger*.

Coming alongside a ship carrying the Governor of Martinique, Roberts pretended to be a French merchant offering vital information on the whereabouts of a certain Bartholomew Roberts, pirate. Suddenly, he struck his true colours and attacked, boarded, and then hanged the Governor.

The spring of 1721 found sea trade almost at a standstill in the Caribbean because of Roberts, which was a bad thing for trade – but also for Roberts; he had been so successful there was now little left for him to plunder. He switched to raiding shipping off the coast of West Africa instead.

The *Royal Fortune* was leaking so, in April 1721, she was abandoned near the Cape Verde Islands with her captain and crew switching to the *Sea King*, renamed the *Royal Fortune* to keep up with tradition. Off the Guinea coast, they were chased by two French ships but Roberts turned the tables and captured them instead, one being renamed *Ranger* the other *Little Ranger* (at least pirates were consistent).

Roberts spent the summer doing what pirates do best, took his time to careen and repair then in January 1722 sailed into Ouidah where ten of the eleven ships at anchor surrendered. Enraged at the failure of that eleventh ship to give way, some members of Roberts' crew boarded her during the night and set her ablaze.

Their luck was to run out in February.

Taking their ease, with the pirate ships *Royal Fortune* and *Ranger* at anchor, the pirates saw the Royal Navy ship, HMS *Swallow* appear. She veered away from the shore avoiding shoals but the pirates assumed she was a merchant fleeing from danger, so some of them set off in hot pursuit – taking *Ranger*, under the command of James Skyrme. Once far enough out to sea, *Swallow* opened fire killing ten pirates outright with Skyrme losing his leg to a cannonball. Although he refused to leave the deck, *Ranger* was forced to surrender and strike her colours. The surviving crew were arrested.

Returning on the 10th February, *Swallow* was to find the *Royal Fortune* still at anchor. Roberts had captured a ship the previous day and the men were well into their drink, celebrating their success. Initially, there was no alarm for the crew thought the ship on the horizon was the *Ranger* returning, but one of the pirates who had deserted from *Swallow* several months previously, recognised the ship and raised the alarm.

As he always did before entering battle, Roberts dressed himself in his finest, wearing a crimson damask waistcoat and a red ostrich feather in his hat, a diamond encrusted crucifix dangling from a gold chain around his neck, and was armed with his well-honed sword and two brace of pistols. He must have had a dashing appearance as he strode on to the deck of the *Royal Fortune*.

The plan was to sail straight past *Swallow* and make a run for it, but the right course was not achieved and *Swallow* was able to deliver two broadsides. Bartholomew Roberts was killed outright by grapeshot striking his throat. The battle continued for almost two hours, ending with the *Royal Fortune*'s mainmast toppling and crippling her. Only two other men had been killed and 272 men were captured. Of these, sixty-five were black and they were sold as slaves. The rest were transported to Cape Coast Castle where fifty-two were hanged, two were pardoned, another twenty agreed to indentured servitude with the Royal African Company, which amounted to a fate worse than a quick death. Seventeen men were taken to Marshalsea Prison, London, where some had the fortune to be acquitted by pleading that they had been forced into piracy. The rest died, or their fate has not been recorded.

The *Swallow*'s Captain, Chaloner Ogle, was rewarded with a knighthood, the only British naval officer to be specifically so honoured for action against pirates. He also personally profited by pocketing some gold dust from Roberts' quarters, and went on to become an admiral.

Roberts' death marked the end of the Golden Age of Piracy, perhaps because if the invincible could be defeated there was little hope for anyone else. With piracy waning, trade increased. As far as African waters were concerned, shipping was now made relatively safe so more trade could commence. The end of piracy meant the expansion of the slave trade.

Fulfilling his wish to be buried at sea, before they were boarded by the Royal Navy the pirate crew wrapped Roberts' body in a sail, weighed the makeshift shroud with cannonballs and committed him to the deep. His bones lie at the bottom of the ocean.

His death sent repercussions around the pirate world as well as the navies of the world because he was believed to be invincible. Many a sailor had regarded him as something of a hero, and he has the prestigious honour of being mentioned by name in *Treasure Island*.

<br>

28

# Trade, Tobacco and Slavery

Successful trade could only result from producing something to successfully sell, or with which to barter. The vast expanse of land in the New World was seen, to the various governments in Europe, as the ideal potential source to provide a viable economic trade. It was a pity that kings, queens, governments and settlers alike had no right to the land, but the native populations of the Americas, as the continent came to be called, were of no consequence to any of those first white Europeans, be they English, Spanish, French, Dutch or Portuguese. And it was a bit of a nuisance that the source of this enormous potential wealth happened to be several thousand miles away on the far side of a vast ocean. Still, ships were being built bigger and faster, and settlers were eager to emigrate with high hopes of starting a new life. It is fascinating, knowing the size of North America as we do today, to realise that these first settlers had no idea of what they had actually got. With the colonies being established all along the many miles of the eastern seaboard during those first years of the 15th century, it was not until the early 1700s that explorers began to head inward, and not until the 1800s that the vast expanse of the American West opened up to wagon trains and further settlement.

Initially, for those first intrepid adventurers, things did not quite go to plan. The first English settlement of Jamestown in Virginia was not successful. The settlers died of starvation. What a pity they did not take more notice of the natives who fished for lobsters in the Chesapeake waters at Hampton Roads. (It seems ironic that one of today's luxury foods could have been a staple diet of those early settlers, had they but known it.) More settlers arrived, settlements were built and expanded and the trade, after more than a few years, began to boom. At least, until the pirates moved in on the action.

## Tobacco

Sir Walter Raleigh is renowned for introducing tobacco to England in the 16th century during the reign of Elizabeth I, but the Spanish Conquistadors had seen the Aztecs using it well before his 'discovery'. The French ambassador to Portugal, Jean Nicot, introduced tobacco to France. To him goes the honour of giving the plant species its name: *Nicotiana tabacum*.

As early as 1604, King James I had been so repulsed by the disgusting habit of smoking that he produced *A Counterblast to Tobacco*, three years before Jamestown was settled. But come the middle of the century, settlers there cared more for the price of tobacco than for a king's opinion. Virginia primarily owed its development and subsequent wealth to growing and exporting tobacco. The early colonists saw the Native Americans growing it and soon adopted the idea to produce it for sale, not for personal use. Since 1613, until the 21st century, the tobacco industry has provided more income than any other farmed crop.

Smoking – using a clay pipe, not the modern cigarette – was already popular in Europe before Virginia was colonised. John Rolfe, an Englishman, was sent there in 1612 to scout for trade possibilities. He found that tobacco would grow well there and sell with a high profit margin. Throughout Virginia and the Chesapeake area, the potential cash value of tobacco soon became apparent.

In 1613, rather than the strong tobacco native to Virginia, Rolfe grew sweet-scented tobacco (which came to be the most popular Virginia tobacco) from seeds imported from the Caribbean. England was prepared to pay a handsome price for this less harsh tobacco, and the race to plant and harvest it took off with settlers growing it on every available patch of soil. Anyone and everyone whose main occupation was not already growing tobacco, cultivated small areas of land as a hobby farmer.

By 1650, Virginia was able to rely on tobacco as a primary means of currency. Wealth was tallied by an estate owner's tobacco harvest, reckoned in pounds weight of tobacco. Tobacco was used as currency to buy and sell, to pay the vicar to perform a marriage, christening or burial, to pay fines and to pay taxes. Rolfe's original shipment of four hogsheads (wooden barrels) had sold in England at three shillings per pound. In 1680, duty levied at two shillings per hogshead yielded Virginia £3,000, and from 1758 to 1762 around £6,000 per year. Was it any wonder that the pirates found it a good commodity to plunder?

Initially, tobacco was exported direct to England, France, Holland, the Caribbean Islands and South America, with Virginia providing more tax revenue to England than any other colony. To ensure all profit remained in England, in 1651, King Charles II initiated the Navigation Acts that prohibited the export of tobacco except to English ports. But of course, smuggling was rife and trade continued, with sea captains highly skilled at evading both the revenue men and the exportation fees. This skill eventually led to the American Revolution and Independence in 1775.

Tobacco leaves were harvested and cured (dried) by suspending bunches on hanging racks in covered sheds. Once dried, tobacco was sorted and pressed into wooden hogsheads with weights, or a lever and screw, the process repeated until each barrel was tightly packed then sealed to prevent the leaves from rotting or being spoilt by weather or seawater.

Those first hogsheads produced in the mid-1600s weighed something like 500 pounds each. But gradually the size of the barrels increased with the capacity for storing and shipping the tobacco. By the 1800s, a typical weight would be nearer 1,300 pounds, and towards the close of the century, England was importing in excess of 20,000,000 pounds weight of tobacco every year.

Plantation owners shipped their hogsheads to agents in London, Bristol, and Bideford in Devon, and a few other smaller cities, often in exchange not for money but for mercantile goods such as guns and gunpowder, linens and fabrics, wool, wigs, hats, iron including pots, pans, nails, hoes, axes, spades and all manner of tools and equipment. Pewter, earthenware, cutlery and tableware – especially quality silverware – were sought-after. China, furniture, glass, paper, leather and leatherwork such as bridles, saddles and harness. Livestock, books – you name it, they exchanged tobacco for it. This was fine, until the price of tobacco occasionally dropped, or the entire cargo was plundered by pirates. Insurance was not, then, the reliable precaution it is today.

To remain safe, merchant ships sailed to England in convoys. When trade, and therefore the wealthy landowners who sat in Parliament, found their pockets were becoming lighter because of piracy, the Royal Navy was soon expected to provide an escort. This meant merchant ships did not need to take up space with weaponry, thus allowing room for more cargo. The convoys started gathering in the spring with the intention of sailing by late May, unless bad weather delayed the departure until June. The presence of the Navy must have been a bitter blow to the pirates, but there was always other shipping to prey upon – those ships returning with the goods exchanged for the tobacco for instance. Another method was making use of officially appointed corrupt governors at various ports to whom they could sell the garnered plunder. These patrons were wealthy men, and on occasion women, who were able to fund illegal enterprises. A few sponsored vessels and a crew, others controlled the buying and selling alone, or within a syndicate. Whichever way it was done, it was a lucrative business based on pirate plunder.

Governor William Markham of Pennsylvania gave his approval for his daughter to marry James Brown, who had sailed as a pirate. William Kidd was assisted by New York entrepreneur, Robert Livingston, and Blackbeard had a highly successful trade agreement with the governor of North Carolina until another governor who had a higher moral stance, Alexander Spotswood of Virginia, put an end to the illegal alliance in 1718.

And all this flowed from the growing and selling of tobacco.

*Slavery*

Historical fiction novelist, Anna Belfrage, on her informative and interesting blog, www.annabelfrage.wordpress.com, says:

> Let's face it; the first English attempts to set up a successful colony in the New World failed dismally. That first outpost of English culture, Roanoke, mysteriously disappeared. The proud little settlement of Jamestown suffered through starvation and indigenous attacks. In general, people who went to the colonies in search of a better life ended up dead, and for some odd reason this made it difficult to recruit new colonists. Without people to work the land and expand the English dominion, the Colony of Virginia was pretty much doomed, so I suspect the directors of the Virginia Company perked up substantially when someone came up with the bright idea to use indentured servants to populate their land.

It took more than a year to grow a crop of tobacco, it was extremely labour intensive and the trade demanded cheap labour. All these factors eventually resulted in the rise of the African slave trade. In addition to adults, children were exploited for their small, nimble fingers were more adept at picking worms off the leaves, weeding the beds and stringing the harvested tobacco to dry. The hours of toil were long, hot and enforced. The original settlers did not have slaves and until the early 1700s, voluntarily indentured white people were the major part of the workforce, exchanging their labour for an agreed period for a promise of land or financial reward. Many of them never saw either because they died before they reaped the benefit. White convicts formed the rest of the labour-force – at least until Australia was discovered and used as a penal colony.

Indentured service was not as cosy a deal as it sounds – for all its nicety of dressing-up the truth, it was enforced labour, amounting to slavery. The practice of volunteering to work for someone else for almost next to nothing in return was nothing new, but the situation in the embryonic colony of Virginia was slightly different. The 'volunteers' signing their agreed contracts of X number of years labour had to be shipped from England, and someone had to pay the cost of the journey. Landowners swallowed the bill by paying the expenses, but they did not foot that cost for they received anything up to fifty acres as compensation from the government, which was invaluable as tobacco plants ate up the ground, poisoning it after a few years of growth to the extent that nothing would grow there again. (Nicotine, as we are now discovering to our cost, has a lot to answer for!) Add to that little perk for the landowner, the indentured 'servant' with his (or her) signed contract of employment, would need to pay off the debt of travel expenses. The lure for these poor unfortunates was the promise of land at the end of their contracted period. Which was good in theory, the downside being, if they gave up, or died, there was no payment forthcoming. For some reason not too many people were keen on this idea: hard toil for years with the prospect of getting little in return, assuming you survived that long? So another, not so legal, solution was set in placer. Labour was taken by force. Just as the navy would press gang sailors when war ships needed to be manned, unfortunates were snatched off the streets and coerced into putting their X mark beside written words they had no comprehension of. They had no way of getting out of the predicament, especially once they arrived on the other side of the Atlantic. For almost all of that first century of the Colony's existence, just as with Australia, most of Virginia's labour force comprised kidnapped victims, convicts and ne'er-do-wells.

As Anna says in her article 'Indentured Servants – An Alternative to Slavery':

Whether forced or voluntary, the life of an indentured servant was no walk in the park. For a woman, there was the constant risk of being raped – these were societies with a chronic shortage of women – and should she become pregnant her term of service would be extended. The men ended up in the fields, disposable beasts of burden that were often worked until they dropped.

A disobedient (or 'wilful') servant was punished – in some cases so severely as to permanently maim the servant. Trying to run away was a serious offence that could lead to beating so brutal the person in question died, and on top of this the reluctant immigrants had to cope with food shortages and unknown ailments. On average, four out of ten indentured servants died in Virginia during the 17th century. No wonder the colony had problems recruiting them!

The first black slaves were introduced in 1619 and by 1680, there was only a small percentage more – but come the turn of the century, with insufficient labour to produce the tobacco, owning and using slaves was becoming an accepted economic solution. With the first census taken in 1790, just under a quarter of the people living in Virginia were African slaves. Even importing slaves was a risky business, however, for where there was a profit to be made, there too would be the pirates.

Anna Belfrage's *Graham Saga* series of timeslip novels set in the 17th and 20th centuries, although not about pirates, nevertheless encapsulate this period of extreme change to great effect, especially in the second book of the series *Like Chaff in the Wind* where the male protagonist, Matthew Graham, has been kidnapped and enslaved into indentured servitude:

Excerpt: *Like Chaff In The Wind* by Anna Belfrage

Five unbearable days, and on the afternoon of the sixth day he was so tired that he accidentally upended the sled, tipping the load of tobacco plants into the dirt. Jones flew at him.

'Fool! Look at what you've done!'

Matthew got to his feet, an effort involving far too many protesting muscles. His shoulders were permanently on fire, the harness had left broad, bleeding sores on his skin, and no matter how he tried to use his worn shirt as padding, the sores deepened and widened, a constant, flaming pain.

'I'll just load them back.' He bent to pick up an armful. His arms were clumsy with weariness, and it took far too long to reload the sled, with Jones an irate, vociferous spectator. Matthew leaned forward into the straps, bunching his thighs. Dear Lord! He couldn't budge the load, the leather cutting even deeper into his lacerated skin. He tried again, and still the sled wouldn't move. Matthew looked back across his shoulder to find Jones sitting on the sled.

'Go on,' Jones sneered, 'get a move on.'

'You're too heavy,' Matthew said, 'you can walk.'

Jones raised a brow. 'Of course I can. But now I want you to pull.'

Matthew felt his pulse begin to thud. Wafting curtains of red clouded his vision.

'I'm a man, aye? I'll work as you tell me to, but you can move of your own accord, fat though you may be. I won't be your yoked beast, I'm a man.'

There was absolute silence around him, his companions staring at him with a mixture of admiration and exasperation.

29

# Stede Bonnet, The Gentleman Pirate

There is one thing I am curious about: the pronunciation of Captain Bonnet's name. Was he 'Bonnet' as in a lady's hat, or 'Bonnay' with a French-sounding twist to it? I am reminded of the UK TV comedy series *Keeping Up Appearances* with Hyacinth Bucket, who insisted her name, Bucket, was pronounced *Bouquet*. Stede 'Bonnay' has much more of a pirate-macho ring to it that Bonnet, don't you think?

Born on Barbados some time in 1688, Stede was christened on 29th July of that year. He was to become a gentleman, a landowner, and a pirate.

An educated man, he inherited the family's Bridgetown estate when his father died in 1694. He married Mary Allamby in 1709 and the couple produced three sons and a daughter. But the marriage was a failure, apparently because of Mary's constant nagging. To escape her, Bonnet cleared off to sea in 1717 despite not having any experience as a sailor. He held the rank of Major for the island's militia but it does not seem that he saw any action with the commission, it was probably held as a traditional right because he was a landowner.

He had a sloop built, called her *Revenge* (well there's a surprise!) and enlisting seventy men as crew and went off to harass shipping along the notorious pirate hunting grounds in the Chesapeake Bay area, along the coast of Virginia and up towards New York. One cannot help wondering how bad his marital problems were to have taken such drastic action. Although divorce was not easy in the 18th century, you would have thought a man of wealth could have come to some sort of agreement with his wife. What a wonderful novel this disastrous relationship, and its consequences could make!

On his way to Nassau in September 1717, Bonnet ran into trouble with a Spanish man o'war. *Revenge* was damaged and Bonnet injured, with more than half of his crew killed or wounded. He refitted and repaired at Nassau, adding extra guns and recruiting more men – unlike all other pirates he paid his crew a wage, not taking the usual course of splitting the profits.

While at Nassau, he met up with Edward Teach, Blackbeard, and because his injury partially incapacitated him, Bonnet handed temporary captaincy to him. So with Teach in command, they plundered ships along the American east coast until Blackbeard took a French ship, renamed her *Queen Anne's Revenge* and parted company with Bonnet in mid-December.

Continuing on his own in the Western Caribbean, in March 1718 Bonnet's *Revenge* met the merchant ship *Protestant Caesar*, which escaped the pirate attack to the annoyance of what remained of Bonnet's crew. Meeting again with Teach, and tired of Bonnet's incompetency, his crew went over to the *Queen Anne's Revenge*. Deserted, surprised at being abandoned, Bonnet remained as a guest aboard *Revenge*, under the command of Captain Richards, one of Teach's henchmen, to form one of Blackbeard's expanding fleet. They sailed to Topsail Inlet, and *Queen Anne's Revenge*, either by accident or on purpose, ran aground. If on purpose, there was something else going on between the pirates that we do not know about. An argument, a falling-out? Jealousies? Disagreements?

Heading for Bathtown, North Carolina, Bonnet acquired a pardon from North Carolina's governor Charles Eden, and applied for permission to obtain a Letter of Marque for *Revenge*, in order to raid Spanish shipping as a legitimate privateer. When he returned to where *Revenge* had been anchored, he discovered that Blackbeard had taken everything of value and cleared off in *Adventure*, headed for the Ocracoke. Bonnet set off in outraged pursuit, but was not to find the man who had stolen everything from him. It does seem to make it clear that all Teach wanted from Bonnet was his financial input.

Short of supplies, and with the hurricane season upon them, Bonnet had no choice but to return to piracy in order to restock his ship. He changed his name to Captain Thomas, the ship to *Royal James* and resumed the role of a pirate. The choice of the ship's name is an indication that Bonnet was probably a Jacobite, hoping to see James Stuart on the throne of England, not George of Hanover.

Anchored in the estuary of the Cape Fear River to careen and wait out the hurricanes, Bonnet, unfortunately, met with pirate hunter Colonel William Rhett, who was working for South Carolina's governor, Robert Johnson. A bitter fight lasting several hours ensued but the pirates, heavily outnumbered, eventually surrendered. Bonnet and his crew were taken to Charlestown in early October where Bonnet was held prisoner at the more comfortable provost marshal's house. Once again, money talked. On the 24th October Bonnet managed to escape. His renewed freedom lasted for only a short while, however, for he was recaptured and went to trial on the 10th November, charged with acts of piracy against the *Fortune* and the *Francis* because these were the only two vessels whose commanders were available to testify in person. Bonnet claimed innocence, arguing that he had been a mere passenger and that he had urged the crew to desist from plundering these ships. He even claimed that he had been asleep during one raid which, given his inefficiency as a captain, is more than likely true.

Sentenced to hang, he wrote a letter to Governor Eden pleading for clemency but Eden obviously did not want to get involved in anything that could draw attention to his own dishonesty and he abandoned Bonnet. The London papers reported that the execution was delayed seven times because of Bonnet's unstable mind, but eventually he was hanged at White Point Garden, Charlestown, on 10th December 1718.

Divorce would have been a far simpler option.

30

# A Sailor's Life For Me: At Least Until Dinner Is Served

*Life Aboard*

There is very little written, with reliability, about day-to-day living aboard a pirate vessel. Presumably they undertook the necessary maintenance to keep the ship in good repair, kept her sailing upon a steady course and kept a very watchful eye for an unwary ship appearing on the horizon. If their ship developed leaks, needed a new anchor cable, mast, or sails they simply captured a Prize that was of better quality and either upgraded or took what they needed. It sounds idyllic, carefree and do-as-you-please interspersed with the occasional fight with another ship and bouts of drinking and whoring ashore. A short life but a merry one. However, that is probably looking at life as a pirate through very heavily-tinted rose-coloured glasses.

For the life of a sailor in the British Royal Navy, there are chestfulls of written information, some as official records written as logbooks by captains, others as supply lists, repair invoices and such, and individual sailors' diaries. Most information comes from the latter part of the 1700s, notably during the seafaring high point of the Navy, the era when Admiral Lord Nelson commanded his flagship, HMS *Victory*. Is it because this period – and Nelson – is so important that these bits of curly-edged yellowing paper or musty-smelling books have been preserved and, in some cases, cherished?

On a pirate ship, the captain and the 'officers', those responsible for various duties, were usually elected by the men. Not so in the Navy.

Pre-mid 1700s promotion to officer status meant being commissioned by the Admiralty, or private sponsorship, to take command of a ship or an expedition; it goes without saying that such people had already shown a degree of knowledge and competency. The lowly seamen who began a life aboard started as 'landsmen' and were ordinary men, often not much more than youths, perhaps sons of fishermen or other seafarers. Younger lads became cabin boys, servants, or aboard a fighting ship, 'powder monkeys' quick, nimble children who took pots of gunpowder from storage to the guns during battle. It is a somewhat horrifying thought that young children, aged about ten years or so, were running about carrying gunpowder while a battle with all guns blazing raged around them. After serving twelve months a landsman could become an ordinary seaman, with another three years on top of that he would become an able seaman, a rank where he usually remained.

Technically, the 'sailors' were the men who attended the sails, the rest were seamen or foremast jacks – Jack Tars. The word 'tar' predates the 1600s and derives from the heavy tarpaulin sheets of black, waterproof cloth the men wore in order to attempt to keep dry. Tarpaulin itself may come from 'tar' and 'paul' referring to the black cloth resembling a mourning shroud. The sticky black tar, or pitch, used to waterproof and preserve things was used everywhere aboard ship, from caulking the decks to coating the ropes. A sailor was easily recognised by tar grimed hands and nails. Stockholm tar was the favourite, obtained from (you've guessed it,) Stockholm. It would be transported in barrels.

The phrase 'Jack the Tar' appears at the start of the Seven Years War in 1756, on an engraving, so it would have been in use well before this date. Officers were nearly always gentlemen, although a few humble men did manage to rise through the ranks – or became pirates where they could, if capable, become a captain. To become an officer or petty officer required technical skill, an education and, to a degree, especially for higher ranks, some financial security.

The lowest rank was a midshipman, usually boys of thirteen years old and upwards. Their place aboard ship could be purchased by rich fathers or, in some cases by relatives wishing to be rid of orphaned kindred. The boys were given training and were expected to move up the ranks. Many a captain began life at sea as a snivelling midshipman cowering below deck, wishing for home and his doting mother.

Commissioned officers required royal or admiralty approval, a degree of competency and a certificate from the lieutenant's examination board, official testing introduced in 1677. Before then, captains could appoint who they wanted to serve beneath them, which led to favouritism, abuse of the system and, all too often, gross incompetency. A lieutenant's seniority was numbered as a first lieutenant, second lieutenant and third lieutenant, and so on. Until 1741, a lieutenant's commission only applied to the ship he was serving upon; after this date, the rank was held in perpetuity.

The lieutenants, particularly the first lieutenant, more or less ran the ship. Get a bad or mean and nasty lieutenant, and you were in trouble; get a good one, and he was likely to be quickly promoted to captain of his own ship. It was to the lieutenant that the crew looked for their safety, for it was to him that decisions often fell. One who dealt over-harshly or alternatively too softly with the men was, either way, looking for trouble.

A commander was a first lieutenant given the acting commission of command, while a captain could only advance to become an admiral when a position became available, through the retirement, resignation or death of an existing officer of that rank. The rating of the vessel also determined the ranking of a captain, so a first-rate ship outranked that of a sixth-rate.

## What They Wore

As with any man or woman from this period, pirates dressed according to their social status. The higher up the ladder, the better quality the clothing in material, style and tailoring. Whatever socio-economic class, clothing for a sailor had to be practical and robust – and waterproof. The latter was achieved by tarring canvas or, in colder climates, making use of seal or otter skins. Chamois and moleskin for breeches and waistcoats was durable, but expensive. A new blue-coloured fabric that originated in a little place in Southern France called *Nîmes,* with the material being called '*serge de Nîmes*', did not become popular and known as 'denim', until the mid-18th century. It was highly regarded for its durability, especially in North America.

Underwear was rarely worn – except by the well off, 'drawers' being made from fine linen or silk. Women rarely wore drawers but when they did, the seam was not joined at the crotch. Nor did they have pockets in their gowns. Instead, there was a slit in the seam and a small poke, or pocket-bag, suspended inside. Unscrupulous (or adventurous) men could easily slip a hand into a woman's gown and have a surreptitious grope through those crotch-less panties.

The gold braid that adorned naval officers' uniforms from the latter part of the 18th century was not the typical dress of a pirate. The distinguishing braid, or lace as it is sometimes called, that decorated the front, cuffs, pocket flaps and skirt of the coat was introduced in 1748, specifically to differentiate the various ranks. The more gold braid, the higher the rank.

By contrast, pirate captains going ashore often dressed as the equivalent of merchant gentlemen wearing knee-breeches, white stockings, lace-trimmed linen or cambric (cotton was not yet in wide use) shirts, with richly embroidered waistcoats, long coats and silver-buckled shoes. This was topped by a three-corner hat – they were not called tricorns until later in the century – and possibly a powdered wig. Men wore bright colours and clothes that nowadays, we would think of as garments for a fop or a dandy. For their own death by hanging, the clothes pirates wore were often stepped up a notch: damask or velvet coats, silk shirts and hose, fine linen breeches.

Black Bart was noted as being one of the well-dressed pirates, favouring a crimson damask waistcoat and a red ostrich feather adorning his hat. Jack Rackham preferred simple calico, hence his nickname. Many pirates also liked to wear gaudy jewellery and trinkets or brightly coloured braids and ribbons laced into their hair – all designed, of course, to impress the ladies or intimidate the foe.

For ordinary pirates, as opposed to their captains, short jackets called *fearnoughts*, or canvas coats were favoured, as well as coloured waistcoats, plain or sometimes checked shirts, and wide-legged canvas trousers that ended at low-calf level. Usually, aboard ship they went barefoot, all the better to climb rigging quickly and safely. Bandanas, three-corner hats or woollen caps protected their heads from the sun or rain. For waterproofing, coats and breeches were coated in tar, whale oil or fat, hence the term 'oilskins'. Their clothes would not be purchased, or made, but stolen. When a Prize had been captured, the 'wardrobe' was the first place to be raided after the rum store.

At sea most men, and women if they were aboard masquerading as men, wore the same clothes until they fell apart. In the Royal Navy the crew were expected to change into clean shirts at least once a week on Sundays, although doing laundry in salt-water with nowhere to dry it could not have been much of an agreeable task. Soap was made from animal fat and tallow, but most laundering was done by soaking in a mixture of ash and urine, for which collecting pots were always available.

The men were often not concerned with where they peed, apart from ensuring the wind was blowing away from, not towards, them. The scuppers (drainage holes out to the open sea) were a favoured place, but anywhere would do. Another suitable area was where shrouds were secured to the sides of the ships; here there were wooden ledges called chains, and on the leeward (downwind) side, the ship would often be leaning over, allowing a clear drop to the sea below.

The Royal Navy, did not have a regulated dress code until 1748. When officers requested something to make them easily identifiable as men of importance, an embroidered blue uniform with white facings, breeches and stockings was introduced for formal occasions, with a less elaborately embroidered outfit for everyday wear. In 1767, the 'best wear' was abandoned to be replaced by the more practical work uniform, with a plain blue simpler coat with gold-lace stripes being used by 1795 as a work-day outfit with epaulettes added to denote rank. The white collar for a midshipman came into use by 1758. Uniforms for ratings were not introduced until the mid-1800s.

## Textiles

Linen: from the Latin for the flax plant, *linum*. A textile made from flax, linen is highly absorbent and valued for its coolness in hot weather.

Silk: a natural fibre produced by insect larvae that form cocoons. Silk's beautiful shimmer is due to the prism-like structure, which refracts light. Known and in use from before Christ, it was traded along the Silk Roads from the Far East. By the 15th and 16th centuries, the more expensive silks were manufactured in Italy and France. England developed a flourishing silk industry after the 1680s, when the Huguenots were expelled from France. As skilled weavers, they established and expanded the industry with English Huguenot silk soon becoming distinct from continental silk by an increased variety of colours.

Cambric: a fine, plain weave white linen cloth originating from Cambrai, which became incorporated into France in 1677. The word is derived from *Kameryk* or *Kamerijk,* which is the Flemish version of Cambrai. It is a fabric noted for its lustre and weight. It was used for ecclesiastical wear, shirts, underwear, frills and ruffs, collars and cuffs, cravats, handkerchiefs and infant wear. After imports into England from France were prohibited in the 18th century, Indian cotton became popular followed by American cotton grown on thousands of acres in the expanding Colonial settlements, and farmed by intense slave labour. Import bans, however, meant little to the smugglers who also traded in fine-quality French and Spanish lace. Highly profitable, light to carry and easy to hide.

Calico: It was in use in England from about 1505, and is a type of muslin, very plain-woven fabric made from unbleached and partially processed Indian cotton. Less coarse or thick than canvas, it was a cheap but fairly robust material. The name came from the original fabric of the city of Kozhikode – to the English, known as

Calicut, in south-western India. Dyed in bright colours as a raw fabric, Calico Print became highly popular throughout Europe.

Dimity: initially, dimity was woven from silk or wool but from the mid-18th century, it became a lightweight cotton. With at least two warp threads, it was mostly used for upholstery and curtains.

Damask: produced as one of the five weaving techniques used in the Byzantine and Islamic weaving centres during the early Middle Ages, (the others are tabby, twill, lampas, and tapestry). The name derives from Damascus. It was known and prized in Europe from the Crusades onwards. Damasks appeared as a European textile in the mid-14th century when it was woven on draw-looms in Italy, with a pattern of one colour in a gloss satin, against a duller background. These bi-coloured damasks had warps and wefts in contrasting hues and some had gold or silver threads. Expensive damasks were woven in silk, but were also produced from wool or linen.

Velvet: an expensive, rich man's fabric, costly to produce and to buy. Probably introduced to the Middle East from the Far East, although it was known it did not appear in England much before the 14th century.

Hats were usually worn to keep off the sun, wind or rain. Woollen caps for the ordinary men, leather or beaverskin two- or three-corner hats for the captain and officers. In the Royal Navy the three-corner hat became a two-corner hat worn at right angles to the shoulders, this transferred to being worn parallel with the shoulders. Lesser officers, lieutenants and midshipmen wore what looked like a short top hat.

For the seamen, the jack tars, hair was often worn long and plaited into a tail or queue. Being clean-shaven was the norm, very few beards and moustaches were on display – whether the pirates adhered to this is, apart from noted gentlemen such as Blackbeard, is not known. By the time arrested pirates came to trial, they were all unkempt, dishevelled and in need of a wash and a shave.

Lice and fleas were always a problem, but so too were other insects brought aboard with the stores. Tarantula spiders, cockroaches, centipedes and scorpions... Ugh! No thanks!

## What They Ate

Officers aboard Royal Navy ships had their own meals, which were of better quality than those served to the crew, although even their food went off. A diet of salted meat, hard-tack biscuit and cabbage, day after day, week after week for the men sounds disgusting to us now, but to those of the 1700s serving aboard a ship – be it pirate, merchant or Royal Navy – this would have constituted food superior to anything eaten ashore by the poorer classes. Although men often went hungry because food was tainted or stores were running low or unscrupulous officers kept a good portion for themselves to eat or sell.

The ship's cook was often selected from wounded or maimed seamen who were therefore unfit for other duties. Long John Silver in *Treasure Island* by Robert Louis Stevenson is probably the most famous. In the early days of explorers such as Magellan and Columbus, food was cooked barbecue style on the open deck, but as ships became larger and more robust, a kitchen area known as the galley was added with brick-built ovens. Here, food was prepared and hot meals provided for the entire crew.

With bread not becoming a part of daily diet aboard ship until well after 1850, the staple diet for any sailor was the ship's biscuit, or hardtack, 'tack' being the slang word for food. Samuel Pepys was responsible for standardising the rations and provisions – the ships victuals. He introduced a table of rations which, although meagre, and often of poor quality, did at least provide a 'square meal' – a term which comes from a sailor's square-shaped wooden platter. In this respect, the navy was a better option than the army, for a meal, at least once a day, was guaranteed. It is not known how often pirates ate, but it is a fair bet that their stomachs fared better on stolen rations than did their navy or merchantmen counterparts.

Made from stone-ground flour, water and salt, hardtack was inexpensive to produce and had a long 'shelf-life'. It would be made by mixing the ingredients into a dough, which was baked in a hot oven for at least half-an-hour and then left to harden. The variety of derogatory names give an indication of what it was like to eat: *molar-breaker, tooth-duller, worm-castle* ... Add to this, hardtack was always full of weevils. Sailors would tap the hard biscuits on the table or deck before eating to rid the things of livestock. One of the most looked-forward to delights of any sailor was to go ashore and purchase fresh, soft, bread.

Fresh fish, including tuna and dolphin, was easily caught and in the Caribbean, turtles were snared and kept alive down in the bilge water of the cable tier. Turtle eggs were a delicacy, while hens were always kept aboard for their eggs – and meat if they stopped laying. Jamaican cuisine included Solomon Gundy or Salmagundi, a concoction of various marinated ingredients of fish, turtle or meat with added herbs, spiced wine, hard-boiled egg, onion and cabbage – or anything that came to hand. For pirates in the Caribbean, there were also yams and pineapples or any fruit and vegetables that grew in the tropical heat.

The importance of Vitamin C, the preventer of scurvy, was not appreciated until much later. Not until 1747, was James Lind to prove that this awful disease could be treated and prevented by supplementing the diet with citrus fruit. For this reason, eventually, British sailors who sucked on lime fruit were called Limeys, while German sailors who ate plenty of sauerkraut (cabbage) became Krauts, and the French with their frogs' legs, Froggies.

Meat was salted or smoked, everything was stored in watertight barrels, butter went rancid, jam went mouldy, flour had weevils. Bread, when available, was usually toasted because it went stale so quickly, although such fare was usually reserved for the better-off captains of navy ships.

Fresh water was preserved for drinking. Washing, either personal or laundry, was done in salt water only. But even then, unless it was fresh, water was dangerous to drink. Water butts were made of wood that soon became slime-stained and contaminated, with the water within quickly turning sour. Cholera outbreaks and dysentery are caused by foul water. Ale or beer was the preferred drink, alongside rum and gin and with brandy, port and wine for the more well-to-do captain and crew. Water had to be collected, barrels filled and hauled aboard, then stored. When filling a glass of fresh, clean water from the kitchen tap, spare a thought for the common sailor from the past aboard a tall ship.

Livestock would be aboard ships, ready for the taking by the pirates: pigs, goats, cattle, rabbits.

We do not know what type of rations the pirates had (if there were any – was it just a free-for-all?)

According to Navy Regulations of 1818, the rations per week, per man, included:

1 gallon beer
2 lb beef
1½ lbs of flour plus 4ozs of raisins plus 2ozs of suet
1 lb of bread
2 lbs potatoes or yams
1 pint of oatmeal or 1pint of wheat
2 ozs butter
2 ozs oil

The food sounds dull, and eating mouldy, contaminated and weevil-ridden meals sounds abhorrent, but poor families on land, unless they grew their own crops or raised their own livestock, fared little better.

Rye bread, the commonest poor-man's bread, was often contaminated by a mould growth called ergot. It was a potent hallucinogenic, so combined with the rum and the gin, I don't suppose many people, landlubbers or sailors, were sober enough to notice the standard of the food. It is thought that the hysteria that precipitated events such as the Salem witch trials and the Pendle Witch accusations were the result of a glut of ergot. In other words, they were all as high as kites.

Have you ever wondered why coffee is an all-American favourite, while tea is for us Brits? Prior to the American War of Independence (and the famous Boston Tea Party) tea was a common drink in the American Colonies, but the British Government taxed tea imports heavily. This led to the commodity being highly prized as smuggled goods, but again the British Government intervened by sending the Royal Navy to intercept the smugglers. One of the most successful ships was HMS *Rose* – the replica of which is now moored at San Diego and is more widely known as HMS *Surprise* of novel and movie fame, (and the ship I base my *Sea Witch* on).

With the tea smuggling trade almost closed down, the Colonists retaliated by refusing to pay the tax and drink tea. They switched to untaxed coffee instead.

The habit stuck.

31

# Thomas Tew

Not all pirates were a bloodthirsty cruel lot. Thomas Tew, for instance, went on only two expeditions, came back from the first one a very rich man, but did not return from the second. He is known as the 'Rhode Island Pirate', as it is widely believed that his family settled there in the early 1640s, although other theories suggest he was born in Northamptonshire before his parents emigrated to the Colonies. Apparently, he was married with two daughters. It does make you wonder where these rumours and ideas come from, however, when there is barely a scrap of evidence to support them – fiction is not always confined to novelists.

Moving to Bermuda in 1691, he engaged in government-backed privateering, obtaining his Letter of Marque in 1692, with a variety of sponsors supporting his intended expedition by providing him with a sloop, *Amity*, which was crewed by forty-six men and carried eight guns. His mission was to attack and destroy a French territory in the Gambia, West Africa.

Leaving Bermuda in the December, and at sea only a few days, possibly after an encounter with a severe storm, Tew turned to piracy telling his crew that it would be more profitable than blasting away at a few French buildings. Either he was most persuasive or they readily agreed with his misgivings about bothering with the French.

They sailed to the Red Sea, taking a ship heading from India in 1693. With their victim offering no resistance, Tew's men ransacked the hold, acquiring treasure worth something in the region of £100,000 for the gold and silver, ivory, gemstones, spices and silks. Tew amassed £8,000 for himself while the crew netted between £1,200 and £3,000 per man. Definitely a better prospect than that abandoned attack on the French.

They set a course to return home, stopping to careen at the pirate haven of St Mary's on Madagascar, and reached Newport in the spring of 1694. He paid off the men who had sponsored the *Amity* and pursued an amicable friendship with the Province of New York Governor.

The common perception of a pirate. (© jgroup)

The fate of most pirates.
(© stocksnapper)

The terror of the seas – run out the
guns! (© etienjones)

*Right*: A pirate's most important asset: his ship. The *Lady Washington*, better known as HMS *Interceptor* in the movie *Pirates of the Caribbean*: *Curse of the Black Pearl*. (© Ifistand)

*Below*: The Ocracoke, scene of Blackbeard's last stand. Does his ghost still haunt the shallows? (© Cathy Helms)

B 43

# LT. ROBERT MAYNARD

Of the Royal Navy. Sent by Gov. Spotswood of Virginia, in the sloop "Ranger," killed the pirate Blackbeard off shore, 1718.

ARCHIVES AND HIGHWAY DEPARTMENTS

*Left*: Blackbeard remembered.
(© Cathy Helms)

*Below*: A forbidding place: Colonial Williamsburg Gaol.
(© Cathy Helms)

The Capitol Building,
Colonial Williamsburg,
where trials took
place before the
Courthouse was built.
(© Cathy Helms)

Governor's Palace,
Colonial Williamsburg.
The impressive entrance
hall and armoury.
(© Cathy Helms)

A place of learning
financed by pirate loot.
(© Cathy Helms)

*Left*: *Sea Witch*. (© leonido)

*Below*: Two more sea witches, in the eyes of their victims; the infamous Ann Bonny and Mary Read. (Author's collection)

*Above*: Life aboard for merchant seamen, Royal Navy ratings or pirates alike was hard work, whatever the weather. (© razyphoto)

*Right*: A dramatic illustration by the marvellous American artist Howard Pyle (1853–1911). (Author's collection)

The ultimate prize that haunted the dreams of all pirates. For practically all of them, that was all it ever was – a dream. (© gl0ck)

By the coming of winter that year, Tew sought another Letter of Marque and sailed off again with about thirty to forty men, increasing the crew to nearer sixty when he reached Madagascar.

At the Bab-el-Mandeb Strait, the entrance to the Red Sea, Tew came across several more pirates all with the same intention as he, one of them being Henry Every and *Fancy*. They joined forces and in either June or September 1695, they came across a Mughal convoy. Overtaking one ship, the *Fateh Muhammed*, the *Amity* attacked. In the battle that followed Tew was killed by a cannon ball hitting his belly and disembowelling him. Shocked and disheartened, his crew surrendered. One version of the tale states that Henry Every caught up, captured the *Fateh Muhammed* and freed the men held prisoner in the hold, while another claims that those who had not been immediately executed died in an Indian prison. Tew's resting place is unknown, as he would have been buried at sea.

William Kidd was commissioned to hunt Tew, and bring him to justice, but Kidd himself turned pirate, although at the time of setting out neither Kidd nor his sponsors knew that Tew was already dead.

The exact details of Tew's flag is uncertain, but it is thought to have been a white arm clutching a scimitar sword on a black background.

His family is rumoured to have lived a pleasant life of luxury from his plundered fortune.

32

# Good Enough For Grown Ups

*Treasure Island* has topped the list of pirate-based stories for several generations of young adult readers, but is it a book for *girls* to enjoy? There is, after all, a distinct lack of female role models in the tale. Are girls interested in this sort of story? One that has no romance or connection with the fast pace of 21st century life? The lure of the sea, exciting adventures involving pirates should satisfy any avid reader, but are teenage girl characters necessary, needed or even wanted in the sort of fiction that is geared to a male-orientated genre? The quick, simple answer is yes. As with toys and sport – cars and football are no longer just for boys – books are for everyone, no matter what gender, but books have to compete with TV, computers, on-line games and other modern-day interests. Getting *any* school age youngster to read a book for pleasure – boy or girl – is a challenge in itself. To have a strong female protagonist is to provide a focus for a girl to identify with, and it is rather nice for us girls to break into the traditionally male-dominated areas of fun and excitement. That is not to say that the boys should be shouldered aside of course. There are some very good young adult novels out there, books that are just as good for grown-ups as well as the boys and the girls. Here are five of my particular favourites:

## PIRATES!, Celia Rees

When two young women meet under extraordinary circumstances in the 18th century West Indies, they are unified in their desire to escape their oppressive lives. The first is a slave, forced to work in a plantation mansion and subjected to terrible cruelty at the hands of the plantation manager. The second is a spirited and rebellious English girl, sent to the West Indies to marry well and combine the wealth of two respectable families. Fate ensures that one night the two young women have to save each other and run away to a life no less dangerous but certainly a lot more free. As pirates, they roam the seas, fight pitched battles against their foes and become embroiled in many a heart-quickening adventures.

Nancy Kington and Minerva Sharp are from very different backgrounds. They find themselves united, and then firm friends, through the common cause of survival. The story deals unashamedly with the plight of slaves and young women, who even of higher status were, beneath it all, just as much slaves to the whims of their fathers, brothers and husbands. The delight of this adventure story are the characters themselves, a story to become engrossed in and enjoy. It may not have the accuracy of shipboard life as would a Patrick O'Brian or C.S. Forrester, but it has adventure, relationships and pluckiness that is well suited to a teenage reader, or an adult looking for something engrossing to enjoy.

## DEAD COOL, *Peter Clover*

A pet dog would be nice. Sammy would like a dog; instead, he is given a parrot. A pretty but boring parrot. All Polly does is squawk, but then, mysteriously, there are two parrots; Polly has a friend, Crabmeat, who can and does, talk. Except only Sammy can see and hear him. Then a red cat turns up, and a boy, Smitty; then some pirates join the boy. Except, they are not ordinary everyday swashbuckling scoundrel pirates, these are the ghosts of pirates who ran afoul of Red Beard the Really Rotten. And that name in itself explains just why this story is such great fun.

## THE BOOK ARK, *Janis Pegrum Smith*

> There is a place where every book you have ever read, every story you ever heard, really exists … Want to go there? When nineteen-year-old Joshua Ridley inherits his grandfather's second-hand book business it proves to be the perfect escape from his extremely miserable home life, but little does he know how it will completely change his life, forever. A story of new versus old; a story of books, but most of all a story about a boy who just really misses his granddad …

Imagine if every character that has ever appeared in a novel were to exist in a parallel universe. Imagine if there was a method of being able to travel from this world to that world. A world where characters from every story ever written, from Odysseus to Little Nell, from Captain Flint to Captain Acorne, continue with their adventures. Then imagine that these characters are in danger of fading away because real books are being shoved aside by electronic ones. A frightening thought for avid readers. The *Book Ark* is a bookstore aboard a barge, and this story is a fascinating start to a series, made all the more enjoyable because it centres around the fascination of books – and some rather cool pirates.

These particular pirates, created to feature as characters in a children's storybook (and therefore become real in the alternative Book World), are great fun despite the worry of a missing granddad, the sadness of a lonely boy and the danger of books disappearing because no one is reading them anymore. Written for older children, but just as enjoyable for adults, the fun blends well with the chilling prospect of technology overtaking traditional print books.

A taster excerpt:

*Not yet realising that what is happening to him is real, Josh Ridley believes he is dreaming. He has stepped into the plot of the pirate story his grandfather wrote for him several years ago when he was an eight-year-old boy. He is soon to discover that the fictional character is alive and well, but 'elsewhere'. Who can resist the lure of a talking dog and a crew of jolly pirates who use jelly and blancmange in battle, instead of cannon balls?*

'So, you're the real Josh Ridley,' said Little Josh, with a broad grin.

'Yes, but how do you know about me?' Josh asked, whilst considering how very similar this young boy looked to himself as an eight-year-old.

'Because your granddad told us all about you,' said the boy, turning the ship's wheel to bring them alongside the shore so Captain Granddad could board the ship via the rope ladder over the side, as people cheered him from the riverbank. 'I'm based on you.'

'I know,' said Josh, 'but how do you know my grandfather?' It was all so real Josh was beginning to forget it was just a dream.

'He's our Creator, of course we know him,' said Captain Granddad, clambering onto the deck and waving his hat to his fans crowding the shore. Putting his hat back upon his head he lifted his eye patch and changed it to the other eye, as Josh remembered was his habit in the book, and the parrot flew down onto his shoulder. 'We're one of the lucky few whose Creator walks amongst us, for he is also a Keeper, the Master of the Books himself, no less.'

Josh was bemused by the captain's words and felt certain it was time to wake up. He tried hard to will himself awake, closed his eyes and then opened them again, but his feet were still solidly on the deck of the *Maria Ave*, and Captain Granddad and Little Josh were still standing in front of him, staring at him.

'He said you might come through one day. He's as proud of you as I am of my Little Josh here.' The captain ruffled the young boy's hair affectionately.

'Is it all over, then?' came a voice coming up the steps from below deck, 'Can I come out?' Argos, or at least a dog that looked like Argos, padded out onto the deck. Josh remembered Argos was also the name of the dog in the book, but this Argos was a talking dog. 'All this mess, just look at it,' Argos said, sniffing the jelly and blancmange-strewn deck. 'Why you can't use actual cannon balls like real pirates I don't know.'

'Because someone might get hurt if we used the real thing,' said Captain Granddad.

'You're a shame to your profession, you know,' said the dog, with great distain. 'To think I could have been a proper pirate's dog, but no, I had to be lumbered with you. Did no one ever tell you it's rude to stare?' The last remark was aimed at Josh. 'Not seen a talking dog before, I'll wager? Never mind, it happens to me all the time. I'm Argos, pleased to meet you.' The dog held out a paw for Josh to shake, which he dutifully did. 'And you are?'

'Josh... Josh Ridley.'

'Ah, Master Warwick's boy, interesting. Then you will know my counterpart in your universe. We're named after Odysseus' faithful hound, you know.'

'I know, the one who waited twenty years for his master's return and then died just after Odysseus finally came back.'

'Yes, though I wouldn't wait twenty seconds for my master,' the dog snorted.

'How d'you fancy walkin' the plank?' the captain replied to the slur.

'That's your answer to everything,' sighed the dog.

'Well, perhaps it is high time that I carried out my threat; teach you a lesson that would.'

'Don't be so ridiculous, we haven't even got a plank.' Argos stretched and yawned.

'I could always get one,' retorted the captain.

The dog looked at the captain witheringly, 'We're on a river. I would simply swim to the bank, not quite the same as being on the high seas with real pirates.' He strode haughtily away and sniffed a pile of green jelly, pulling a face of disgust.

## THE BLACK BANNER, *Helen Hart*

At last tomboys have got a book about pirates for themselves.

Penniless Becky Baxter crops her hair, dresses in breeches, and leaves the dangerous backstreets of Bristol for a life of adventure and fortune on the high seas. But she quickly discovers that there are far more dangerous enemies than her drunken Ma and evil Mr Crudder ... Pirates!

A taster:

*Becky Baxter – disguised as a boy – meets her (his!) first Prize...*

Logan put his eyeglass up and squinted at the horizon. 'Spanish,' he murmured. 'She'll be loaded to the gunwales with gold. Slow. Easy to catch.' He rubbed his chin thoughtfully. 'And alone, too. She must have got separated from the flotilla on her way home.' He smiled. 'Well, she's one ship that won't be topping up King Felipe's royal coffers. Not today.'

He lowered the eyeglass and nodded briskly. 'We'll take her.' He caught me staring at him and flashed me a grin before I had time to look away. He said to me, 'Although I dare say it barely counts as piracy. Spaniards have been plundering Mexico for nigh on 200 years, so us taking from them isn't really stealing. Redistribution of assets – that's what we'll call it, eh lad?' The diamond cross at his throat glittered in the sun as he raised his voice: 'All hands! Arm yourselves!'

The cry was taken up the length and breadth of the ship and men raced to get ready. The *Bonny Marie* tilted and turned, cutting her way across the ocean. I stood still, not sure what my new role as a pirate entailed, and Logan grasped my shoulder. 'No fighting for you, lad. You're not ready for blood just yet. Stay here and Reuben will take care of you.'

Reuben turned out to be the raffish-looking pirate with lace-frothed cuffs who'd challenged Flubb during the battle for the *Bonny Marie*. He still wore the lace shirt, and now high-waisted green silk pantaloons billowed about his legs before disappearing down into salt-stained leather boots. He'd slung three or four belts around his hips and tucked in a gleaming mother-of-pearl inlaid dagger. His blond hair was plaited at the nape of his neck and tied with a red ribbon.

Grinning, he swapped his plug of chewing tobacco from one cheek to the other. 'Let's find a spot where you can see everything. For your first time you need a grandstand view. Come on!' He grasped my hand and hauled me up onto the quarterdeck. 'See that banner we're raising? Spanish. We fly a friendly flag to lure them in. We get close enough to see the whites of their eyes – softly, softly. At the last minute the black banner goes up.' He spat a stream of brown liquid onto the deck. 'One glimpse of those crossed cutlasses and most don't even bother to fight.'

Reuben and I must have stood there for an hour, watching the purposeful movements of our crew. All of them filled their pockets with musket balls and checked the sharp edges of cutlass blades. Some stacked stinkpots and apple-sized grenades inside coils of rope. Others lay flat in the bulwarks, ready to pounce.

The stark white sails of the Spanish ship grew ever closer and when we were near enough to make out her name – the *Magdalena* – our men began to disperse, ducking down out of sight. Reuben and I did the same.

As we waited for the black banner to go up, he tossed me a handful of cloth strips. 'Stuff your ears and wrap something around your head, eh?' he said. 'The blast from the guns is deafening.'

He was right. A heart-stopping *Whoompf* barrelled through my chest as the deck cannons were fired. My ears rang. As the Spaniards realised their fate a series of agitated cries echoed across the water. For the first time I felt icy fear trickle through my veins, but the fear was for them not us. After all, only a couple of days ago I'd been on the other side of a fight like this and I knew how fearsome we looked.

Logan leapt up onto the quarterdeck rail and yelled, 'Gold and Glory!'

The pirates took up the chant. 'Gold and Glory! Gold and Glory!'

Instantly our men surged from their hiding places, weapons primed. A volley of stinkpots rained down on the *Magdalena's* decks as grappling irons clattered against her sides. Murdoch, our Scottish piper, began his cacophony. Between snatches of smoke and billowing sulphurous fumes I caught glimpses of fighting – Logan and three others, blades glittering in the sunlight, sweat sticking shirts to chests. Musket shot whistled through the air and splintered the deck timbers. A dozen pirates became two dozen, and then three as Logan's men massed on the deck of the *Magdalena*.

Panic broke out among the Spaniards as they realised they were outnumbered. Great spumes of water splashed up as men jumped overboard to escape. Those remaining on the decks pointed and grabbed at each other, jabbering incoherently, the whites of their eyes almost luminous now. I felt sick as I recognised the sheer terror in their rigid stance. Beside me, Reuben sneered. 'See how they run away? Yellow dogs. They deserve to die.'

*The Buccaneers, Iain Lawrence*
An ideal book for boys, (or girls) the third in a trilogy, but it can be read as a stand-alone. It is 1803 and John Spencer, aboard the *Dragon*, sights a lifeboat adrift in the ocean with a single passenger aboard. *The Buccaneers* is not a run-of-the-mill pirate adventure, it has warts-an-all realism that portray what life was really like on a wooden ship powered by wind and sail. Not for the squeamish or younger readers, but aimed at older teenagers, adults too will enjoy the nautical adventuring that contains action and entertainment, but without the usual 'romance' of the more common pirate novel.

If you like realism, this one is for you.

33

# Will The Real Author Stand Up?

In 1724, Captain Charles Johnson published a book entitled *A General History of the Robberies and Murders of the most notorious Pyrates*. From it we get our concept of pirates and piracy in the 'golden age' of the early 18th century and it is our main source of information about the more notorious rogues. It has what we take as typical pirates with missing limbs, eye-patches, parrots and burying their treasure. Originally published as two volumes, the first more or less respecting recorded detail although with a few exaggerated fictional flourishes, covered the 1700s pirates, while the second delved into the earlier 1600s buccaneers and harder to believe for accuracy is more fiction than fact.

Because its publication is contemporary with the height of piracy, the 1700s section is usually regarded as being fairly accurate, although one man's view can be biased and who is to say what is fact and what is fiction? There is one enormous difficulty with the book, however. We have no idea who Charles Johnson was, as the name is a pseudonym. There was no Captain Johnson recorded as a ship's master (nor anyone in the military). The author obviously had a good knowledge of all things nautical, so must have been a sailor (or a pirate?) and he shows a detailed knowledge of the pirates, their lives and their exploits. There was a writer called Johnson who produced a work entitled *The Successful Pirate* about Henry Avery in 1712, but he did not write *The General History*. Maybe the writer did not want his name linked with piracy? Which leads to the question, why not?

There have been various attempts to identify his (or her) true identity, but to date nothing definite has materialised. There are several candidates, some suggestions put forward by various scholars and a couple of my own theories.

You can come to your own conclusions.

NATHANIAL MIST: a sailor, journalist and printer and who had his own printing press is a popular candidate. Arrested and tried for sedition on several occasions, he was fined £50 in 1720, was sent to the pillory and spent three months in jail for his passionate Jacobite tendencies. (Democracy and freedom of speech were not embraced in the 18th century.) Bitterly opposing the Whig government, he used the pages of his highly successful *Mist's Weekly Journal* to attack Robert Walpole and King George of Hanover. He frequently published his articles using a false name for the person he was condemning, although all his readers knew who he was talking about. (For example, if I were to mention Anthony Bare and Greg Bosh, the political leaders involved in the Iraq War, I think you would know who I meant.)

He also used a variety of authors who employed pen names. Daniel Defoe was one of them, despite being a known Whig supporter, an established spy and placed by the government to keep an eye on Mist, a fact which Defoe himself later confirmed. In 1727 Mist went a step too far by libelling the King and he fled to France, although his newssheets continued to be printed. A year later, his presses were vandalised and destroyed. The journal was subsequently renamed and the still exiled Mist was spurred into supporting the Jacobite cause as much as he could. Maybe his efforts went too far because by 1734, he had been ostracised by his fellow Jacobites and in due course he was permitted to return to England. He died in September 1737.

So what might connect him to *The General History*? It was first printed by Charles Rivington, who had produced several of Mist's books prior to 1724. The book was registered in Mist's name at Her Majesty's Stationery Office. This does not mean he wrote it, merely that he was the publisher. The book you are reading now is 'registered' with the modern equivalent to HMSO – the British Library – via its ISBN, the International Standard Book Number, which is a unique number issued to every edition and variation (except a reprint) of *every* UK book published. Authors, particularly self-published writers, can purchase these numbers themselves but usually it is the publisher who does this. Therefore the 'owner' of the ISBN for *Pirates: Truth and Tale* is Amberley Publishing, but ownership does not make them the author; that (dubious?) honour is mine.

As a sailor, Mist may well have personally encountered some of the men and actions related in the book. But why would an anti-government activist who was determined to ridicule and lampoon the Whigs suddenly decide to write a two-volume part-fictional book, under an assumed name, about pirates, a work that had absolutely nothing to do with politics?

DANIEL DEFOE: Born 1660 in London is famous for the novels *Robinson Crusoe* and *Moll Flanders*. He has often been cited as being Charles Johnson because he was a writer of that era and produced several similar works in a similar style. Yet he published none of his other most interesting works under a made-up name, so why would he do so for this one?

His family name, of Flemish background, was Foe. His father was a tallow chandler. As a boy he would have experienced some of the most fearful events of London's history, such as the Great Plague of 1665, when over 70,000 Londoners died; and the Great Fire of London in 1666. In the area where he lived, the Foes' house and two others were left intact.

Well educated, he had initially been expected to join the Presbyterian Ministry but he preferred to become a merchant, dealing in various goods and travelling widely to purchase and sell them. Unfortunately, he went bankrupt to the tune of £17,000. In his early thirties he travelled to Europe and by the time he returned to England, around 1695, he had changed his name to 'Defoe'. Perhaps to escape more debtors? Another business venture failed while he was in prison in 1703 for political offences. He had written several politically-based pamphlets, writing against Catholic James II, and had joined the ill-fated Monmouth Rebellion, escaping the disastrous result of Sedgemoor by the skin of his teeth. With James fleeing into exile three years later, Defoe heartily welcomed William of Orange and Queen Mary, becoming the leading royal pamphleteer. (He would have made a good modern-day political spin-doctor.) In 1701, he published *The True-Born Englishman*, a witty poem about racial prejudices that he confessed to be extremely proud of.

War with Europe, Spain in particular, was again looming. In 1701, five men from Kent called for better defences of the coast by handing a petition to Parliament and the then Tory government. They were immediately, and illegally, sent to prison. Showing great courage Defoe confronted the Speaker of the Commons, Robert Harley, with a document reminding the politicians that 'Englishmen are no more to be slaves to Parliaments than to a King' referring, of course to the days of English Civil War, King Charles I and Cromwell. The Kentishmen were released and Defoe proclaimed a hero, except, of course, by the Tory government who thereafter regarded him as a Whig supporter and a great danger.

As a Dissenter, Defoe then became embroiled in religious matters, which at this time were barely separate from political issues. He was accused of sedition and in May 1703, was arrested, fined and sentenced to endure three days in the pillory. His literary popularity won out however, for instead of pelting him with the traditional rotten rubbish, the crowd garlanded the pillory with flowers and heartily drank to his health. When he was sent back to Newgate prison to complete his punishment, his business collapsed and his wife and eight children suffered. He appealed to Harley, who eventually agreed to his release, which meant Defoe had to work for him in return. Harley was the government spymaster, which meant Defoe became a spy. (You are permitted to hum the James Bond theme here.)

Defoe seems to have enjoyed his new role as it meant doing the things he enjoyed: travelling and writing reports and pamphlets. In 1704, he re-produced eyewitness statements in what is believed to be the first piece of modern journalism when he wrote in detail about the Great Storm of the previous year, which devastated miles of southern England, uprooted thousands of trees, destroyed hundreds of homes and killed more than 8,000 people.

The Act of Union with Scotland in 1707 gave him the opportunity to travel North of the Border and keep his new master, Harley, informed of events and public opinion. Between 1724 and 1726, Defoe published three volumes of his *Tour Through the Whole Island of Great Britain*.

Not all his writing was political; he originally anonymously published several works of a spiritual and moral nature and it is believed that in all, he produced more than 500 titles as novels, satirical poems, essays, articles and religious and political pamphlets. He does not seem to have written much about ships, shipping or nautical matters though. Nor pirates.

During Queen Anne's reign, from 1704 to 1713, he produced *The Review* a serious and in-depth newspaper which he almost entirely wrote himself. Initially a weekly publication, it appeared three times a week, even continuing while Defoe was, again, imprisoned by his political opponents. It unashamedly discussed politics, religion, trade and morals and was a forerunner of the modern press. No pirates though.

With the crowning of George of Hanover after Queen Anne's death in 1714, the Tory government gave way to the Whigs, who in turn came to value Defoe's writing and 'intelligence' talents. He produced various other works, most notably in 1722 with the appearance of *Moll Flanders, A Journal of the Plague Year,* and *Colonel Jack,* his last work of fiction being *Roxana* published in 1724. He died on 24th April 1731, but his most famous book, *Robinson Crusoe* had been published in 1719, based on the real marooning of Andrew Selkirk, with information supplied by Governor Woodes Rogers. *Robinson Crusoe* was not about *pirates,* though was it?

There does not seem to be much in Defoe's life to connect him with the in-depth detail and knowledge of the sea, sailing and sailors explored in Johnson's book. Where would Defoe have found the time to write something he knew very little about? He was a political, religious and moralistic writer who followed the common writer's advice of 'write what you know.' Admitted he knew nothing about being marooned on a desert island for four years, but he did meet Selkirk, and like all good journalists, he would have squeezed every bit of the story out of him then turned it into an exciting, and highly profitable, read.

As for pirates, though... there is absolutely no connection.

WOODES ROGERS. My favourite candidate is Governor Woodes Rogers. Here is why:

He was in England, having temporarily retired as Governor, and facing debtor's prison.

He knew a lot about sailing and pirates.

He claimed that he was approached by a man who intended to write a history of piracy, and dutifully supplied him with detailed information. This man, he claimed, was Johnson.

*The General History* was a 'best seller' on both sides of the Atlantic and Rogers found himself a national hero for the second time. Why? All he did was talk to a man who was writing a book ...

His connection with the book, and presumably Johnson, made him rich again.

Because of the nature of the book, and being, no doubt, concerned that someone might take offence, not least some of the still living pirates, he used the pen name and kept his identity secret.

Rogers knew Daniel Defoe.

Daniel Defoe knew Nathanial Mist.

Therefore, Woodes Rogers was Charles Johnson.

Naturally, I have absolutely no proof of this, but does it not make sense? Q.E.D.

More fancifully, we do not know what happened to Anne Bonny. Perhaps she wrote the book as a memoir of her days at sea?

Henry Jennings had retired to his Barbados plantation. Could he have been the author? My money is on Woodes Rogers.

## 34

# Gaol

The word 'gaol' is the old spelling and use of today's 'jail'. Pronunciation and meaning is exactly the same *jay-l*, but however it is spelt the word means prison.

Men, women, and children, were sent to gaol for what now seems to us, the most trivial of reasons. Stealing a loaf of bread or an apple; for sedition, speaking out against the government or monarch; for differences of religious beliefs; for poaching a rabbit or falling into debt. Higher crimes, murder, treason and piracy usually carried the penalty of hanging. As did acts of homosexuality. If you were gay and discovered, you would be hanged so men and women of the eighteenth century stayed very firmly hidden and did not 'come out'.

Gaol was not a nice place to be.

Until the 1800s, prisons were not regarded as places of punishment but as a building where debtors were held until they repaid what they owed, or a trial resulted in sentence. These ranged from a ducking in the river (more unpleasant than it sounds; the River Thames was an open sewer,) to a spell in a pillory, a flogging, transportation to the Colonies as an indentured slave, or execution. Debtors consigned to gaol often took their families with them – where else were they to live? The State would not support them, indeed prisoners even had to pay rent for the privilege of being locked up in filthy, stinking conditions.

London's two famous prisons were Newgate and Marshalsea. Few who went into these awful places expected to get out again if they had to endure long sentences or had no money. The rich could buy luxuries, like food or pay for a private room.

*Marshalsea*

To be incarcerated within the walls of Marshalsea Prison in Southwark, to the south side of the River Thames, was dreaded. If a prisoner had money he, or she, could afford access to luxuries and pleasantries such as a shop and a restaurant, and they were even permitted to leave the prison during the day (for a fee of course). Those who did not have any financial means found themselves squashed into small rooms with many other prisoners.

The poor were likely to starve as they could not afford food. In 1729, 300 prisoners in three months starved to death within Marshalsea's walls. Prostitution was rife as it was a way to earn a few meagre pennies in order to survive.

Prisoners were beaten and tortured, the worst punishment was to be locked in the 'strong room' which was a shed, originally built to hold pirates, without fresh air or light and situated next to where bodies awaited burial, the gaol's sewer and where the night soil was piled for disposal. The place was never cleaned, had no drain and was overrun by rats. Prisons had to lie or sit on the filth of the floor as there was no stool, chair, bed or bench.

The Admiralty, responsible for Royal Navy discipline, which included stamping out piracy and smuggling, sent sailors found guilty through court-marshal for desertion and 'unnatural crimes', a euphemism for homosexuality, to the Marshalsea.

The prison was closed in 1842, and the buildings and land were sold by auction a year later. They were bought by a Master Hicks for £5,100. All that remains now is one wall.

Notorious as it was, Marshalsea's fame increased because of a certain novelist whose father was interred there for debt in 1824. His son was forced to leave his education at the age of twelve to earn enough money by working in a shoe-blacking factory to pay the debt off and set his father free. He used the experience for many of his subsequent novels.

His name? Charles Dickens.

## Newgate

It was once a gate, although by the 1700s not a very new one, for it was originally built as the western gateway for the Roman wall, was rebuilt in the 12th century, with various following re-builds, most notably in 1672 after the Great Fire of London had destroyed it in 1666. This notorious place of terror, squalor and cruelty was finally demolished in 1904. Prisoners awaiting hanging at Tyburn were held at Newgate, although it was not reliably secure because the thief, Jack Sheppard, escaped twice before he went to the gallows in 1724. Accommodation consisted of three wards; the Master's for those who had the money to afford to pay their way, the Common Side for the poor, and the Press Yard for special prisoners. Entering, prisoners would be chained by leg irons and taken to the dungeons, which were unlit and rank with fetid detritus. Those awaiting execution were held in a cellar beneath the Keeper's house, which was nothing more than an open sewer with chains and shackles affixed to the dank walls. Daniel Defoe was imprisoned at Newgate for debts. The protagonist of one of his novels, *Moll Flanders*, was born in Newgate. Pirate William Kidd was held at Newgate prior to being hanged at Wapping in 1701, and Newgate has a legend of a Black Dog, a ghostly canine which represented the cruel treatment of inmates.

The Cockney slang '*as black as Nookie's [Newgate's] Knocker*' refers to the doorknocker on the prison's front door.

### Colonial Williamsburg's Public Gaol

When Lt Maynard defeated Edward Teach, Blackbeard, at the Ocracoke in 1718, the remainder of the pirate crew were taken to Williamsburg, then the capital of Virginia. They were incarcerated in the public gaol until their trial, and subsequent hanging several months later. The gaol that can be seen there today is an accurate replica.

A two-storey building of red brick, it is located towards the east end of Nicholson Street. It was originally built in 1704. Initially it was assumed that small and simple would be sufficient, for large numbers of criminals were not expected to be a problem, therefore only three rooms were built, one for the gaoler's use and two for prisoners. But to house runaway slaves, thieves, spies, pirates and other such miscreants a twenty-by-thirty-foot building soon proved inadequate. An exercise yard was added in 1703, a debtor's prison room in 1711, and a house for the gaoler and his family in 1722.

As with any other gaol, the conditions were foul. In winter, the cells were so cold some prisoners froze to death. In summer the humidity and heat was like an oven. At least there was a window and a grill on the door for air and light, unlike Newgate and Marshalsea, and there was a lavatory built as a wooden box with steps up to the 'seat of ease'. It probably stank.

Women prisoners were housed in an upstairs room, and it is claimed two female ghosts still haunt the building, the thud of their shoes can occasionally be heard on the wooden flooring.

35

# Hanging on to Dance the Hempen Jig with Jack Ketch

Curtains are 'hung', a person is 'hanged'; such are the quirks of the English language. Hanging is not a pleasant way to die. No execution is pleasant, but until the 'long drop and the short stop' was introduced, it could take anything up to twenty minutes to slowly strangle to death, with the bowels and bladder emptying. Death could be quicker if weight was added, so family and friends would 'hang on' to the victim's legs and torso to speed up the process. This is where the term 'hangers on' comes from.

The 'hempen jig' refers to the body jerking in those last moments of life suspended from a hemp rope, and Jack (or John,) Ketch became a name synonymous with hanging. Employed by Charles II in the late 1600s he is first mentioned in London's Old Bailey proceedings as a public executioner in 1676. In addition to hangings, he was responsible for overseeing burning and beheadings, two of which he bodged so badly he later had to publish a public apology. He executed Lord William Russell by beheading in 1683, the accused sentenced to death at Lincoln's Inn Fields, London, in July 1683 for plotting against King Charles II. Ketch struck the axe four times before finally decapitating him. Then in July 1685, following the failed rebellion against King James II, he similarly botched the beheading of James Fitzroy Scott, the Duke of Monmouth, Charles II's eldest illegitimate son, at Tower Hill, taking between five to eight repeated blows in a brutal manner to do the task. Ketch is mentioned in several novels (including my own) and in Dickens' *Oliver Twist, Pickwick Papers* and *David Copperfield*.

The most well-known places of execution in London were Tyburn, located near the current position of London's Marble Arch; Tower Hill, close to the Tower of London; and Wapping, next to the River Thames, used for pirates, as was Port Royal in the West Indies. An estimate of more than 60,000 souls were executed at Tyburn between the end of the 12th century and the close of the 18th, most being under the age of twenty-one.

The purpose of public executions was to discourage crime and to demonstrate the power of the law to the populace. Hangings at Tyburn took place eight times per annum and were conducted in a sombre and severe way to enhance the deterrent to committing crime. In other places, notably Port Royal, Nassau, and Williamsburg, in Virginia, the sentence could be carried out within four-and-twenty hours, if not immediately.

Execution day was a public event, an entertainment. Crowds would gather, entire families – children too. Pie-men, cake sellers, drink sellers were there and every seat was taken in the taverns and coffee shops. Prostitutes touting their wares would be busy, their employment heightened by the air of excitement. Pamphlets of written confessions would be on sale, no one bothered to ask if they were fact or fiction. Think of your local outdoor event, a fair or County Show maybe, with the press of people out to enjoy themselves and tradesmen hoping to make a nice profit. The cutpurses and street entertainers would be there; lots of noise and bustle, shouting, laughter. An argument or two with pushing and shoving for a front row view. For that is the main attraction, the thing they have all come to see. Not a pop or film star, not Royalty passing by in a gold coach, not the latest-trend magician attempting some seemingly impossible trick, but the wooden frame of the gallows was the centre of attention, and the man, or woman, who was about to 'dance' beneath it.

On execution day, the prisoner would be released from the shackles that had restrained him or her, possibly for many months, so wrists and ankles would be sore, the flesh swollen. The tethering would be replaced with a leather cord or wrist chains. A leather halter would be fitted around the neck and he or she would either walk, or be taken by cart (depending on the distance), to the place of execution. If the procession passed a church or chapel, the condemned would be permitted an opportunity to pray. Crowds would line the route, jeering and yelling. The more unpopular the criminal, or his crime, the louder the noise.

Making a brave end was essential for good will. The crowd could turn nasty against those who showed fear, while the brave-faced, especially those who uttered subversive, derisive or bold speeches, were admired. Those who displayed an air of showmanship by jesting with the crowd, or offering a confession that contained lurid and graphic detail, went down well. To provide a good entertainment meant obtaining immortality through a pamphlet or column in the newssheets. Glory is a strange thing.

What the condemned wore was also important. They were permitted to wear what they chose. The better the quality, the better for the executioner because he would later sell the clothes for a profit, unless the victim was to be gibbetted in an iron cage after death. Even then, it is doubtful that anything flamboyant would be displayed for many months on a rotting corpse. The fine clothes would be surreptitiously swapped for something less ostentatious. Many pirates loved colour and trinkets, wearing jewellery – brooches, rings, necklaces, earrings, and ribbons in their hair, they hoped to convey a dashing, rich and successful figure. King Charles I of England chose to wear several shirts for his public beheading so he might not be seen to shiver, for it was a cold day and he did not want to be thought of as shaking from fear.

Hannah Dagoe cheated the hangman out of his extra money by stripping off her clothes as she walked to the gallows, tossing bits of finery to the admiring crowd, arriving at the place of execution with very little on. She then further insulted the hangman by kneeing him in the groin and jumped out of the cart, breaking her own neck as she hanged. Many of the condemned, far from showing remorse or proving crime did not pay, became celebrities.

Hanging in Britain had been a capital punishment since the days of the Anglo-Saxons in the fifth century. Duke William of Normandy preferred castration and blinding, unless you were caught poaching one of his deer, in which case you were put to death. (Take note if ever time-travel is invented: from 1066 to the mid-1100s you could kill a commoner and live to see another day, well maybe not *see* exactly… but you would be hanged for killing a deer you poached in order to feed your starving family.) William's son, Henry I, brought hanging back as a quicker way to deal with a large number of offenders, although boiling in oil, burning at the stake and beheading were equally as popular.

Nice lot, our ancestors!

By the 18th century, hanging was the most used death sentence. 1770 saw the first start of pleas for the death penalty to be more humane, but it was not until 1868 that public hangings were stopped in favour of private execution within the prison walls.

Children as young as seven could be hanged for a capital crime, of which there was no less than 222, including damaging Westminster Bridge! The number was reduced to four offenses in 1861, these being murder, arson in a royal dockyard, treason and piracy. The death penalty in Britain was not abolished until 1969 but this was only for murder, the other three remained until the European Convention on Human Rights in 1999 ratified a law that all death penalties were to be abolished. The last public hanging outside Newgate Prison was in May 1868, and the last public execution of a woman was at Maidstone that same year.

Popular belief is that witches were burned at the stake, although in England they were more usually hanged. Burning was reserved for religious sedition and treason.

The change to the drop and the rope being knotted in such a way that the neck is broken and the jugular vein ruptured is not necessarily a 'kinder' way to kill, although it is quicker. The truth is there is no way of knowing how long or short a time the person feels pain. Death by hanging is supposedly 'almost instantaneous.' The word 'almost' is a little alarming. Sentencing carries the words 'hanged by the neck until dead.' A Canadian in 1919 took over an hour to be hanged by the neck until he was dead. There were also cases of the head being snapped off. Nasty.

Anything could be used for a gallows, often a sturdy bough was ideal for the job with the unfortunate victim being 'turned off' from a ladder, stool, back of a cart or a horse. Most towns erected a gallows either in the town centre, or at a crossroads just outside, the conventional structure being a single upright with a beam cross-braced at a right angle, or two upright posts joined by a beam for dispatching more than one person at once. Both required a ladder, stool, barrel or cart for the hanged person to stand on.

The 'triple tree' was erected at Tyburn, a triangular-shape from uprights of about twelve feet high and crossbeams, where up to twenty-four could be hanged at once.

The 'drop' gallows came into use at Newgate in 1783, consisting of a box that the victim stood on, then it dropped down leaving him or her suspended and strangling. The 'box' was eventually replaced by a trapdoor. Until 1892, the prisoner's hands were usually bound in front, with the cord around the wrists and a second one encircling the body and arms. This was so that they could pray until that final moment and it was not until the 1890s that arms were restrained behind the back. Hoods to obscure the face from public view were not used until the 1800s. The noose was initially a hemp loop, but when the end was threaded through a brass eyelet, it became easier to run, and therefore tighten quicker. The position of the eyelet, beneath the angle of the jaw, was vital in order to ensure the head moved backwards to break the neck, not forwards to constrict the throat.

The rope itself, after it had done its job, would be cut into short lengths by the hangman, and sold as souvenirs. Also on sale were the dead person's body parts, or even the entire cadaver, to be used by medical men and students for dissection. One body thus disposed of, was laid out on the dissecting table only to 'come alive' as proceedings began. This was not a one-off occurrence. Anyone who was found to still be alive was reprieved, as survival was seen as God's intervention. From the 1st of June 1752, mandatory dissection for murderers, men or women, came into being with an Act of Parliament. The Act was abolished in August 1832. The family of the deceased were also able to buy the body if they had enough funds to bribe the hangman. In the 1600s and 1700s, he was more often than not a criminal himself, reprieved on condition that he executed others who had been condemned. For this reason, it is very rare to have the hangman's name or identity recorded.

At Tyburn on the Christmas Eve of 1705, John Smith was turned off from the cart and dangled from the noose for a good fifteen minutes. The crowd shouted for his reprieve and he was cut down, taken away and made a full recovery. Apparently when asked what the experience had been like he answered: 'I was, for some time, sensible of very great pain occasioned by the weight of my body and felt my spirits in strange commotion, violently pressing upwards. Having forced their way to my head I saw a great blaze or glaring light that seemed to go out of my eyes in a flash and then I lost all sense of pain. After I was cut down, I began to come to myself and the blood and spirits forcing themselves into their former channels put me by a prickling or shooting into such intolerable pain that I could have wished those hanged who had cut me down.'

Where an example had to be made, particularly in the case of pirates, gibbeting, or hanging in chains was an additional sentence. After death, the criminal would be stripped naked, the body coated in hot pitch or tar and when it had set hard, be re-dressed and secured in an iron cage. The entire structure was then attached to the gallows from which the culprit had 'swung' or a gibbet that had been erected in a prominent place especially for the purpose. The idea was to display a stark reminder of the fate awaiting the lawless. It does not seem to have worked very well as a warning. The corpse remained there until it was either eaten by birds and rats or rotted away. The risk of having your corpse gibbetted, or dissected, made no difference to the manner of execution but for the religious, hanging in chains and dissection meant a great deal, for it was believed a body was needed to be able to reach heaven. Even if not especially religious in life, belief in God and an afterlife often meant a great deal when someone was about to meet his or her maker. The punishment signified no reprieve even after death but continuous torment for the soul. I wonder how many pirates actually cared about that?

36

# Are You Kidding?
# Hanged *Twice*?

1701. May. The tarred corpse of a pirate hangs in an iron cage from the gibbet at Tilbury Point, Wapping, beside the River Thames. It is to remain there until it rots. Thus ended the days of William Kidd, Captain, and as he claimed, a privateer not a pirate.

Scotsman William Kidd was born in Dundee in January 1645, according to his testimony at his trial for piracy in 1694 or 1695. His father, John Kyd, had been lost at sea, although there have been some claims that he was a Minister of the Church. It seems William became a sailor well before his privateering days, and that he took up residence in the young city of New York.

In 1689, he was a member of a crew that mutinied, threw out the captain and sailed for Nevis, a small Caribbean island that is part of the Leeward Islands. Kidd became captain and the ship was renamed *Blessed William*, presumably for William of Orange, not William Kidd, although there are any number of Williams from saints to sinners who could have been the object of the accolade. It is possible Nevis's governor, Christopher Codrington, gave William Kidd the captaincy because the ship became one of a fleet that was to defend the island against the French – due to another war, of course. Unable to pay the crew a fee for their services as sailors, Codrington offered a Letter of Marque and expected the men to take their wages out of the potential French Prizes. Whether his instructions included attacking the French island of Marie-Galante, and destroying its town, is unclear but the profit gathered from this escapade was in the region of £2,000. Kidd and the crew went on to capture other Prizes, for which they were rewarded. In May 1691, William married Englishwoman Sarah Bradley Cox Oort, who had been widowed twice and was one of the wealthiest women in New York.

Governor Bellmont of New York, Massachusetts and New Hampshire commissioned Kidd to go pirate hunting, seeking out the rogues of those early years of piracy in the Caribbean along with any French ships. Travelling to England to obtain financing for the venture, Kidd managed to find sponsorship from the Earl of Orford, the Baron of Romney, the Duke of Shrewsbury and Sir John Somers, all notable and powerful Englishmen. Kidd was given a Letter of Marque, signed by King William III, the deal being any Prize was to be distributed with ten percent for the King and the rest divided between the crew and the sponsors. Kidd financed some of the expedition and named his new ship the *Adventure Galley*. She was a fast, sleek vessel equipped with oars as well as sail.

Setting out along the Thames, perhaps not being aware of the custom, Kidd failed to salute a Royal Navy vessel anchored at Greenwich. Affronted, the captain ordered a shot to be fired to draw attention to this lack of respect. Kidd's crew responded with even more disrespect by exposing and slapping their buttocks. Furious, the Navy captain had many of Kidd's crew pressed into service, leaving him short-handed. However, he still managed to capture a French ship on the crossing back to New York, where he replenished his crew.

By September 1696, Kidd was ready to set sail for Africa and the Cape of Good Hope. Cholera diminished his crew, the *Adventure Galley* sprung several leaks and the pirates he was supposed to be hunting were not to be found. Undeterred, Kidd sailed for the Strait of Bab-el-Mandeb, the southern entrance of the Red Sea, where pirates notoriously laid in wait for the rich Moghul ships heading to Mecca. He was out of luck. He must have been desperate to find a Prize or two to cover the heavy financial outlay but he passed several non-French ships while sticking to the rules of the Letter of Marque he carried, even though the dispirited crew were close to mutiny. When a Dutch ship was hove into view and Kidd again refused to attack it because King William III was Dutch, an argument broke out. Kidd killed one of his own crew, possibly by accident; he snatched up an iron bucket that he threw at the man, fracturing his skull. He died that same day. This could be regarded as a murder but Kidd appeared unconcerned.

One of the small Prizes they took later reported acts of indecency, torture and cruelty with Kidd's crew ransacking ships while he sat in his cabin talking to the captain of the captured *Mary*. Kidd was outraged when he found out and forced the crew to give the plunder back.

He took a hefty Prize in January 1698 when he captured the richly laden *Quedagh Merchant*, her captain being an Englishman carrying a pass from the French East India Company promising him protection by the French Crown. Kidd attempted to persuade his crew to desist from ransacking the ship, but failed, the crew maintaining that their commission was to take French ships, even if one was captained by an Englishman. Kidd relented to avoid mutiny, or worse, but when news eventually reached England, Kidd was branded a pirate and a warrant was put out for his arrest.

Kidd kept the ship, renaming her the *Adventure Prize*. Back in Madagascar, he encountered his first pirate, however, the crew refused to attack and threatened to shoot Kidd instead. Another nail in the coffin for the accusation of piracy. Pirates did not usually attack other pirates. Most of the crew, now disloyal and against Kidd, deserted and he returned to the Caribbean with only thirteen remaining men. He soon discovered that he was a wanted man, abandoned the *Adventure Prize* and completed his journey to New York as a passenger aboard a sloop, apparently burying some of his plunder with the intention of coming back for it later. He is one of the very few pirates who buried their treasure. His backers, unfortunately, had decided that they would rather not be associated with piracy; Kidd was arrested when he reached Boston in July 1699.

Held for over a year, mostly in solitary confinement in Stone Prison, he was eventually transferred to England and brought before Parliament to explain himself. He was nothing more than a scapegoat used by the Tories to discredit the Whigs who had backed him, but Kidd remained silent and refused to give details of names, confident that his sponsors would come forward on his behalf. They didn't. Would he have been spared if he had talked? We will never know. Sent to trial before the High Court of the Admiralty, where he had no friends, he was charged with piracy and murder (that iron bucket, remember?) He wrote a series of pleading letters to the King while imprisoned in Newgate, presumably all of which were ignored. Found guilty of murder and five counts of piracy, he was sentenced to hang at Execution Dock, Wapping, on 23rd May 1701.

Still protesting his innocence, he was pushed off a barrel, the drop the usual short one that should have meant slow strangulation, but the rope broke. Another noose was fashioned and slung around his neck. (You can't help but feel sorry for the poor man who was probably innocent of the charges and now faced this terrible ordeal.) A second time a noose was set around his neck and he stood upon a barrel – if a rope broke again, it would be deemed an Act of God and he would be reprieved ...

The rope didn't break.

His body was coated in tar and secured in an iron cage to dangle from a gibbet for more than three years. The members of his crew, who had also been arrested, were all granted pardons. He was abandoned and blamed for no other reason than he failed to deliver a fortune in loot to those who had backed him.

If William Kidd had buried a significant amount of treasure, it has never been found. Claims that the wreck of his ship had been found have not been substantiated, and a silver ingot supposedly recovered has been proven to be of a much later date. The legend of Captain Kidd lives on in many films, songs and novels. Of all the pirates, he deserves sympathy. I believe he was the wrong man in the wrong place, and paid the ultimate price.

37

# A Reign of Terror: Charles Vane

(Spoiler alert.) When in the TV drama series *Black Sails*, Charles Vane (played by New York born actor Zach McGowan) was killed off there was an outcry from the show's fans, which is a little baffling as the real Charles Vane was hanged in 1721 so his death was not exactly a secret or a surprise.

Born between 1680 – 1690, I assure you it is as annoying for me as it must be for you to not have the exact dates, Vane was an English pirate who terrorised the Caribbean from 1716 to 1719. He was one of the pirates who was part of the self-named Flying Gang based at New Providence, Nassau. Vane had a notoriously violent career and reputation. As with most of the Golden Age Pirates, the information we have about Vane comes from Captain Charles Johnson's *A General History of the Pyrates,* which may, or may not, be accurate.

With no documented evidence about his early life, it can only be speculated that Vane served somewhere as a seaman, either in the Royal Navy or as a merchantman. Wherever it was, he gained much knowledge and experience of ships, sailing and fighting at sea. He is first recorded as sailing with Henry Jennings and Samuel Bellamy in connection with Jennings' daring raid to steal the treasure from the Spanish Fleet that went down off the coast of Florida in 1715. These men had amassed a fortune and Nassau was, then, a safe harbour for ne'er-do-wells so Vane and his colleagues probably lived a life of relative luxury with money enough to spend on wine, women and song. Committing various pirate attacks, Vane plundered ships from all nations throughout the West Indies bringing trade almost to its knees. By April 1718, Vane had a small fleet under his command with men such as Edward England and Jack Rackham serving as crew. During that April, he took twelve vessels as Prizes, treating the captured crews with horrific cruelty despite their early surrender – usually if a Chase gave no resistance, it would be plundered for the goods it carried, but with no violence against its crew.

Vane brutally tortured his victims, making them tell where the valuable cargo was hidden. He worked to his own rules: he stole from his crew and committed acts of violence against them. When he captured a ship, he would often abandon the previous vessel and exchange it for the new one, calling most of them *Ranger*. In July 1718, he took a twenty-gun French sloop – which was to meet an explosive end. Vane and his fleet returned to Nassau, took possession of the town and hoisted his colours above the dilapidated fort. His ruling authority was short lived. Enter Governor Woodes Rogers, who had sailed heavily armed from England with a Royal Navy escort to put an end to the shenanigans of pirates like Vane and company. Offering an amnesty to all who agreed to give up the pirate life, Rogers knew he was on to a winner where most of the scoundrels were concerned, but it is doubtful that he expected the likes of Vane and Edward Teach to surrender to a life of peace, and no doubt, boredom. Charles Vane certainly had no intention of doing so.

Boldly sailing into Nassau's harbour, Rogers' Navy escort had blockaded the entrance offering an ultimatum to sign the agreement or face the gallows. There were to be no half measures. Among those who signed were Henry Jennings and Benjamin Hornigold.

Vane, however would bow to no man, especially one representing the British Government and King George of Hanover. Using his captured French ship as a fireship, he set her adrift to head straight for the blockading vessels. With ships being made of wood, fire was the dread of all sailors. When the gunpowder packed within the magazine exploded, the noise must have been incredible. The act of defiance, as bold as it was, failed. The Navy captains were experienced seamen and quickly cutting their anchor cables, drifted out of danger. Vane and his crew got clean away to fight another day – which they did with gusto.

He did was not always a good leader, making his own decisions and not listening to the opinions of his crew. Sailing with Captain Yeates in tandem, the two men fell out and Yeates, taking most of Vane's crew and a shipload of slaves they had captured, left Vane to get on with it himself. It is possible that Yeates surrendered, handed over the slaves and took the King's Pardon, which would explain the cause of the disagreement. Vane, however, seems to have had in mind a plan to retake Nassau, for in October he met with Blackbeard on the Ocracoke Island off the coast of North Carolina where they held a week-long party, with lots of alcohol, and Vane attempting to persuade Blackbeard to join his retaliatory enterprise. Blackbeard refused, and within a month he was dead, attacked by a Navy crew sent at the express orders of Governor Spotswood of Virginia.

By February 1719, Vane was hunting in the waters around the coastline of New York, where he and the crew encountered what turned out to be a French warship. Vane considered it to outgun and outmatch his own vessel, so he called off the Chase – much to the chagrin of his crew. Annoyed, and led by Rackham, they deposed Vane and sent him off in one of the smaller boats with the fifteen men who remained loyal to him.

His luck was running out as swiftly as sand through an hourglass because in March 1719, his ship was wrecked and with only one other survivor, Vane found himself marooned on an uninhabited island in the Bay of Honduras. They were to be there for several months. When a ship did come by, under the command of a Captain Holford, he recognised Vane and chose to leave him where he was for he felt (quite rightly) that Vane could not be trusted and was not willing to risk the pirate inciting the crew to mutiny and taking over the ship. A second ship came by a short while later, and this time, not being recognised, Vane and his fellow maroonee were taken aboard as foremast jacks. Vane's cache of luck had completely emptied though, for this captain met up with Holford who came aboard invited to dine. About to return to his own ship after a pleasant evening he spotted Vane and spilt the beans. Vane, and the other survivor were instantly arrested, put in chains and transferred to Holford's ship.

Holford handed the two men over to the British authorities at Port Royal, Jamaica. Vane was tried for acts of piracy, was found guilty and sentenced to hang. He was executed at Gallows Point in Port Royal, not expressing any remorse or regret. The dates for his death vary between March 1720 and March 1721. Whatever the correct date, his corpse was left in an iron gibbet to rot next to the remains of Jack Rackham, who had been hanged in November 1720. Given that the area quickly came to be known as 'Rackham's Cay' I would hazard a guess that Rackham was executed first, and Vane followed in 1721. The discrepancy could be because Vane had been marooned longer than realised, or the trial could have been delayed in order to gather evidence. Either way, I cannot feel sorry for the man.

38

# Black Sails

Famous names such as Charles Vane, Calico Jack Rackham, Anne Bonny and Blackbeard elicit a thrill of excitement and adventure, along with a shiver of apprehension. The TV-drama series *Black Sails* proves the point that pirates are as popular as ever, and we are not talking about the family entertainment buffoon-type character of Jack Sparrow here, but the nearer-reality warts an' all type.

Set twenty years before the events of Robert Louis Stevenson's *Treasure Island, Black Sails* is television's version of the pirate genre. Captain Flint, played by British actor Toby Stephens, son of actress Dame Maggie Smith, is lord of his ship, the *Walrus*, and is terrorising the Caribbean. After successfully capturing a Prize, one of the defeated crew turns out to be a very young, naïve and with all-limbs accounted for, John Silver (Australian actor Luke Arnold) who is intent on survival. Bargaining his life by proclaiming, untruthfully, his status as cook, the partnership between Flint and Silver, as depicted in *Treasure Island,* is set in motion. The series, consisting of four seasons, is not for the faint-hearted. It is sexually explicit and contains a lot of violence. The introduction of real-life characters interwoven with the fictional *Treasure Island* names is well done. So alongside Billy Bones and Ben Gunn there are Charles Vane, Benjamin Hornigold, Jack Rackham, Anne Bonny and Governor Woodes Rogers. The superb visual effects and idyllic scenery, mostly filmed on location in Cape Town, South Africa, resulted in the series being nominated for Prime Time Emmy awards each year, eventually claiming the prestigious accolade in 2014.

The relationship that develops between Flint and Silver is cleverly done, with Flint becoming more obsessed and Silver turning into a darker character as the series progressed. The show is not for viewers hoping for light entertainment and a romantic romp through the fictional adventurous world of the *Treasure Island* pirates. It is a more realistic portrayal of the gritty life these rough thieves and murderers lived. It shows the filth of daily life and the degradation of living on the edge, with a lust for treasure, drink and sex sharing prime objectives. It shows too, the political machinations between individual pirates, the greed of merchant traders and the corruption of governor and crown representatives alike.

The women of the period have their part to play in this drama series. Eleanor Guthrie, played by Hannah New, is determined to show her father – and the pirates – that she is more than capable of running Nassau as a profitable trading post, albeit trading in pirate loot. Anne Bonny (Clara Paget) lurks menacingly in the background, and Max, who starts out as a prostitute of little consequence ends up running the place when Eleanor finds herself in trouble.

The series, because of its sexual and violent content is not to everyone's taste, but the exploration of the characters, both real and fictional, blending fact with fiction is cleverly done. Added to that, the sailing sequences are superb. *Black Sails* convincingly sets the scene for the action depicted in *Treasure Island*, seamlessly blending real history and real pirates with Stevenson's fictional ones. You will not find Captain Flint in the pages of *Treasure Island*, for in the story he is long dead from a surfeit of rum. He is immortalised, however, as Long John Silver's talkative parrot is named after him.

The novel *Treasure Island* was written by Robert Louis Stevenson for his invalid stepson while holidaying in the Scottish Highlands. He was urged to publish it, which he did by serialising it in the *Young Folks Magazine* from October 1881 to January 1882 with the title *Treasure Island or, the Mutiny of the Hispaniola* and using the pseudonym Captain George North. It was published in book form a year later in 1883 through Cassell & Co. Stevenson himself described the tale as 'a story about a map, and a treasure, and a mutiny, and a derelict ship... and a sea-cook with only one leg.'

Narrated by young Jim Hawkins, *Treasure Island* has a straightforward plot with every possible pirate cliché going – except it was this story that started the clichés in the first place. The tale is full of adventure, derring-do, dastardly pirates and page-turning excitement – needless to say, it is up to young Jim Hawkins to sort everything out and, eventually, save the day.

Jim meets up with an old sea captain, Billy Bones, who is afraid of being discovered by a one-legged seafarer. Billy dies of fright and Jim discovers his old treasure map (complete with X marks the spot) and soon finds himself involved in a sea voyage to unearth the treasure, along with a crew of former pirates led by that one-legged man, Long John Silver. In the book, Silver speaks with a heavy West Country accent, which was richly developed by actor Robert Newton in the 1950 film version.

Arrr! Jim lad!

<br>

39

# Sing Along a Shanty

My thanks to John Fitzhugh Millar of Newport House, which is within walking distance of Colonial Williamsburg, Virginia, for his splendid information about sea shanties. If you would like to know more about music and dance of the 17th and 18th century I can heartily recommend a stay in John's Colonial Style B&B.

*What shall we do with a drunken sailor?*
*What shall we do with a drunken sailor?*
*What shall we do with a drunken sailor, early in the morning?*

*Heave Ho and up she rises,*
*Heave Ho and up she rises,*
*Heave Ho and up she rises, early in the morning.*

*Put him in the longboat and make him bail her,*
*Put him in the longboat and make him bail her,*
*Put him in the longboat and make him bail her, early in the morning.*

*Heave Ho and up she rises,*
*Heave Ho and up she rises,*
*Heave Ho and up she rises, early in the morning.*

Most of us know this famous shanty, which is thought to date from the 1820s. We are possibly familiar with '*Farewell and Adieu to You Fair Spanish Ladies*' as well, but there were many more rich and varied songs that sailors, and pirates, would have sung as entertainment, amusement or to keep time and rhythm during various strenuous shipboard tasks. Officially, the Royal Navy only permitted a fiddle or fife and drum to be played while the monotonous tasks were performed, there was no singing, as it was thought that orders might not be heard clearly, but I wonder how many captains turned a deaf ear to the official rules? Pirates certainly never conformed to them.

The term 'shanty' is of uncertain origin but was first mentioned in the mid-1800s. Two other variations are chanty or chantey, so it possibly derived from the French *chanter* which comes from the Latin *cantare*, both meaning 'to sing', and which, in turn, resulted in the term 'chant'. Another source – and my favourite – could be derived from the bagpipes, which come in several forms and were pumped beneath the elbow. The Chanter is the pipe, played with two hands, that supplies the melody much as in a recorder or tin whistle. It is more often than not open-ended, causing a constant on-going sound, which is not easy for the player to stop – very similar to the steady rhythm of a chant, or shanty.

Although the term is of relatively modern usage, the actual singing precedes the 1840s by a long shot. The words are often humorous or nonsensical, and as with the plaintive chants of the medieval monks and nuns, it was the steady unbroken rhythm that was important. Many had interchangeable lyrics, which could be inserted as the singers chose, or the task they were doing required. The lead singer for these work-songs and sing-outs was always referred to as the Chanty Man, both for on board and among the dock-bound stevedores who also used shanties to complete the hard, arduous task of hauling cargo on and off the dockside ships and wharves. Similar chants and songs were used by the slaves in the cotton, tobacco or sugar-cane fields, except these usually had a religious slant.

In 1865, concerning the heavy and hard work of weighing anchor, G.E. Clark wrote in his *Seven Years of a Sailor's Life*: 'The cheerful chanty was roared out, and heard above the howl of the gale…and the men, soaked and sweating, yelled out hoarsely, "Paddy on the Railway" and "We're Homeward Bound," while they tugged at the brakes, and wound the long, hard cable in, inch by inch.'

Several of the songs are linked to the drink 'grog' but the term only came into use after 1742, so pirates in the Caribbean during the Golden Age would never have heard of the word.

### A SHIP AND A MAID (1683)
18th century. To the English country dance tune *Mock Hobby Horse*

A ship she rides anchor, safe upon her bitts.
A maid must have a young man to kiss her on her ****.
*Top and t'gallant, a ship she sails trimly,*
*But maids if they be not pleased, they'll frown and look most grimly.*

A ship she has some buntlines to gather in her sail.
A maid must have a young man to tickle her on her ****.
*Top and t'gallant, a ship she sails trimly,*
*But maids if they be not pleased, they'll frown and look most grimly.*

A ship must have a mast, a long and trusty stick.
And a maid must have a young man with a long and lusty ****.

*Top and t'gallant, a ship she sails trimly,*
*But maids if they be not pleased, they'll frown and look most grimly.*

A ship must be well vittled with meat without the bones.
And a maid must have a young man with a stout good pair of ****.
*Top and t'gallant, a ship she sails trimly,*
*But maids if they be not pleased they'll frown and look most grimly.*

When a ship is under sail, we do wish her very good luck.
And a maid under a young man, we wish her a good ****.
*Top and t'gallant, a ship she sails trimly,*
*But maids if they be not pleased, they'll frown and look most grimly.*

## SAM'S GONE AWAY
1700, infinitely expandable

I wish I was a cabin boy aboard a man of war.
*Sam's gone away aboard a man of war,*
*Pretty work, brave boys, pretty work, I say.*
*Sam's gone away aboard a man of war.*

I wish I was a seaman aboard a man of war.
*Sam's gone away aboard a man of war,*
*Pretty work, brave boys, pretty work, I say.*
*Sam's gone away aboard a man of war.*

I wish I was a topman aboard a man of war.
*Sam's gone away aboard a man of war,*
*Pretty work, brave boys, pretty work, I say.*
*Sam's gone away aboard a man of war.*

I wish I was a gunner aboard a man of war.
*Sam's gone away aboard a man of war,*
*Pretty work, brave boys, pretty work, I say.*
*Sam's gone away aboard a man of war.*

I wish I was the bo'sun aboard a man of war.
*Sam's gone away aboard a man of war,*

*Pretty work, brave boys, pretty work, I say.*
*Sam's gone away aboard a man of war.*

I wish I was a marine aboard a man of war.
*Sam's gone away aboard a man of war,*
*Pretty work, brave boys, pretty work, I say.*
*Sam's gone away aboard a man of war.*

I wish I was an officer aboard a man of war.
*Sam's gone away aboard a man of war,*
*Pretty work, brave boys, pretty work, I say.*
*Sam's gone away aboard a man of war.*

I wish I was the captain aboard a man of war.
*Sam's gone away aboard a man of war,*
*Pretty work, brave boys, pretty work, I say.*
*Sam's gone away aboard a man of war.*

## SPANISH LADIES

Early 18th century. *The tune can be either minor or major (or both)*
The words have varied over the years, but this set may be one of
the earliest.

Farewell and adieu to you, Spanish ladies.
Farewell and adieu to you ladies of Spain,
For we've received orders to sail for old England,
But we hope very shortly to see you again.

*We'll rant and we'll roar like trueborn young sailors,*
*We'll rant and we'll roar on deck and below,*
*Until we sight Lizard on the coast of old England,*
*And straight up the Channel to Portsmouth we'll go.*

Now, I've been a topman and I've been a gunner's mate.
I can dance, I can sing, I can walk a jib boom.
I can handle a cutlass and cut a fine figure,
Whenever I'm in a longboat's standing room.

*We'll rant and we'll roar like trueborn young sailors.*
*We'll rant and we'll roar on deck and below,*
*Until we sight Lizard on the coast of old England,*
*And straight up the Channel to Portsmouth we'll go.*

I went to a dance one night in Gibraltar
Plenty of girls as fine as you'd wish.
One pretty maiden was chewing tobacco,
Just like a young kitten a-chewing on fish.

*We'll rant and we'll roar like trueborn young sailors.*
*We'll rant and we'll roar on deck and below,*
*Until we sight Lizard on the coast of old England,*
*And straight up the Channel to Portsmouth we'll go.*

We hove our ship to with the wind at sou'west, boys,
We hove our ship to for to strike soundings clear.
Then we filled our main tops'l and bore right away, boys,
And straight up the Channel our course we did steer.

*We'll rant and we'll roar like trueborn young sailors.*
*We'll rant and we'll roar on deck and below,*
*Until we sight Lizard on the coast of old England,*
*And straight up the Channel to Portsmouth we'll go.*

So farewell and adieu to you, Spanish ladies,
Farewell and adieu to the girls of Cadiz.
Now, be you all merry; don't be melancholy.
I'd marry you all, but me wife won't agree.

*We'll rant and we'll roar like trueborn young sailors.*
*We'll rant and we'll roar on deck and below,*
*Until we sight Lizard on the coast of old England,*
*And straight up the Channel to Portsmouth we'll go.*

## THE TOPMAN AND THE AFTERGUARD
18th century (an afterguard is a marine)

A topman and an afterguard were out walking one day,
Said the topman to the afterguard, I mean for to pray,
For the rights of all sailors and the wrongs of all men,
And whatever I do pray for,
You must answer, *Amen.*

First we'll pray for our bo'sun with his nasty stick.
He calls out 'All hands, boys' and he gives us a lick.
He beats many a brave fellow and kicks him amain.
May the devil double-damn him.
Said the afterguard, *Amen.*

Next we'll pray for our paymaster, who holds back our due.
We are owed three years' wages and prize money too.
It's 'You can't have it yet, Jack; try next voyage again.'
May the devil double-damn him.
Said the afterguard, *Amen.*

The next thing we'll pray for will be some fresh beef.
And if we ever get some we will eat with relief.
And if we get one pound, may we also get ten,
And never want for beef, boys.
Said the afterguard, *Amen.*

Next we'll pray for our purser who brings us to eat,
Salt pork, rancid butter, and rotten horsemeat,
With weavilly biscuits, so he gets the gain.
May the devil double-damn him.
Said the afterguard, *Amen.*

Now the last thing we'll pray for is a mug of good beer.
The Lord sends us liquor our spirits for to cheer.
And if we have one pot, may we also have ten,
And never want for grog, boys.
Said the afterguard, *Amen.*

*Note: the original song would have used ale or rum in place of the word grog.*

## BOSTON HARBOUR
Mid-18th century, to the tune *Derry down, down, down derry down.*

From Boston Harbour we set sail.
The wind it blew a devil of a gale.
With a ring-tail set all abaft the peak,
And a Rule Britannia, boys, ploughing up the deep.
*Derry down, down, down derry down.*

The captain comes up from down below.
It's 'Lay, aloft, lads, look alow.'
And it's 'Look alow' and it's 'Look aloft',
And it's 'Coil up your ropes, lads, fore an' aft.'
*Derry down, down, down derry down.*

Well, down to his cabin next he crawls,
And to his poor old steward next he bawls:
'Go fetch me a drink that will make me cough,
For it's warmer down here than it is up aloft.'
*Derry down, down, down derry down.*

Now there's we poor sailors on the decks,
With the blasted rain pouring down our necks.
Not a drop of grog would he to us afford,
But he damned our eyes at every other word.
*Derry down, down, down derry down.*

Now there is one thing that we do crave:
That our captain he meets with a watery grave.
We'll throw him right down into some dark hole,
Where the sharks'll have his body an' the devil have his soul.
*Derry down, down, down derry down.*

Now that dirty old bugger is dead and gone.
Damn his eyes, he has left us a son.

And if to us he doesn't prove frank,
We'll very soon make him walk the plank.
*Derry down, down, down derry down.*

## ALL THINGS WERE QUITE SILENT
18th century

All things were quite silent, each mortals at rest,
When she and her true love lay snug in one nest.
And a bold set of ruffians they entered her cave,
And they forced her dear jewel to plough the salt wave.

She begged hard for her true love as she'd beg for her life,
But they'd not listen to her, although a fond wife.
Saying, 'The king must have sailors, to the seas he must go,
And they left her lamenting in sorrow and woe.

Through green fields and meadows they oft-times did walk,
And with sweet conversations of love they did talk.
And the birds in the woodlands so sweetly did sing,
And the lovely thrushes' voices made the valleys to ring.

Though her love has left her she'll not be cast down.
Who knows, but some day her love may return.
And will make her amends for her sorrow and strife,
And she and her true love may live happy for life.

## THE FEMALE SAILOR
18th century

It is interesting that there were songs about women sailors in use during the 1700s. This particular song is one of maybe ten period songs about female sailors, all with different angles. If a thirteen-year-old girl were left an orphan, there were few options for her to survive. What could she do that did not involve prostitution? She could easily pretend to be a boy, and as long as the ship were in northern waters where the sailors had to wear so many layers of clothing, no one would ever know and she could get away with it.

John Fitzhugh Millar says: 'If she were to be found out, they would segregate her from the crew and put her ashore at the next port with all her back pay, and there would be nothing stopping her from doing it again on a different ship – no computer records in those days. It is possible that maybe one percent of the crews of all Royal Navy ships in the 18th century were women in disguise. One female sailor song even claims that a woman got promoted all the way to captain of a Royal Navy ship, which is at least possible, although probably the only time it happened.' (What a fantastic series of novels that would make!)

When Sally was a young lass, a pretty little thing,
She 'listed in the navy for to serve the king.
She 'listed in the navy a sailor lad to stand,
To hear the cannons rattle and the music so grand.
*The music so grand, the music so grand,*
*To hear the cannons rattle and the music so grand.*

The officer who 'listed her, he was a handsome man.
He said, 'You'll make a sailor, so come along, my man.'
Her waist was long and slender, her fingers long and thin,
The very things they learn-ed her she soon exceeded them.
*She soon exceeded them, she soon exceeded them.*
*The very things they learn-ed her she soon exceeded them.*

She slept in a hammock instead of a bed.
To lie with a sailor, she never was afraid.
In buttoning up her blue coat it often made her smile,
For to think she was a sailor and a maiden all the while.
*A maiden all the while, a maiden all the while.*
*For to think she was a sailor, a maiden all the while.*

I think she might still be here until this very hour,
But in guarding of prisoners they ordered her ashore.
A young girl fell in love with her, she said she was a maid,
So she went unto the captain and the secret she betrayed.
*The secret she betrayed, the secret she betrayed.*
*So she went unto the captain and the secret she betrayed.*

The captain he sent for her and asked if this were so,
And Sally being honest she dared not answer no.
'It's a pity we should lose you, such a sailor lad you made,
it's a pity we should lose such a handsome young maid.'
*Such a handsome young maid, such a handsome young maid,*
*It's a pity we should lose such a handsome young maid.*

Now, fare thee well dear captain, I'm sad to part with thee,
And likewise my shipmates, you've been so kind to me.
If e'er the navy needs a lad, a sailor I'll remain,
I'll take off my hat and feathers and I'll run the rigging again.
*I'll run the rigging again, I'll run the rigging again.*
*I'll take off my hat and feathers and I'll run the rigging again.*

## HAUL AWAY, JOE
18th century

When I was a boy I learned, or so me mother told me,
*Way haul away, we'll haul away Joe,*
That if I didn't kiss the girls their lips would all grow mouldy.
*Way haul away, we'll haul away Joe.*
*Way haul away, we'll haul for better weather, way haul away, we'll*
*haul away Joe.*

King Charles he was a bonnie king before the revolution,
*Way haul away, we'll haul away Joe,*
But then he got his head cut off, which spoiled his constitution.
*Way haul away, we'll haul away Joe.*
*Way haul away, we'll haul for better weather, way haul away, we'll*
*haul away Joe.*

The cook is in the galley, a-making duff so handy.
*Way haul away, we'll haul away Joe,*
The captain's in his cabin, a-drinking wine and brandy.
*Way haul away, we'll haul away Joe.*
*Way haul away, we'll haul for better weather, way haul away, we'll*
*haul away Joe.*

Once I had an Irish girl, but she was fat and lazy,
*Way haul away, we'll haul away Joe,*
But now I have a Boston girl, she damn near drives me crazy.
*Way haul away, we'll haul away Joe.*
*Way haul away, we'll haul for better weather, way haul away, we'll haul away Joe.*

Once in me life I married a wife, her name was Kitty Flanagan.
*Way haul away, we'll haul away Joe,*
She stole me watch, she stole me clothes, she stole me plate an' pannikin.
*Way haul away, we'll haul away Joe.*
*Way haul away, we'll haul for better weather, way haul away, we'll haul away Joe.*

Went out all night, and oh what a sight, and where do you think I found her?
*Way haul away, we'll haul away Joe,*
At the back of the bar with the sheets all off and twenty men around her.
*Way haul away, we'll haul away Joe.*
*Way haul away, we'll haul for better weather, way haul away, we'll haul away Joe.*

Saint Patrick was an Irishman, he lived in Dublin City.
*Way haul away, we'll haul away Joe,*
He chased the snakes from Ireland, then drank up all the whisky.
*Way haul away, we'll haul away Joe.*
*Way haul away, we'll haul for better weather, way haul away, we'll haul away Joe.*

Saint Patrick lived in Ireland, he came from decent people.
*Way haul away, we'll haul away Joe,*
He built a church in Dublin Town, and on it put a steeple.
*Way haul away, we'll haul away Joe.*
*Way haul away, we'll haul for better weather, way haul away, we'll haul away Joe.*

## BLOW THE MAN DOWN
17th or 18th century

Come all you young fellows that follow the sea,
*To me way hey blow the man down,*
Pray pay attention and listen to me,
*Give me some time to blow the man down.*

*Blow the man down, bullies, blow the man down,*
*To me way hey blow the man down.*
*Blow the man down, bullies, blow him away,*
*Give me some time to blow the man down.*

As I was a-walking down Paradise Street,
*To me way hey blow the man down,*
A pretty young damsel I chanced for to meet.
*Give me some time to blow the man down.*

*Blow the man down, bullies, blow the man down,*
*To me way hey blow the man down.*
*Blow the man down, bullies, blow him away,*
*Give me some time to blow the man down.*

She was bowling along with the wind blowing free.
*To me way hey blow the man down.*
She clewed up her courses and waited for me.
*Give me some time to blow the man down.*

*Blow the man down, bullies, blow the man down,*
*To me way hey blow the man down.*
*Blow the man down, bullies, blow him away,*
*Give me some time to blow the man down.*

Where she did hail from, I can't tell you much,
*To me way hey blow the man down.*
Her flag wore three colours – I think she was Dutch.
*Give me some time to blow the man down.*

*Blow the man down, bullies, blow the man down,*
*To me way hey blow the man down.*
*Blow the man down, bullies, blow him away,*
*Give me some time to blow the man down.*

She was round in the counter and bluff in the bow,
*To me way hey blow the man down.*
So I hauled in all sail and cried, 'Way enough now!'
*Give me some time to blow the man down.*

*Blow the man down, bullies, blow the man down,*
*To me way hey blow the man down.*
*Blow the man down, bullies, blow him away,*
*Give me some time to blow the man down.*

I gave her me flipper and took her in tow,
*To me way hey blow the man down,*
And yardarm to yardarm away we did go,
*Give me some time to blow the man down.*

*Blow the man down, bullies, blow the man down,*
*To me way hey blow the man down.*
*Blow the man down, bullies, blow him away,*
*Give me some time to blow the man down.*

## QUEER BUNG-YOUR-EYE
18th century

Now Jack was a sailor and he come to town,
And she was a damsel, she skipped up and down.
Said the damsel to Jack,
'Would you like for to buy what I have in this basket, some old
Bung-your-eye?'
*Ruddy rye; folla-diddle-eye ruddy rye, ruddy rye.*

Says Jack to himself,
Now what can this be but the finest of whisky from far Germany,

Wrapped up in a basket and sold on the sly,
And the name that it goes by is old Bung-your-eye.
*Ruddy rye; folla-diddle-eye ruddy rye, ruddy rye.*

Jack gave her a shilling, well pleased with the exchange.
'Hold the basket, young man, while I fetch you your change.'
Jack peeked in the basket and a child he did spy.
'I'll be damned!' did he cry, 'This is queer Bung-your-eye!'
*Ruddy rye; folla-diddle-eye ruddy rye, ruddy rye.*

To get the child Christened was Jack's next intent.
To get the child Christened to the parson he went.
Said the parson to Jack, 'What will he go by?'
'I'll be damned!' did he cry, 'Call him 'Queer Bung-your-eye!"
*Ruddy rye; folla-diddle-eye ruddy rye, ruddy rye.*

Said the parson to Jack,
'That's a mighty queer name!'
'I'll be damned!' did he cry, 'Twas a queer way he came:
Wrapped up in a basket and sold on the sly,
So the name that he'll go by is 'Queer Bung-your-eye.'
*Ruddy rye; folla-diddle-eye ruddy rye, ruddy rye.*

So come all you young sailors when you come to town,
Beware of them damsels who skip up and down,
And look in their baskets as they pass you by,
Or else they may sell you some queer bung-your-eye!
*Ruddy rye; folla-diddle-eye ruddy rye, ruddy rye.*

### SAUCY LITTLE TRIM-RIGGED DOXIE
18th century

As I walked out one May morning along the London river,
A handsome maid I chanced to spy, her topsails all a-quiver.
Her cheeks they was like roses red; she had a little bonnet all on
her head.
I put the hard word on her but she said she was a maid.
*That saucy little trim-rigged doxie.*

'I can't and I shan't and I won't go with thee, thou saucy rambling sailor.
Me parents they would not agree – I'm promised to a tailor.'
But I was hotshot eager to rifle her charms. 'A guinea,' says I,
'for a roll in your arms.'
So we went upstairs in the old King's Arms.
*That saucy little trim-rigged doxie*

It was heave and haul and let the stays'ls fall, and yardarm to
yardarm bobbin'.
Me shot's all gone, asleep I falls, and she soon fell a-robbin'.
She robbed me pockets of all that I had; she took the boots from
the end of the bed.
She even took the gold watch from underneath me head.
*That saucy little trim-rigged doxie*

And when I found that she had gone, I started to roar like thunder.
Me gold watch and me money, too, she'd borne away for plunder.
But it ain't for me watch, nor me money too. Them I don't value,
for I tell you true:
I fear a little fire-bucket burned me bobstay through.
*That saucy little trim-rigged doxie*

## THE MAID OF AMSTERDAM
1608

In Amsterdam there lived a maid,
*Mark well what I do say.*
In Amsterdam there lived a maid,
And she was mistress of her trade.
*I'll go no more a-roving with you, fair maid,*
*A-roving, a-roving, since roving's been my ru-I-in,*
*I'll go no more a-roving with you fair maid.*

Her eyes were like two stars so bright,
*Mark well what I do say.*
Her eyes were like two stars so bright.
Her face was fair, her step was light.
*I'll go no more a-roving with you, fair maid,*

*A-roving, a-roving, since roving's been my ru-I-in,*
*I'll go no more a-roving with you fair maid.*

I asked this maid to take a walk,
*Mark well what I do say.*
I asked this maid to take a walk,
So we could have some private talk.
*I'll go no more a-roving with you, fair maid,*
*A-roving, a-roving, since roving's been my ru-I-in,*
*I'll go no more a-roving with you fair maid.*

I put my arm around her waist,
*Mark well what I do say.*
I put my arm around her waist,
Says she, 'Young man, you're in great haste.'
*I'll go no more a-roving with you, fair maid,*
*A-roving, a-roving, since roving's been my ru-I-in,*
*I'll go no more a-roving with you fair maid.*

Then a great big Dutchman rammed me bow,
*Mark well what I do say.*
Then a great big Dutchman rammed me bow,
And said, 'Young man, dis bin mein vrow!'
*I'll go no more a-roving with you, fair maid,*
*A-roving, a-roving, since roving's been my ru-I-in,*
*I'll go no more a-roving with you fair maid.*

Hear now, lads, this warning from me,
*Mark well what I do say*
Hear now, lads, this warning from me,
With other men's wives don't make too free.
*I'll go no more a-roving with you, fair maid,*
*A-roving, a-roving, since roving's been my ru-I-in,*
*I'll go no more a-roving with you fair maid.*

I gave this maid a parting kiss,
*Mark well what I do say.*
I gave this maid a parting kiss,

When I walked away, my money I missed.
*I'll go no more a-roving with you, fair maid,*
*A-roving, a-roving, since roving's been my ru-I-in,*
*I'll go no more a-roving with you fair maid.*

## THE CREW WE ALL ROW IN THE JOLLY-BOAT

This song may well be 20th century, but it is such fun, I had to
include it.
To the tune *My Bonnie Lies Over The Ocean*:

The crew we all row in the jolly-boat;
The captain he rides in a gig.
It don't get him there any faster,
But it makes the old bugger feel big.

The crew we all eat on the gundeck;
The captain won't eat with the mob.
It's not that he eats any better –
He don't want us to know he's a slob.

The crew we all row in a jolly-boat;
The admiral he rides in a barge.
It don't get him there any faster,
But it gives the old bastard a charge.

The crew we all sleep in our hammocks;
The admiral he sleeps in a bed.
It's not that he sleeps any better,
But it's twenty feet nearer the head.

## SO I'LL DO YOURS WHILE YOU DO MINE

I made a shanty up for Jesamiah in *Sea Witch*. I wanted something
cheeky and a little rude to fit his character...

The Captain's a bugger, but I bugger better.
*So swab out yer gun and we'll get the job done.*
*Heave ho, heave ho, heave ho, m'lads.*
The bosun's a daisy, we know 'e's 'alf crazy.

*So swab out yer gun and we'll get the job done.*
*Heave ho, heave ho, heave ho, m'lads.*

The bilges are stinkin', who cares we're a'drinkin!
*So swab out yer gun and we'll get the job done.*
*Heave ho, heave ho, heave ho, m'lads.*

We'll sit in the sun an' might get the job done.
*So swab out yer gun and we'll get the job done.*
*Heave ho, heave ho, heave ho, m'lads.*

Then I'll do yours, while you do mine, an' we'll do 'alf the crew of
a ship o' the line!
*So swab out yer gun and we'll get the job done.*
*Heave ho, heave ho, heave ho, m'lads.*

Although sounding lewd the song is innocent – many a shanty had
a double meaning, the last line here alluded to men helping each
other plait and tar their long hair into the single braid of a queue,
favoured by many sailors. Why? (shocked expression) What did
you think it meant? Here's how that scene ended:

Jenna batted at him with the cloth that was in her hand, he
ducked beneath it and planted a kiss on her lips. 'You're pretty
when you smile, love,' he said. 'Do it more often, an' I'll give you
another kiss.'

From across the room, Tiola laughed, her head back, delighted.
He was so absurd!

Lifting the bucket, swinging it in his left hand he set off again to
fetch the last.

*'The lieutenant's a baby, 'e's got two – well maybe...*
*So I'll 'old yours while you 'old mine.*
*And we'll do all the crew of a ship o' the line!'*

40

# Pirates of the Caribbean:
# *Not All Treasure Is Silver And*
# *Gold, Mate*

*The Curse of the Black Pearl* (2003)
*Dead Man's Chest* (2006)
*At World's End* (2007)
*On Stranger Tides* (2011)
*Dead Men Tell No Tales* (2017)

When Disney's *Pirates of the Caribbean: The Curse of the Black Pearl* first hit the big screen in 2003, their expectations were not only shattered but blasted into smithereens as if a broadside of cannons from a Royal Navy man o'war had opened fire. The broadside came from one actor, Johnny Depp, in his role as Jack Sparrow. Intended as a family film to draw more interest to Disney's theme park *Pirates of the Caribbean* ride, Depp broadened the horizon, quite extensively, to touch the humour and imagination of children and adults alike. Add to that, Captain Sparrow is fun. He is also handsome and very sexy.

The series as a whole – four movies released between 2003 and 2011, with a fifth on the way (presumed release date summer 2017) – is swashbuckling fantasy adventure starring some big name actors: Orlando Bloom, Kiera Knightly, Jack Davenport, Lee Arenberg, Martin Klebba, Mackenzie Crook, Jonathan Pryce, Geoffrey Rush, Bill Nighy, Penélope Cruz, Ian McShane and even Keith Richards of Rolling Stones fame. With some off-screen names just as big; producer Jerry Bruckheimer, who rejected the original screenplay which, without the supernatural element was a straight pirate adventure. Directors include Gore Verbinski, Rob Marshall, Joachim Rønning and Espen Sandberg.

The writers are Ted Elliott and Terry Rossio, Stuart Beattie, Jay Wolpert, and Jeff Nathanson. The film franchise has grossed not far short of $4 billion worldwide, and is the 11th highest-grossing series.

The general gist of the plots are variations of quest themes: the search for Aztec Gold, the Dead Man's Chest and Jack Sparrow's magic compass, the quest for power, the Fountain of Youth and Poseidon's Trident. As back story, there is rivalry between Jack Sparrow and Captain Barbossa, and for the first two movies, all blacksmith William Turner wants is to get his girl, Elizabeth Swann, and all she wants is the excitement of adventure – oh, and true love.

The setting is the Caribbean, with no specific date just a general early 1700s, with a slight nod to accuracy regarding the British Navy and the East India Company. Prior to release, however, the media was convinced *The Curse of the Black Pearl* would be an enormous flop as pirate films and fiction had held no interest for years. Isn't it nice when these 'know-it-all' media people are proved wrong?

To the fans, the first movie in particular meant more than just a film to watch for entertainment, and a handsome eye-candy hunk to drool over. Over the internet, social media and chat room forums sprang up to bring people from around the world together. Initially, these were fan groups to discuss the movies, but many quickly expanded into something else. One in particular was not necessarily unique, but it had something very special that lasted through the years to become an internet connected 'crew' of firm friends.

As these fans of *The Faithful Bride* say:

The POTC movies (or more specifically the first POTC movie) brought me out of post-marriage depression and back into society. A friend had almost to literally drag me to see the movie the first time. The one thing I can point out as having the biggest impact is the absolute sense of *fun* throughout the movie! Yes, there was a plot; yes, there was drama; yes, there were scary elements, but the whole thing – the whole movie – re-introduced me to the concept of play and enjoyment. Heck,

I was only forty years old, and I had felt more like sixty! Captain Jack Sparrow called me out to play, and I played with a vengeance. I now have friends I would never have met if not for their interest in a pirate movie. I don't know that there is *anything* I disliked about that first movie. Or the second or the third (though the stories began to become a bit gritty by number three!) Number four – *Fountain of Youth* – ehhhh ... not the *best* POTC by a long shot. Maybe it was the introduction of new characters that threw me off, but number four simply did not grab my heart like the first three had done. Overall, and I know my pirate friends will not believe this, I became an outgoing person with a firm desire to enjoy life and all it has to offer. During and after my marriage but before POTC, I was shy, quiet, self-effacing, and mousy. I worked and took care of my family, because that is what I thought I was supposed to do. Now, I do what I *want* to do and have fun with everything. Bring me that horizon!

*Rear Admiral Bloody Brianna*

I had no idea, that warm July evening in 2003 that going to a pirate movie with my cousins would change my life. That sounds melodramatic I know, but it did. I've always had kind of a *thing* for pirates, but this pirate, in this movie, knocked me off my feet. The movie was a joyride for me, from start to finish and I think I may have actually done a little skipping as I left the theatre. The movie was over, but I wanted more, so I charted my course (used the internet) and set sail. I found others who shared my enthusiasm for this movie and this pirate, and through the kind offices of two of these amazing ladies, a small group of us found a home and a family on our own little website. We came from different places, different life experiences, we were of different faiths, but we shared a common love of this movie and its pirate captain. Through daily interaction, we got to know and love each other. We had fun, of course, but we also shared ups and downs, sickness, personal challenges, death and loss. We found friendship and support on this 'pirate crew' of ours, and for me, personally, the whole experience – the movie, the friendship – seemed to open me up somehow. I was living a fairly quiet life. I was fifty-one and single, working full-time for a private university, and living with and caring for my elderly father. I had friends and a few hobbies, but life was pretty staid. Then suddenly I discovered my 'inner pirate,' and found my somewhat sedate self, throwing caution to the winds and embarking on all kinds of adventures. The first I'll admit was pretty scary. I flew to Portland and met, face to face, some of these people who I'd only known as names on the internet. We sailed (in pirate regalia!) on the ship used as *The Interceptor* in the first movie. It was an amazing experience and it made me want more. So then there were more trips, more meetings, more adventures in Canada, Tennessee, Louisiana, Mississippi, Florida, California, Utah. We held interactive viewings of the movie as fundraisers. We met some of the incredible actors who had created those fearsome pirates, and even one of the screenwriters. There were parties and dinners and premieres for the second and third movies, and the ultimate fan-girl experience of seeing and touching the man who created our beloved Jack Sparrow. Through all this I started writing again, trying to put into words how my heart had changed because of this pirate. I have fabulous photos and indelible memories from my trips and my adventures, but more than that I have lifelong friends who have become more precious than silver and gold. I owe it all to Jack Sparrow, who taught me about freedom and taking risks, and how to head for that horizon.

Jansy

Have you ever been on an amusement ride – think roller coaster in particular – and felt such joy and excitement that you wanted to rush back to where the queue began and do it all over again? That was my reaction upon seeing the first *Pirates of the Caribbean* movie, and even after eighteen more viewings in the theater in 2003, that feeling remains. I probably would have gone back that often anyway, but the fact it made me smile and laugh while enduring a summer of multiple surgeries for breast cancer and the chemo that followed... well, it was more than just escapism; it was therapy! Once the movie left the theater, I was adrift, so to speak, but then I stumbled upon the POTC Interactive Project website (now, alas no longer active) and the many wonderful pirate pals aboard the forum, who I'm blessed to call friends to this day. They were the best cancer support group ever, and continue to give loving support and encouragement. Last, but certainly not least, tricorn hats off to the actor who took on a movie role without a script because – according to him, it felt right to do so. Oh, and did I mention that it did not dawn on me till almost six months had gone by that the character's name in the movie, Captain Jack Sparrow, matched up perfectly with the name of the hospital and cancer center where I was being treated? Aye, 'twas Sparrow! (In Lansing, Michigan). What are the chances of that happening? I don't know if 'that's what you call ironic' but the discovery certainly put a huge smile on my face. I, too, have traveled far in the last thirteen years: to New Orleans, Biloxi, Salt Lake City, and to Tobermory, Kitchener, and Hanover in Ontario, Canada, to make memories, tell tales, and share much laughter with my fellow pirates. You can't put a price on that kind of treasure!

'Ramblin' Chaplain Red'

I have happy memories of flying halfway round the world to Salt Lake City to be with these wonderful ladies and gentlemen, which included the great pleasure of meeting 'pirates' Lee Arenberg and Marty Klebba. Happy days, happy memories. For the record, I also met Johnny Depp at the premier of *Dead Man's Chest* in Leicester Square, London. And, yes, he is as good looking in real life as he is on the big screen.

With the success of the first film, the franchise was rapidly turned into a trilogy, the idea being to continue the story with the same core characters, as was done in the *Back To The Future*, *Indiana Jones* and the *Star Wars* series. The fourth movie starred some of the main characters, but included new ones such as Penélope Cruz as Jack's romantic interest and Ian McShane as the notorious Blackbeard. This fourth instalment lacked the sparkle of the first episode, the locations were limited, the stunts not so spectacular and the plot far from gripping. The fifth film, yet to be released at the time of writing, has been dogged by various delays including problems with the script, a legal case between Mr Depp and the Australian Government concerning him bringing his dogs into the country, followed by a difficult divorce for Mr Depp.

Will it be ready for 2017? Will it be a good movie?

Time and tide will tell.

## Best Quotes

'You are without doubt the worst pirate I've ever heard of.'
'But you have heard of me.'

'This girl... how far are you willing to go to save her?'
'I'd die for her.'
'Oh good. No worries then.'

'Take what you can, give nothing back.'

'Me? I'm dishonest, and a dishonest man you can always trust to be dishonest. Honestly.'

'You cheated.'
'Pirate.'

'Why is the rum gone?'

'Now, bring me that horizon.'

41

# Pirate or Privateer? Captain Benjamin Hornigold

Pirates have been called terrorists, murderers, thieves, rogues, scallywags and when he was interviewed for the first *Pirates of the Caribbean* movie, *The Curse of the Black Pearl,* Johnny Depp referred to them as the rock stars of their day. Benjamin Hornigold could possibly belong in all these categories.

Nothing was known of him until after the War of the Spanish Succession in 1713, although there is speculation that he came from Norfolk, England, perhaps the busy ports of Kings Lynn or Great Yarmouth. He always considered himself a privateer, not a pirate, as he only attacked enemy ships – or so he claimed. There is some evidence to refute this but to be fair, Hornigold did, eventually, return a captured ship to its owner.

Governor Spotswood of Virginia certainly did not agree with Hornigold's claim. In a letter he wrote: '…There is so little trust to be given to such a People, that it is not to be doubted they will use all Nations alike whenever they have an advantage.'

Hornigold moved his original base from Jamaica to Nassau where there was many another pirate, and several of them adopted a group name of 'The Flying Gang' consisting of the most notorious pirates, including Edward Teach, Sam Bellamy, Charles Vane, Stede Bonnet and Henry Jennings. Hornigold's intention was to become the leader of the pirate fraternity and establish Nassau as a Pirate Republic. He was almost successful, but underestimated the greed of the young men he expected to follow in his wake. Odd that if he truly considered himself a privateer, he was happy to associate with men who had a hefty pirate price on their heads.

He commanded a variety of ships: the *Happy Return, Adventure, Ranger* … well at least *Happy Return* had a different name …

Did these pirates not get confused between which *Adventure*, *Revenge* or *Ranger* was which? I am almost beginning to wonder if, in fact, there was only a handful of ships and they merely took turns at sailing them.

Hornigold more-or-less taught Edward Teach, his second-in-command the 'craft' of piracy, while Henry Jennings and Benjamin Hornigold were rivals to a small degree, as in 1716 Jennings tried to steal one of Hornigold's ships. Samuel Bellamy, Paulsgrave Williams and their crew joined with Hornigold, who, impressed that they had stolen some loot from Jennings, made Bellamy the Captain of the *Marianne*. With his growing fleet and claiming they were privateers, Hornigold took forty-one Prizes within one year – although Hornigold cautioned against attacking anything English. He might have had honourable intentions; his fellow shipmates did not. Maybe it was because Hornigold was attempting to stick to his own code that men like Teach voted him out of the role as captain and broke away to sail their own course under their own rules.

When Woodes Rogers arrived at Nassau with his offer of amnesty from King George, Hornigold took the royal pardon and turned pirate hunter. He accepted a commission from Rogers to go out after Teach & Co, maybe to prove his point that he was, and always had been, a legitimate privateer – or perhaps because he had felt betrayed by those he had trusted for turning against his authority and advice? For the next eighteen months, he pursued Stede Bonnet and Jack Rackham. In 1718, Rogers commended Hornigold to the Board of Trade for his efforts, even though he did not actually catch anyone.

The date of his death is uncertain, for he merely disappears in 1719. Most probably, he was lost at sea, rumour has it that his ship was wrecked on a reef during a hurricane. This is more than likely, although the fictional side would be more interesting and exciting if someone like Teach had attacked and blown Hornigold's ship to pieces. Far better to go out in a blaze of fictional glory.

42

# An Important Accessory: The Ship

What would a pirate be without a ship? Presumably the answer would be a thief, or perhaps a highwayman, although for that he would need a horse.

Pirates usually stole the ships they needed, although the technical term is *commandeer*. Stede Bonnet and William Kidd are the exceptions because they legally obtained their first ships. A ship was more than just a wooden hulk to sail about in, to the men aboard it (she!) was home, the community where they lived and worked all with the same purpose: to survive whatever the sea and the weather threw at you. Or in the case of pirates, to get rich quick with as little effort as possible. The best ships to acquire were sloops, schooners and brigantines, although in the pre-1700s, galleys were also favoured because they had oars as well as sails.

So what is the difference between a ship and a boat? Simple. A boat has one or two masts, a ship has more than two, but this only applied to sailing vessels pre mid-1800s, for modern ships/boats powered by an engine it gets more complicated: 'the difference is about the way a vessel heels (tips to the side) when going around a corner. A vessel is turning to port, and you are standing on deck facing the bow. If it heels outward during the turn (i.e. leans so your right foot is lower than your left) it's a ship. If the opposite is true, it's a boat.' Or at least, that is what my engineer nephew tells me, but I think the two or more masts rule is a lot easier to work out.

Most pirates preferred smaller boats because they were easier to handle – not so many sails and fewer men required, which in turn meant more profit per person. The disadvantage was it was more difficult to attack larger vessels, there were fewer men available to use in a fight and not so many guns.

More often than not, a Prize did not suit the pirates who had captured her. They would head for the nearest careening place, or a safe harbour like Nassau, and customise her by removing unwanted decks, particularly raised quarter or poop decks, shortening masts and removing bulkheads and cabins. Extra gunports and gun mounts would be added, then Bob's your uncle, Fanny's your aunt … you have a fully-functioning, fast and efficient pirate ship.

## Canoes

Sometimes these smaller vessels, which were also called piragua or pirogue, were found useful, especially for exploits in rivers or narrow waterways. Buccaneers, in particular, used canoes to great advantage. They were ideal for attacking towns from a river as they were powered by oars or paddles, which made them manoeuvrable and quiet. Made from cedar wood, cypress, or the kapok 'cotton tree', one could be made within a fortnight and it would be light enough to carry over land. A large canoe could take up to forty men, with huge war canoes accommodating over 100 crew.

## Galley

Propelled by sail and oar – officially called sweeps. A galley is long and slender with a shallow draught, they were extremely versatile and did not need to rely on the wind. Used as warships in the Mediterranean by the Greeks and Romans, they remained a useful vessel until the 1700s, when superior types of ships began to be built.

## Sloop

The single deck sloop was fast, agile and relatively easy to sail, even with not many men, although they could carry up to 150 crew. They had one mast rigged with a jib sail and a main fore-and-aft sail. The sails could be attended to from the deck, which meant there was no need to climb aloft, except for 'look-out' duty. Most were thirty-five to sixty-five feet in length and often required less than ten feet depth of water. They appeared in the Caribbean at the start of the 1700s when the design of vessels was rapidly improving, many being built in Bermuda or Jamaica.

### Schooner

Schooners only needed a minimum of two men to sail her, as she was rigged similarly to a sloop but with two masts, not one. They were fast, capable of maintaining over ten-knots in a good wind. The length was between forty and seventy feet and a schooner required only five feet of water beneath her keel. As with the sloop, the boats built towards the first half of the 18th century were from Bermuda and Jamaica, but later the Baltimore Flyers were built in Maryland with designs improving through the turn of the century.

### Brigs and Brigantines

These were sturdy enough to cope with the rough seas of the Atlantic. Originating from Europe, they were the main class of vessel used for merchant shipping. In 1704 they had two masts with square-rigged sails and fore-and-aft on the mainmast. Length averaged around eighty feet and needed about 100 men to manage them. They were also fast and manoeuvrable.

### Frigate

Usually of the Royal Navy, three-masted full-rigged frigates were larger than brigantines and designed as a fast and efficient warship, often with one or two gun decks, with at least twenty-eight cannons deployed. Commonly they were used as patrol boats or for escorting convoys of either merchant or navy vessels. They were the 'work horse' of the Royal Navy, and if in the hands of a capable captain could out-gun almost any ship.

### Man o'War (Man of War)

As the name suggests, a fighting ship of the British Royal Navy. With three masts each carrying three or four square-rigged sails. Reaching up to 200 feet in length and with anything up to 124 cannons usually arrayed over at least three decks, they were strong, tough, and formidable weapons of war. Compared to a sloop or schooner they were clumsy, slow and bulky, making only a maximum of nine knots, but no one got in range of those guns when they fired a full broadside.

## Galleon
A 17th-century Spanish vessel used for battle and to carry treasure from Mexico and South America back to Spain.

## East-Indiaman
These were large three-masted merchant vessels designed for the long voyages from England (the East-India Company) or the Netherlands (the *Vereenigde Oost-Indische Compagnie)* specifically to carry cargo. They were usually heavily armed.

## What Is a Ship?
She is made of wood, well-seasoned oak being preferred by the English: note that the English oak tree is different to the American one, ours is the familiar broad-trunked, wide canopied monarch of the forest, the American oak is taller and narrower. There are the tall masts stretching upwards and another pointing forwards. She has decks, a hull, and a keel. A pointy bit at the front, a blunt end at the back. There are acres of canvas sail and a lot – a lot – of rope for the rigging. She is powered by the wind, or by oars too, and the tall ships we are familiar with, such as the *Cutty Sark* and *HMS Victory* that are seen in dry dock as visitor attractions are steered by a steering wheel – the helm.

To steer a ship in the early centuries, pre-1500s, a large oar-like paddle was suspended over the side and the helmsman turned it as required to steer by altering the amount of drag pushing against it. Located on the right-hand side when facing forward this became the steerboard side, which later corrupted into starboard and starb'd. The opposite side, the left, was larboard or larb'd, with the term port coming into use by admiralty orders in the late 1700s (we think) to avoid confusion. It is easy to remember which side is which. Port, in addition to rum, is a sailor's favourite tipple: ergo, when entering harbour, especially after a long voyage, 'there is no port left'.

A hinged rudder at the stern and below the waterline replaced the steerboard towards the end of the 12th century, with a tiller or whipstaff in order to move it left or right. This enabled ships to become bigger, higher and longer. By means of ingenious late Medieval technology, a long, thin pole, the whipstaff, was connected to the rudder at one end and the tiller at the other, which the helmsman steered possibly from one or two decks above the level of the rudder, but not out on the open deck. He would view the way ahead through a porthole or hatchway called a 'companion'. To move the ship he would push the connecting pole to left or right. Steering was now better but it was difficult for the man at the helm to see the set of the sails, and there was a limited range of movement for the controlling tiller, no more than15 degrees.

The steering wheel-shaped helm came into common use at the turn of the 18th century, around 1700-1705. This invention meant the man at the helm stood on the quarterdeck so he could see behind and to either side, but not always ahead if the lower main and fore sails were set, as they would impede his view. He could, however, actually *see* the sails, which meant he could steer with far more accuracy. I wonder if those first mariners complained about the helm being out in the open? With an inside tiller they were at least dry, if not necessarily warm. Standing at the outside helm, they were at the mercy of the elements and the danger of storm-driven waves washing over the deck to drag them overboard. That problem was solved by the helmsman lashing himself to the wheel. When it was very hot, he risked getting sunburned and maybe even sunstroke; but such was the way in the age of sail.

So why is a ship called a 'she'? The legend goes that she is capricious, likes to do as she pleases and often has ideas of her own. She has a waist and stays, and it needs a lot of paint to keep her looking good. There is always a gang of men around her and it takes experience to handle her whims. She proudly shows her topsides, demurely hides her bottom, and when entering harbour she heads straight for the buoys. So now you know.

Nearly all the larger pirate vessels had a main deck, below it was the living space and the cargo hold. The larger the vessel, the more decks it would have. Space, particularly height, was limited with sturdy beams supporting the overhead deck, often with less than five feet of headspace. Light was provided through gratings and hatchways which were battened down in stormy weather and covered by tarpaulins or oiled sailcloth. For the Great Cabin at the rear (the captain's quarters) there would be windows across the stern and sometimes at the sides for small quarter cabins, which would house a bed on one side and a latrine, which was nothing more than a hole leading to the outside, with a wooden surround, in the other. For the men, the latrine, known as the Head, would be up towards the bow, and again, mere holes cut in a plank suspended above into the sea. More often than not, they would merely urinate over the side – which side depended on which way the wind was blowing. The crew, especially on merchant ships lived mostly towards the front of the vessel at the forecastle (pronounced fo'c'sle). Here they would eat, sleep and pass the day when not needed on deck. The captain and officers aboard a merchantman would have wooden box-beds, usually slung on ropes at each corner from the overhead beams. The crew had hammocks, which would be taken down during the day, or slept on the open deck.

Some of the vessels had a galley, a kitchen, which would have a secure brick-built oven set on a flagstone floor. Gunpowder would be stored below deck away from there, and usually protected by a wetted canvas curtain instead of a door.

Conditions below deck would be dark, cramped, damp at best, wet at worst, would smell of mildew and mould and be infested with rats, lice and fleas. In heat, it would be sweltering; in cold weather, freezing. The hold was amidships; supplies, sails, cargo, or treasure if there was any, would be stored here. Beneath this deck was the bilge, a space filled with ballast that could be stones, rocks, gravel or sometimes timber if this was part of the cargo. It was always damp and stank; the anchor cable was also stored here.

Cannons would be placed according to the size of the vessel, and fired round-shot, grapeshot, langrage and chain-shot. The size of a gun was measured by the size of the round shot, so a four-pounder ball to a twelve- or eighteen-pounder meant bigger and heavier guns. Swivel guns mounted on the rail were of about two-pounder range and could, as the name implies be swivelled around to take aim or reload.

During action, the decks would be cleared of everything movable, if necessary the bulkheads below deck, that is, the inner walls, were taken down, and the stern windows swung up to be secured on the ceiling above. The galley fire would be doused and the lower sails on a square-rigged vessel 'clewed' up, that is furled away, to give a clear view along the deck and as a precaution to avoid the spread of fire. Sand would be scattered around the guns to prevent the men slipping.

The masts – vertical poles, or for the bowsprit at the front, a horizontal pole – were not one, long solid piece of wood, but had several sections that fitted neatly together, the lower section supporting the topmast, which in turn supported the topgallant. In bad weather these top two sections could be taken down – struck. The sails hung from wooden poles called 'yards', which could be hoisted up and down or turned back and forth by means of hauling on ropes. To 'know the ropes' meant to know what all the various ropes and pulleys did, where they went to and came from. The yardarms were the end of the yards and each yard was known by where it was situated with the fore yardarm being the least popular as it was from here that men were hanged. The sails themselves, made from canvas by sailmakers, with the canvas coming from flax, were hung either in a fore-and-aft vertical line along the deck, or at right angles for a square-rigged vessel. Even on a square-rigged ship, sails were not square but tapered or rectangular, and the bigger the ship, the larger the area of sail. HMS *Victory*, now seen in dry-dock at Portsmouth, had about four acres of sail in total, although smaller ships such as those used by pirates were more likely to be nearer one acre.

Rigging was either running or standing, running being rope that passed through blocks and tackles for moving the yards around, and hauling and lifting, while the standing rigging of shrouds and stays were ropes of various widths and lengths that were in a permanent, fixed position to support the masts and yards. There could be about forty miles of rope on board with over 1,000 pulleys.

The topmen were those who went aloft to the highest yards, they were usually the young, agile men, and were the elite of the crew and valued their position. Working aloft meant they were out of sight of the officers for one thing, and they were left alone to get on with their job. They often had their own mess groups, and thought very little of the waisters, the non-sailors such as marines, sea-based soldiers. Until standard uniforms were introduced, they preferred colourful clothes and jewellery and wore different hairstyles. To be a topman also required courage. To go aloft to manhandle the sails and work dangling from the yards in not just bad weather but storms and gales, often in the dark required a touch of madness as well as bravery.

To ascend the masts the men would climb the rigging, a bit like an assault course rope ladder, and, sorry to say, there was no crow's nest for the lookout to perch in, it is a later term and applies to whaling ships. Lookouts would either be at the bow, the front, or perched in the crosstrees up the mast – or straddling the highest yards. And if all these nautical terms are baffling you, there is a short glossary at the back of this books.

Dangers to ships were shallows, rocks, and storms which could snap a mast in two or be so severe that waves would swamp the below decks, despite all hatches being battened down. Lightning was an unpredictable danger, especially if it were to strike near where the powder magazine was situated. The lightning rod, or conductor, was invented by Benjamin Franklin in 1749, and proved to be most useful for ships with tall masts, except too many conductors were fitted incorrectly and caused more damage than necessary.

If you had managed to cross the Atlantic in one piece, with only a little water and food left, your masts were just about intact despite the lightning, your keel is scraped from getting too close to the shallows and rocks, the hull is covered in barnacles and the sails are worn and patched from the rage of the wind – you have survived all that – only to come face to face with a pirate.

*A Few Pirates and Their Ships*
Howell Davies

| Sloop | *Rover* | 32 cannon |
| Sloop | *Adventure* | 10 cannon |

Edward Teach –Blackbeard,

| Frigate | *Queen Anne's Revenge* | 40 cannon |

**Charles Vane**

| Sloop | *Ranger* | 10 cannon |
|-------|----------|-----------|
| Brigantine | *Ranger* | unknown |

**Bartholomew Roberts**

| Brigantine | *Good Fortune* | 32 cannon |
|------------|----------------|-----------|
| Frigate | *Royal Fortune* | 32 cannon |
| Brigantine | *Sea King* | 32 cannon |

**Samuel Bellamy**

| Sloop | *Mary Anne* | 8 cannon |
|-------|-------------|----------|
| Galley | *Whydah Gally* | 28 cannon |

**Stede Bonnet**

| Sloop | *Revenge* | 10 cannon |
|-------|-----------|-----------|

**Jack Rackham**

| Sloop | *William* | 6 cannon |
|-------|-----------|----------|

### Famous in Their Own Right

Ships such as *Victory, Cutty Sark, Mary Rose, Bounty* and the *Mayflower* are almost household names to tall ship and age of sail enthusiasts, but they all, as beautiful as they are, fall outside the main era of piracy. The *Whydah* and *Queen Anne's Revenge* belong to our golden age sea-wolves, both known because their wrecks have been found and excavated. The *Whydah* is a definite find, as her ship's bell, complete with engraved name, was discovered, while the *Queen Anne's Revenge* remained uncertain until it was concluded that the discoveries made were from Blackbeard's lost ship.

### The Whydah Gally

*Galley*, or *Gally*, both versions are correct. Built in London in 1715 and launched a year later, she was captured by Sam Bellamy in February 1717 and wrecked on 26th April 1717 off Cape Cod, Massachusetts Bay Colony. She was a Galley of 300 tons, 110 ft in length, carrying twenty-eight guns, fully rigged with three masts. She had a possible speed of thirteen knots (15 mph), and could carry a complement of 150 souls, but went down with 145 men and one boy. Her wreck was discovered in 1984, buried beneath the sand between sixteen to thirty feet under water.

### Queen Anne's Revenge
Frigate, launched 1710, England, 200 tons, 103 ft, complement, 125 souls. Captured by the French and renamed *La Concorde de Nantes*, then captured by Benjamin Hornigold on 28th November 1717, near the island of Martinique, but commanded by Edward Teach who renamed her *Queen Anne's Revenge*. She ran aground in 1718 near Beaufort Inlet, North Carolina. Intersal Inc., a private research firm, discovered the wreck in 1996, located by director of operations, Mike Daniel in twenty-eight feet of water, one mile of Atlantic Beach, North Carolina. Thirty-one cannons of various origins have been identified, and more than 250,000 artefacts recovered, which support that the wreck is that of *Queen Anne's Revenge*.

### Lady Washington (Replica)
Not herself a pirate ship, but as HMS *Interceptor* she was commandeered by pirate Jack Sparrow in the first *Pirates of the Caribbean* movie.

The original trade ship, *Lady Washington*, was a ninety ton brig. She left Boston Harbour in October 1787 and sailed around Cape Horn, the first vessel carrying an American flag to do so. Named for Martha Washington, she was the first American vessel to reach Japan. She foundered in the Philippines in 1797.

The replica was built in 1989, and designed by John Fitzhugh Millar of Newport House, Williamsburg, Virginia, who also kindly advised me about sea shanties and the *Bachelor's Delight*. She has appeared in several films in addition to *Pirates of the Caribbean* as the brig *Enterprise*, a namesake of *Starship Enterprise*, in *Star Trek Generations*, in the IMAX film *The Great American West* and in the TV miniseries *Blackbeard*.

### HMS Rose aka Surprise (Replica)
Again, not a pirate ship but, for me, a pirate connection as in her new guise as HMS *Surprise*, from the movie *Master and Commander*,

I commandeered her as the template for *Sea Witch*. The movie is adapted from the novels *HMS Surprise* and *The Far Side of the World* by Patrick O'Brian, the screenplay co-written and directed by Peter Weir, and starring Russell Crowe as Jack Aubrey, with Paul Bettany as Stephen Maturin. It was released by 20th Century Fox, Miramax Films and Universal Studios. For an almost authentic feel of what life was like aboard a ship in the 18th century, watch this movie.

Her specifications are: 500 tons, full rigged ship; overall length, 179 feet; length on deck, 135 feet. Height of main mast, 130 feet. 13,000 sq feet area of sail; draught, 13 feet, beam, 32 feet.

My original intention had been to model *Sea Witch* on the *Whydah* or *Queen Anne's Revenge*, but the plan never gelled. *Rose/Surprise* fitted my imagination like a glove, except she was built several years after the period in which the *Sea Witch Voyages* are set – 1715 to about 1725, but then my series is part fantasy and it is not meant to be taken seriously, so I bent the facts a little.

Moored in San Diego, California, *Surprise* is a beautiful ship, originally built as a replica of HMS *Rose*, an 18th-century Royal Navy vessel that was, in part, responsible for the outbreak of the American War of Independence and cruised the American coast during the Revolutionary War.

The replica was built in Nova Scotia in 1970 by John Fitzhugh Millar, using construction drawings from 1757. The real *Rose* was built in Hull, England in 1757 and her duty was to be a scout ship for the British fleet and to patrol the coasts of any enemy country during the time of war. In 1768, she was sent to America to patrol the eastern coastline where high taxes were causing unrest – and in 1774, commanded by James Wallace, she sailed to Narragansett Bay, Rhode Island to put an end to the extensive smuggling.

On 4th May 1776, Rhode Island initiated the Declaration of Independence from Britain, two full months before the rest of the Colonies. It is often believed, especially here in the UK, that the Boston Tea Party, where a cargo of tea was thrown overboard into Boston Harbour as a protest against the payment of taxes started the American War of Independence. In fact, it was the petitioning to Congress to form a Continental Navy in order to rid Narragansett Bay of the highly efficient *Rose,* which fanned the flames of unrest among the Colonies.

*The Flying Dutchman*

I cannot have a chapter about ships without mentioning the *Flying Dutchman*. She was a Dutch East India Company ship and rounding the Cape of Good Hope, off the tip of Africa, she met with a terrible storm, as often happens in those parts. The captain, instead of running for the nearest safe harbour, maintained his heading, vowing that he would hold his course until Judgement Day if he had to. The ship sank, never to be seen again, with no one from the crew being found, alive or dead.

Since then, there have been many claims that the ghost of the *Flying Dutchman* has been seen at sea, including by the future King George V of England while serving in the Royal Navy in 1881. He described a strange red light surrounding a phantom ship, a brig, with masts, spars and sails. The legend that seeing the ship is an omen of impending doom does not seem to have affected the Prince. Perhaps royalty and future monarchs are an exception to the ghostly legend?

43

# Frenchman's Creek

One of the most famous and familiar opening lines of a novel is, '*Last night I dreamt I went to Manderley again*'. It comes from *Rebecca* by Lady Browning – Dame Daphne du Maurier DBE. She also wrote *Jamaica Inn*, *My Cousin Rachel* and many others, but I wonder how many people know that Hitchcock's thriller *The Birds* is also a Du Maurier story? For myself, my favourite is *Frenchman's Creek*. It ticks all the boxes. It is about pirates, has action, adventure, romance and a handsome hero. The icing on the cake is that it is set in the West Country, Cornwall, where Du Maurier lived. For a holiday treat, try a walk alongside the real

Frenchman's Creek near Helford and imagine a pirate ship hiding there among the leafy glades. There is also a wonderful Riverside Café Victorian Tearoom at the start – or end – of the walk, which is equally worth a visit.

Born in May 1907, Daphne du Maurier's first novel, *The Loving Spirit*, was published in 1931, and while many of her following works may not be regarded as being of great literary merit, they are stories that linger well after the last page has been read and the book closed and set aside. They rarely finish with the expected 'happy ending' but leave the reader wondering how the characters fared afterwards. They are not historically accurate – few novels of before the 21st century are – and they are, perhaps, a little old-fashioned with the plots, characters and style belonging to a bygone era but then they were written in the 1930s and 40s. Nevertheless, Daphne du Maurier was a first-class, first-rate storyteller. She had a gift for writing suspense and the unexpected, with the ability to create a sense of time, place and believability that immerses the reader in the world of the story. She created atmosphere as if it is the easiest thing in the world to do. And still today, her stories capture the heart, the soul and the imagination, most of them having never been out of print. She died in 1989, at home in Cornwall.

*Frenchman's Creek* was published in 1942 and is set in England during the reign of Charles II. Bored with her dull life and her even duller husband, Dona, Lady St Columb abruptly decides to escape from the meaningless and extravagant parties and balls shared with equally dull people with too much money to spend and nothing of interest to do. The king has been restored to the throne, along with frivolity and carefree abandon and Dona is sick of it. Telling her husband that she needs time to be alone and to be able to breathe fresh, clear air, she takes her two children and their nurse and heads for Navron, her Cornish home, which she has not visited for many years.

On arrival, she finds the house all but empty apart from one servant, William, whom she has never seen before. His calm efficiency plus the quiet and the slower pace of life at Navron suits her; she has found an understanding friend in William, her freedom, and now needs to find herself.

She plays with her children in the woods, not caring about staying clean or tidy. As the story progresses, the reader can feel Dona beginning to relax and become more likeable. The woman at the beginning of the book was difficult, she was fraught, cross, sarcastic and uncaring; at Navron she has rediscovered her sense of humour – and adventure, which springs to full life the day she sees a boat, *La Mouette*, anchored in the creek that borders her land.

At once she realises this is the French pirate who has been the talk of the nearby town for his daring raids along the Cornish coast. She soon links William to the pirate, and realises they have been using Navron, and the creek, as a safe harbour and hiding place. It is not long before she meets the pirate, Jean-Benoit Aubéry and discovers he is not a murderer but an educated man who likes to draw birds, and loves the sea and his freedom.

Dressed as a boy, Dona takes her next step into adventure and a life very different from her own by joining his crew to capture a richly laden merchant ship, which belongs to one of her neighbours who is as boring as her husband. The expedition is a success but maybe Aubéry has gone a step too far this time, for the affronted rich locals are now determined to find him and his crew, and hang them.

Harry, Dona's husband and his friend, Rockingham, who desires Dona, arrive spoiling her new life of freedom and excitement. The men plot to capture the pirates, but end up as their prisoners instead. The astute Rockingham quickly realises the emotional and sexual rapport between Dona and Aubéry ... and to tell more would be a huge spoiler. You will have to read the book to find out what happens.

*Frenchman's Creek* is a well-crafted story about the need to escape and find freedom, the motive that drove the desire of most pirates to kick over the traces and roam the seas in command of their own destiny – even if that destiny was more often than not a date with the gallows. Dona is a realist, she understands that fun and adventure cannot last forever, that loyalty and responsibility are also important but it is the doing, and having, the secretive memories that is important to her and to the reader, who shares the secret with her.

The novel is not a romance, but it is romantic. It is an adventure with swashbuckling pirates, but the style is calm and patient, almost languid. There is sexual tension but nothing explicit, and its ambiguous ending leaves the characters lingering very strongly in the mind. Did they? Did he? Did she?

The 1998 film version, starring Tara FitzGerald as Dona and Anthony Delon as Aubéry, was immensely enjoyable, even if in places it was very different from the book. So what? A good adventure is a good adventure, especially when pirates are involved.

When the east wind blows up Helford River the shining waters become troubled and disturbed and the little waves beat angrily upon the sandy shores. The short seas break above the bar at ebb-tide, and the waders fly inland to the mud flats, their wings skimming the surface, and calling to one another as they go.

*Frenchman's Creek* by Daphne du Maurier

44

# Another Frenchman – But a Real One This Time

Alexandre Exquemelin, in his 1684 *The History of the Buccaneers of America*, states that Frenchman François l'Ollonnais prowled the Caribbean in the 1660s. Like William Dampier, he came to Saint Dominque (Haiti) as an indentured servant a decade before that. When the servitude was finished, he turned to buccaneering, preying upon the shipping in the Spanish Main. Some while into his new career he and his crew were shipwrecked and they were attacked by Spanish soldiers who killed everyone except L'Ollonnais who survived by hiding among the dead.

He managed to reach Tortuga, with the assistance of some escaped slaves and, fully recovered, held a Spanish town hostage demanding a ransom for its safe keeping. The Governor of Havana took a dim view of this and sent a ship to have done with this irritating Frenchman. Unfortunate for the governor, l'Ollonnais captured the crew and beheaded the lot of them, save one, who was forced to carry a message back to Havana, the gist of which was to announce that l'Ollonnais would never give any Spaniard quarter.

Sailing from Tortuga with a crew of 440 men and a fleet of eight ships in 1666, they captured a Spanish treasure ship carrying a cargo of cocoa beans, gemstones and 260,000 Spanish dollars. They then went on to sack Maracaibo, in today's Venezuela. They plundered the city, but the residents had fled and the crew found no treasure. The poor people had not hidden themselves very well though, for l'Ollonnais found them, tortured them and discovered where the city's gold had been stashed. L'Ollonnais's 'persuasion' methods were not very pleasant. Few resisted long.

Over the next two months the Frenchman and his crew tortured and raped, then plundered the city, burning what was left of it to the ground. Then they went to San Antonio de Gibraltar, Venezuela, slaughtering 500 soldiers in the garrison and held the city for ransom. This was paid – a sum of 20,000 pieces of eight, along with 500 head of cattle – but l'Ollonnais continued ransacking the place, increasing his total of plunder to 260,000 pieces of eight plus precious gems, silver, gold, rare silks and slaves.

The residents of Tortuga heard about his success and gave l'Ollonnais the nickname 'The Bane of Spain', *Fléau des Espagnols*. Pirates flocked to enlist with his crew when he was ready for a new expedition to pillage Central America, in 1667. Approaching San Pedro, the pirates met Spanish soldiers and l'Ollonnais only narrowly escaped with his life, although he later captured two men. He killed one of them by cutting out his heart, then he proceeded to eat it. Terrified, the second man showed a suitable route to the city – but the attackers were repelled and the few survivors returned to their ship, which foundered on a shoal off the coast near Darién, a province of Panama. According to Exquemelin, while seeking food inland, the men were caught by native Kuna warriors and eaten. One wonders, however, if all the crew were thus killed, and their bones and charred flesh scattered to the wind, how Exquemelin came to know of such a grisly end?

45

# Getting There and Back

Getting from A to B in the days of sail was not easy. Much of the ocean was unexplored; for instance, Australia had not been discovered in the early 1700s. There was no longitude, only latitude. The only thing sailors from the 15th to 18th centuries could do was 'run down the latitudes' – basically, head north or south until they reached a point where they wanted to turn east or west, steer as straight as possible, then hope for the best. In the earlier days of sail, for the Greeks, the Romans and the Vikings, navigation meant sailing close to land taking note of landmarks, rock formations, bays and inlets. There was the path of the sun and the moon, and the patterns of the stars to follow; early sailors knew well enough that the North Star showed north, but what happened on cloudy nights? Landmarks were a necessity; the White Cliffs of Dover, Sugar Loaf Mountain (Monte Christo) in Brazil, Table Mountain in Cape Town, the distinctive shape of various Caribbean Islands, the Needles at the Isle of White ...

Knowledge of the tides and currents were also essential: the Gulf Stream, for instance, played a most important part in sailing across the Atlantic. Weather patterns, too, had to be considered such as the hurricane season, the Monsoons, the regular reoccurring winds. Then there were areas to avoid or to take care when navigating them – rounding Cape Horn and the Cape of Good Hope were both fraught with danger. The Bay of Biscay was, and is, notorious for bad weather and strong currents that can make ships founder on the rocks of Ushant.

Another challenge were the Doldrums, a vast area above and below the equator that could extend from fifty to 150 miles where there was very little to no wind at all with hot, oppressive air that could becalm a ship for days or weeks – unless a storm blew up from nowhere. Even today, the term 'in the Doldrums' means to be stuck, depressed, or out-of-sorts. To either side of this languid area were paths of constant wind, known as the Trade Winds, for obvious reasons. For the pirates, the Windward Passage, between Cuba and Hispaniola, were a good hunting ground. Further north, towards the Pole, the Westerlies were reliable winds that blew from the west; between them and the Trades, were the unreliable winds known as the Variables.

Charts that mapped the sea were highly prized by pirates, assuming they had a navigator who could interpret them. They marked the coast and landmarks, the depth of water, where there were shoals or sandbanks, river mouths, bays, harbours, tides and currents.

In addition to natural features and charts the fortunate pirate vessel had an experienced navigator who had a full set of navigation equipment. Vessels had a magnetic compass fitted in the binnacle, where at night the only light was permissible. The pivoting needle set atop a card with the compass points, known as the compass rose, etched into it was in use from the 1500s.

The lead line took soundings when near land to determine what was beneath the keel. Knots along a length of rope indicated depth, one fathom, which is six feet. Two, three, four... Standing as close to the bow as possible the leadsman would coat the lead weight, weighing anything up to 56lbs, at the end of the line with tallow or wax, then hurl the entire line outward, either counting the knots as the rope went out, or as he brought it in again. He could see what was on the seabed by what was sticking to the wax: a clean weight meant rock, whereas sand, broken shell or mud meant a soft bottom. 'Swinging the lead' is a term assumed to indicate not doing a job properly or shirking duties but it would have been difficult for a sailor to do this as there were always others nearby, and anyway to do so would not only put the entire ship in danger, but that individual sailor's safety as well.

Time was measured by a sand-filled glass, the most familiar one being the half-hour-glass with its nipped-in waist. Sand would trickle from top to bottom at a measured rate. Day aboard a ship, and in the early Medieval period on land as well, began at noon. Twenty-four hours were divided into four-hour 'watches'.

The speed of the vessel was also essential for gauging distance travelled. This was established by use of the Log Line, a length of rope with a weight at one end and knots set at regular intervals – and a thirty-second sandglass. The end of the log-line was hurled overboard and the line allowed to run free, with the sandglass set at the same moment. When all the sand had trickled from the top bulb to the bottom one, the line was immediately stopped from running and hauled in. The number of knots counted indicated the speed, one, two, three, four, five, six, seven, eight, nine, ten knots or more.

Published navigation manuals and tables listed sailing directions. Some date back to as early as 1509, although these – and subsequent publications right up into the 18th century – were not always very reliable.

Telescopes – nicknamed a *Bring It Close*, were essential. So were dividers and parallel rulers with a good knowledge of mathematics. Dividers were to measure distance and to plot a course using whatever sea chart was appropriate. Most navigation was accomplished by dead reckoning – little more than intellectual guesswork really.

The quadrant, a device to ascertain latitude, was a quarter-circle of wood marked in degrees and with a plumb line and sight along one edge. Another similar tool was the astrolabe, both in use in the 15th century.

The cross-staff came into use during the next century. It had two parts to it, a long, graduated staff or pole and a sliding crosspiece. Holding one end of the staff close to his eye, the navigator lined up with where the sun and the horizon could be sighted, moving the crosspiece along until one end became level with the horizon and the other with the sun. The angle marked on the scale on the staff gave the latitude. A variation was the backstaff, in use around 1594, which did the same job but without the need to look directly at the sun. Both were simple, not expensive, but were not effective if the sun could not be seen through cloud, fog or rain. The nocturne was similar but was designed for taking measurements from the North Star to the two pointer stars of Ursa Major – also known as the Plough, Great Bear or, in the US, Big Dipper. Again, a problem on a cloudy night.

In the mid-1600s, John Napier came up with the notion of logarithms, which Edmund Gunter turned into simple calculations for ships' navigators, which in turn led to the increase of intrepid sailors circumnavigating the world. Come the early days of the 18th century, and our pirates roaming the seas for easy prey and the lure of loot, a good navigator could estimate the time within a quarter of an hour, and thus be able to ascertain the latitude within a discrepancy of a handful of miles.

The sextant replaced the simpler instruments from around 1759, and used mirrors to measure latitude. Navigation was still a bit hit-and-miss, however, until longitude was finally able to be measured. To do so, a reliable clock was needed and mariners had to wait for this until 1764. Even then, the chronometer, as it was called, did not come into full use until 1825. Greenwich Mean Time was used as a standard for measuring time but was not made fully effective until 1833.

Sailing the seas was not a quick, easy way to travel. A letter, for instance, could take up to sixty days – assuming there were suitable wind and weather conditions – to reach London from Virginia, or seventy days from the Caribbean. Voyages around the world took several years to complete.

Imagine a wife, mother, or family waiting patiently back home, never knowing how their loved-one was faring from month to month and all too often, never discovering why they would not be coming home. Imagine wondering whether they had become the victim of pirates, or were to hang because they had turned to piracy, although at least with the latter, loved ones would, eventually, learn of their ultimate fate.

46

# The Lowest of the Lowe

One of the last pirates of the Golden Age to be about his piratical business in the Caribbean was Edward, 'Ned' Lowe (and you've guessed it, it could be Low, Lowe or Loe, depending on how you want to spell his name.) Born in 1690 at Westminster, London, he came from a chronically poor background, was illiterate and forever fighting; he probably had to do so in order to survive. He very soon got into pickpocketing and thieving, as was most of his family. His younger brother, Richard, was hanged at Stepney in 1707 for burglary. Lowe's petty crimes escalated as he grew to maturity and he left London for the Caribbean in 1710. You can't but speculate that this was to avoid arrest. Had someone recognised him? Did a burglary go wrong perhaps? Best way to avoid the noose – hop on a ship and head for where the sun shone.

Ned Lowe spent three or four years in different places before settling in Boston, in Massachusetts Bay, where he married Eliza Marble on 12th August 1714. The couple produced a son, who did not survive infancy, and a daughter born in 1719, with Eliza dying in childbirth. Did her loss affect Lowe? He seems to have respected marriage, as he did not force men with a wife and family to join his crew when he turned to piracy, and he ensured that no women were ever harmed. A rare thing, a pirate who was a gentleman? Hmm. Read on.

It appears he did seek an honest living as a rigger and in 1722, he joined a twelve-man crew aboard a sloop heading for Honduras with the intention of purchasing timber to sell back in Boston. Loading the cargo, he got into an argument about rations and shot at the captain with a musket. Unfortunately, he missed (muskets never were accurate) and shot another man instead. Forced to make a run for it, Lowe, with Francis Spriggs and the crew, stole a different ship, murdering another man in order to do so, and headed off into a life of piracy. Spriggs acted as quartermaster as they prowled the shipping lanes between Boston and New York before sailing for the Cayman Islands. There Lowe became lieutenant to pirate George Lowther who had a 100 ton sloop, the *Happy Delivery*, which boasted eight cannon and ten swivel guns. The sloop was destroyed by islanders, but small things like that do not deter pirates, they simply stole another ship called (wait for it...) *Ranger*.

May 1722 found Ned Lowe given the command of a brigantine they had captured, *Rebecca*, and on good terms, he parted company with Lowther to follow his own path with Spriggs as quartermaster again, and a crew of forty-four men.

In June 1722, they blockaded and subsequently plundered thirteen fishing boats at anchor in Port Roseway, Nova Scotia, with Lowe flying his own distinctive colours of a blood-red skeleton on a plain black background, and declaring No Quarter to anyone offering resistance. Sensibly, no one did. With all the ships plundered and then burnt, Lowe abandoned *Rebecca* and took the largest one, an 80 ton schooner, renaming her *Fancy*. The plunder did not include just the cargo of the vessels he sacked, for Lowe also forced most of the fishermen to join his crew. Philip Ashton managed, eventually, to escape in the early spring of 1723 at Roatán Island off the coast of British Honduras. He described his ordeal as being beaten, flogged, kept in chains and threatened with death when he refused to sign the pirate articles.

As a commander Lowe was ruthless, efficient and cruel. (So not a gentleman after all.) During his reign of terror, he captured more than 100 vessels sinking most of them once they had been plundered, and became feared for torturing his victims if they refused to join his crew or put up a fight. One of his favoured methods was to place cord or slow-match (a rope fuse) between the fingers of bound hands and set light to the rope, which would burn slowly roasting the flesh of the hands and fingers to the bone. Another favourite was to suspend his victims by the ankles from a yardarm and drop them to the deck, repeating the process until they died.

Lowe headed out to the Azores, halfway across the Atlantic, where he joined forces with pirate Charles Harris, and captured a warship, which he turned into his new flagship, renaming it *Rose Pink*. (If nothing else, you have to give the man credit for being inventive with naming his ships.) Calling himself 'Commodore' he sailed on to the Canary Islands and Cape Verde, then headed back to Brazil, where he ran into bad weather and was driven towards the Caribbean. Off the coast of Surinam, they decided to careen but Lowe was not an experienced seaman and *Rose Pink* capsized during the procedure. The portholes had been left open, she filled with water and sank taking all the food, cargo, water, ammunition and plunder with her.

So yet again another ship, renamed *Squirrel* (did Lowe have a penchant for nature I wonder?) was commandeered and sail was set for Trinidad and Tobago. They found themselves near French-owned Grenada where Lowe planned to send some of the crew ashore for provisions. The French were not going to permit a stranger into their harbour, however, and sent a vessel to investigate. Lowe captured the ship, renamed her *Ranger* (not unusual) and gave *Squirrel* to Spriggs to command, who promptly renamed her *Delight*. A disagreement a few days later saw Spriggs sailing away one night to become independent of Lowe.

More captured ships came and went. Lowe kept one, calling her *Fortune*. Then a Portuguese ship, the *Nostra Seignior de Victoria* fell into his hands. He had struck rich, for she was carrying a bag of 11,000 gold Portuguese moidores, at the time worth around £15,000, but rather than the treasure falling into the pirate's hands the ship's captain heaved the bag into the sea. Not a good idea. Lowe cut off his lips and boiled them in water, then forced the unfortunate man to eat them. Lowe then murdered him along with the rest of the crew. He was also said to have burned a Frenchman alive. The conclusion has to be Lowe was definitely not a nice man.

Are these stories exaggerations? Perhaps deliberately spread rumours to intimidate possible Prizes? Or was the man a deranged psychopath? The fact that several men from his various crews spoke of him as vile and wicked points to the latter.

By now various governments were interested in putting a stop to Lowe. He headed back to the Azores again, where he joined with pirate Charles Harris. On 10th June, they met with a British man-of-war, HMS *Greyhound*. Her captain, Peter Solgard, had been especially commissioned to capture Lowe. Leaving Harris and the *Ranger* to see to themselves, Lowe fled with enormous losses to his crew and damage to his vessel. The *Greyhound* captured twenty-five men, who were tried and hanged at Newport near Rhode Island, on 19th July 1723. Captain Harris was taken to England and hanged at Execution Dock, Wapping. Solgard was rewarded handsomely.

Furious, Lowe captured a whaling vessel, torturing the captain before shooting him through the head. He set the whaler's crew adrift without provisions, although his intention of them starving to death failed as they managed to reach Nantucket, more or less in one piece. Near Block Island, off the coast of North America, Lowe took a fishing boat as a Prize. He cut off the head of the ship's master with such savagery that his crew refused to take part in any further torture of the unfortunate prisoners. A French vessel with twenty-two guns was next, then a merchantman from Virginia, the *Merry Christmas*.

He met up with his friend, Lowther, again in late 1723 and together they captured the *Delight* near the coast of Guinea with command of her going to Spriggs. Within two days Lowther and Spriggs had again abandoned Lowe, leaving him with just the *Merry Christmas*, and he was never heard of again.

Charles Johnson in his *General History of the Pyrates* published in 1724, related several varying rumours including that Lowe had sailed for Brazil or his ship had sunk in a storm. The National Maritime Museum, Greenwich, records that he was never caught. Another rumour is that his own crew set him adrift, yet another that he was rescued by a French ship, recognised and hanged in Martinique, where few legal records remain, in 1724.

So no one knows what befell Edward Lowe, his fate remains a mystery – which is a delight for novelists like myself, although I am not sure that anyone outside of horror fiction would be too keen on writing about this awful man. However, expect to meet him – and his demise – in a future *Sea Witch* Voyage.

47

# Hoist the Colours

Flags, or Colours as they are correctly called, were important as identification, much like an I.D. card or vehicle number plate is today. Think about Trooping the Colour in London, where a regiment's 'colours' are displayed – trooped – before the reigning monarch. Flags were also used as signals to send messages in the Royal Navy, with different patterns and shapes, square or with a 'swallow tail', meaning different things: the alphabet for spelling out orders, or specific meanings, such as the Blue Peter while in harbour to announce that the vessel is about to set sail.

James VI of Scotland, when he became King James I of England in 1606 after the death of childless Queen Elizabeth I, had a flag designed that combined the cross of St George and the cross of St Andrew, thus joining England's and Scotland's emblems together. The new flag, although known as the British flag, became more popularly known as the Union Jack, the 'Jack' coming from the Latin, *Jacobus*, for James. Ireland was, back then, not represented. From around 1627, ships flew a smaller version of the flag – known by its size as a 'Jack' from the jack staff situated at the bow or on the bowsprit. By the 18th century, with staysails being added between the bowsprit and the foremast on most vessels, the Jack ensign was only flown when in harbour, although the flag itself had, by then, become the main distinguishing flag for the British Royal Navy. Sometimes called the Union Flag, both Jack and Flag are correct terms, although it has been argued that the 'Jack' should only apply to ships at sea. This has been hotly disputed, even by the Admiralty, and 'Union Jack' has always been the more common name, becoming official in 1908 when Parliament approved that, 'the Union Jack should be regarded as the National flag'.

Today's familiar design with the additional cross of St Patrick representing Northern Ireland dates from 1801. Wales was not represented, as the Principality was regarded as already being part of England from Henry VII and the start of the Tudor dynasty.

English privateers would have flown the Jack ensign but with those rascal pirates, they had additional colours to flaunt in the face of their enemies. Flying the colours of a friendly nation would lure the prospective Prize into believing there was no danger – until the last moment when up would come the dreaded Jolly Roger. As with so much involving pirates, there is no indication where the name 'Jolly Roger' came from. One plausible explanation is that 'Old Roger' was a common name for the devil, and several pirate flags depicted a grinning Beelzebub of one sort or another.

The commonest design associated with the Jolly Roger flag is the skull and crossed bones, used by Sam Bellamy and Edward England, while the skull and crossed cutlasses, was Calico Jack Rackham's colours. Both flags had a white emblem on a black background. The symbol of a skull or skeleton was a familiar one long before the days of shipping as they would often be carved on to tombstones. The adaptation into a pirate's clear message of 'heave to or die' would have been well understood.

A plain black flag was flown by several privateers in the early 1600s, with a reference to a skull and crossbones on a red background in 1687, although this has been connected to pirates on land, not at sea. A red flag was used in conjunction with the black; it signified the spilling of blood. If the Chase did not surrender when the black flag was flown, up would go the red one, and woe betide the victim for that red flag signified 'No Quarter', no reprieve; death was the only outcome.

Most privateers, Sir Henry Morgan as example, used English colours, but the pirates' intention was to intimidate and frighten, so their leering skulls and suggestion of death and fierce weaponry was all a part of the Grand Plan. Whether the almost universal use between the pirate brethren of these leering flags was an arranged idea, or it spread in popularity is, again, annoyingly unknown, but by the height of piracy in the Caribbean circa 1720, nearly every pirate captain could boast his own colours.

Edward Lowe: black background with a red skeleton

Edward Teach (Blackbeard): black background with a devil skeleton holding an hourglass in one hand, a spear about to stab a red heart in the other. This may also have been similar to another flag used by Edward Lowe.

Bartholomew Roberts: First flag, black background, himself and the devil holding an hourglass; second flag, black background, himself standing on two skulls.

Jack Rackham: black background, a grinning skull between two crossed cutlasses.

Sam Bellamy and Edward Lowe: black background, leering skull atop two crossed bones.

Whatever the emblem, when ships saw that black flag being hoisted to the masthead it meant only one thing – trouble.

48

# Two More Immortal Captains

Two fictional pirates cling to the mind from childhood, both much-loved for very different reasons.

> *'Have to fly, have to fight, have to crow... Hook is back.'*
> *'I hate, I hate, I hate, I hate Peter Pan!'*

Captain James Hook, or *J.A.S. Hook, Cptn,* as he makes his mark, is possibly the most ruthless (and lovable) pirate villain in the world of storybook and movies – even outdoing Captain Flint and Long John Silver, although in a far different way. Hook is obsessed with making an end to Peter Pan and will stop at nothing to achieve his goal.

This included kidnapping Pan's children in the 1991 Steven Spielberg movie *Hook,* starring Robin Williams and Dustin Hoffman, among other great names such as Dame Maggie Smith, Bob Hoskins and Julia Roberts. The movie, which was nominated for five Oscars, begins with the premise that (spoiler alert, if you have not seen the film, skip the rest of this paragraph ...) Peter has *grown up*. He is married to Wendy's granddaughter, has two children, and has completely forgotten Neverland and his life as The Pan. When Hook kidnaps the children Peter Pan, with the help of Tinkerbell and the Lost Boys, must become Peter Pan again and battle against Captain Hook.

The original character of Peter Pan was a seven-day-old baby created by J.M. Barrie in a chapter entitled *Peter Pan in Kensington Gardens* as part of an adult novel, *The Little White Bird,* published in 1902. After the success of Barrie's play, *Peter Pan, or The Boy Who Wouldn't Grow Up,* which premiered in London soon after Christmas 1904, his publisher, Hodder and Stoughton, took the relevant sections and republished them as an individual story with illustrations by Arthur Rackham.

Barrie himself extended the plot of the stage play and published it as *Peter Pan and Wendy* in 1911. Peter, as a character, was based on Barrie's elder brother, David, who drowned the day before his 14th birthday in an ice-skating accident. David was always remembered, thereafter, as the boy who would not grow up.

Peter Pan can fly with the aid of fairy dust supplied by his fairy-friend, Tinker Bell, and passes his eternal childhood having a variety of adventures with fairies, mermaids, American Indians – and pirates – on the island of Neverland, which you can find by heading for the '*second to the right, and straight on till morning.*'

His appearance was never detailed by Barrie. In the stage play, his clothes were made from autumn leaves and cobwebs, but these were adapted into a dark red tunic and green tights. A costume worn by Pauline Chase for the productions that ran between 1906 and 1913, is exhibited at the Museum of London. The green costume became synonymous with Pan after the release of the 1953 Walt Disney animation.

His name, 'Pan', and his love of playing panpipes seem to be linked to the mythological god, Pan. As a pre- and post-Christmas pantomime, the character has usually been played by a boyish-looking actress.

As a rival to the dastardly Captain Hook, Peter Pan is skilled with a sword, which was the cause of the enmity between them as Pan had sliced off Hook's hand in a duel, hence the hook. Pirate Hook's ship is a brig, the *Jolly Roger*, and Barrie states that he was formerly Blackbeard's bo'sun. His own bo'sun is Mr Smee, and aside from his loathing of Pan, Hook has two fears; the sight of his own blood, and a particular crocodile, which swallowed both the severed hand and a clock, the ticktock of which always announces his immanent arrival.

In the original stage play, Hook was not included as a character, but observing that children loved villainous pirates and pirate stories Barrie expanded the story to include our captain. The character was initially intended for actress Dorothea Baird, but Gerald du Maurier, the father of *Frenchman's Creek* author Daphne du Maurier, begged for the part instead of playing Wendy's father, George Darling. (I wonder if this is where Daphne developed her love of pirates?)

Barrie stated that Hook's obsession with the crocodile echoed Captain Ahab's quest for the white whale in Herman Melville's 1851 novel, *Moby Dick*. He also said that 'Hook' was not the Captain's real name, but to reveal it would be to 'set the country in a blaze', and that the only man Long John Silver from *Treasure Island* was afraid of was Hook. Barrie implied that Hook went to Eton College for in the play his last words are '*Floreat Etona*', Eton's motto, but for the novel, he ends with disapproving of Pan defeating him by throwing him overboard by saying, 'Bad form,' implying dishonour.

In most portrayals of Hook, he wears a black Charles II-type curly wig and he has bushy eyebrows and a moustache. He is good looking and elegant in manner and speech, even when blaspheming. In the play, his hook is on his right hand, in most movie adaptations it is the left, and he often carries a cigar holder which contains two cigars.

In the Disney cartoon version, the character is voiced by Hans Conried, and is portrayed as a foppish comical figure with a streak of cowardice about him – somewhat similar to the lion, Prince John, in the *Robin Hood* Disney adaptation, voiced by Peter Ustinov. Disney insisted on keeping Hook alive at the end of his cartoon animation as he said; 'The audience will get to liking Hook, and they don't want to see him killed.'

Quite rightly spoken sir, Good Form!

Cue a sea-shanty-style jolly theme tune called *The Trumpet Hornpipe* played on an accordion. Roll credits for a much-loved children's TV series that used cardboard cut-outs. Captain Pugwash and his crew aboard the *Black Pig* was one of my favourite childhood delights. Created by John Ryan, the series was shown in black and white on BBC television in 1957. I would have been four years old, and I well remember the tall, wooden box with a tiny screen at the top that took ages to warm up before we could view anything. I recall my Dad being so proud of that TV set, although now, all these years later, I have a sad feeling that he did not purchase it solely so that I could watch the adventures of Pugwash and his crew.

Our hero, Captain Horatio Pugwash, was ably assisted by Tom the Cabin Boy, and pirates Willy and Barnabus, with Master Mate and their enemy Cut-Throat Jake, captain of the *Flying Dustman*.

At one point, scurrilous rumours were spread by the British media claiming the characters were linked to risqué sexual names, such as Seaman Staines, and Roger the Cabin Boy. Completely unfounded, for there were no such names. The newspapers were forced to make a public retraction and pay a settlement fee. Why does the media have to, so often, spoil innocent fun with smutty untruths? I reckon Cut-Throat Jake put them up to it.

Pugwash debuted in *The Eagle* comic in 1950, then as a cartoon strip in the TV programme guide *Radio Times*. The subsequent TV cartoon series of eighty-seven five-minute long adventures was produced by Gordon Murray with the voices provided by Peter Hawkins. The last series was produced in 1975.

Using the cardboard cut-outs, the animation was formed by using levers to move them against a painted background. There are many anachronisms in the stories – none of which were meant to portray historical accuracy – but the king strongly resembles George of Hanover, King George I, although in one TV episode Pugwash wins the Pirate of the Year Contest for 1775, which would have been King George III. Still, that is being somewhat picky.

Pugwash himself is a useless sailor; in the first episode he has no idea what the terms his crew are using mean and he calls for his Nautical Dictionary. He is pompous but likeable, and he often calls himself the bravest buccaneer, although more often than not he gets himself into all sorts of predicaments because he hasn't a clue about anything. He always wins the day, though, usually because of the quiet assistance from Tom the Cabin Boy. He very rarely commits any acts of piracy, despite prominently displaying the skull and crossbones.

Master Mate is equally as clueless, and often uses mispronounced words. He stows a teddy bear in his bunk and has no authority over the crew.

In contrast, Tom the Cabin Boy is quick witted and clever. He is the cook and the only one who actually knows how to sail the *Black Pig*.

Cut-Throat Jake, when not scheming to think up ways to outwit Pugwash, always seems to have a hold full of treasure and is far more competent than his rival. He speaks with a typical pirate West Country accent, and wears an eye patch and a large beard.

Pugwash has several endearing catchphrases, which are guaranteed to raise a smile: 'Blistering barnacles'; 'Coddling catfish'; 'Dolloping doubloons'; 'Kipper me capstans'; 'Nautical nitwits'; 'Shuddering sharks'; 'Stuttering starfish'; and 'Suffering seagulls'. Cut-Throat Jake occasionally utters things like, 'Scupper me Jolly Roger!'

The theme tune, played by Tom Edmundson and arranged by Philip Lane, was popular from the 19th century although the country of origin, and composer, like most shanties, is unknown. In the United States it is called *The Thunder Hornpipe*, not *The Trumpet Hornpipe*.

The pleasure of writing this book, and this chapter, has meant that for research purposes I had to spend a pleasant afternoon watching episodes of Captain Pugwash on You Tube.

Writing can be such a hard taskmaster ...

49

# A Few Not-So-Well-Knowns

Privateer Jan Baert was born in 1650 to a Dunkirk seafaring family. He was Flemish speaking and served with the Dutch Navy. In 1672 there was yet another war and he signed up to support the French. Only those of good birth could become officers, so he enlisted in the Dunkirk Privateers, where he was commended for bravery.

He married sixteen-year-old Nicole Gontier in 1676, and they had four children with their eldest son, François-Cornil, eventually becoming vice-admiral. (Nicole died in 1682).

By 1679, Baert had risen to the rank of lieutenant. His derring-do was a thorn in the Dutch backside and greatly affected their commercial trade. As one example, he managed to break through a blockade with only six ships, destroying several of the enemy's vessels and escorted a convoy of grain safely through to the Dunkirk shore. He then attained the rank of captain, and after that, admiral, achieving his greatest glories during the Nine Years War of 1688-1697.

Things had not begun all that well, though. In 1689, the English captured him and he was escorted to Plymouth. But three days later, he escaped with twenty other prisoners and reached Brittany in a rowboat. During this year, he also married again, to Jacoba Tugghe. They had ten children.

In 1691, he again managed to slip through a blockade at Dunkirk, heading outward this time. He sailed to Scotland where he burnt a castle and several villages. Come June 1694, he even outdid his own prowess by capturing a convoy carrying Dutch grain and saved Paris from starvation. For his reward, he was raised to the peerage on 4th August 1694.

However, he had not finished terrorising the Dutch. In 1696, he defeated them in the Battle of Dogger Bank. The Peace of Ryswick, a treaty signed in 1697, ended his seafaring exploits. During his time as a French Privateer, he captured 386 ships and burned or sank many more. Dunkirk has a statue of him, and the public square bears his name. He died in April 1702 of pleurisy and is buried at Dunkirk, in the Eglise Saint-Eloi.

**WILLIAM FLY** was an English pirate for a total of three months during 1726. His career started in April of that year after signing on as crew with Captain Green aboard the *Elizabeth* with the intention of sailing to West Africa. Tempers flared and Fly instigated a mutiny. Captain Green was thrown overboard and Fly took command after being elected as captain, and renamed the ship *Fames' Revenge*. They headed for North Carolina, taking five vessels as Prizes but were then captured and arrested. Fly was sentenced to hang at Boston Harbour on 12th July1726 but he was disdainful of his fate, refusing to repent, and accusing the hangman of doing a poor job. Fly re-tied the noose correctly and placed it around his own neck; his final words being a warning to all captains to treat their crews with respect: 'Our Captain and his mate used us Barbarously. We poor men can't have justice done us.'

Fly's corpse was gibbeted as a warning against piracy, and two others of his crew, Samuel Cole and Henry Greenville, were hanged on the same day.

**ISRAEL HANDS** was second-in-command to Edward Teach, Blackbeard. Captain Charles Johnson stated that Hands was shot in the knee by Teach, who was aiming at another member of the crew. There is a suggestion the shooting was deliberate in order to save Hands from taking part in the battle with Lt Maynard at the Ocracoke. Seems a bit of a drastic method to me. Added to that, would Blackbeard seriously think that he would be defeated? And anyway, Hands was in Bathtown, North Carolina, at the time, recovering from his wound, although it never healed and it left him disabled.

He was captured and tried for piracy at Williamsburg, Virginia, but in exchange for a pardon, Hands testified against the North Carolina government officials with whom Teach had been working. There is no record of what happened to Hands, although Johnson declares that he died a beggar in London, England. It is more likely that because he turned King's Evidence he changed his identity, recovered a squirrelled-away hoard of loot, and lived a pleasant life in retirement somewhere.

**CAPTAIN WILLIAM LEWIS** had a lengthy career as a pirate from 1717 to 1726, although little is known about him. He captured several vessels off the Carolina coast in his ship *Morning Star*. He was murdered in his bed by his own crew because they thought he was in league with the devil.

**CHRISTOPHER MOODY** was possibly one of Bartholomew Robert's crew, committing acts of piracy off the North and South Carolina coasts between 1713 and 1718. His flag was different to all others in that it was gold on red with an hourglass sprouting wings – depicting to his victims that time, for them, was running out – and a white arm brandishing a dagger. He was captured in 1722, and hanged off the coast of Africa with his body gibbeted at Cape Coast Castle in Ghana.

**PETER PAINTER** retired from piracy to live a quiet life in Charlestown, South Carolina, and became a respected member of the community. However, when he was suggested for the position of public powder-receiver he was turned down on grounds of, 'Having committed Piracy and not having His Majesties Pardon for the same its resolved he is not fit for that Trust.' Who on earth suggested an ex-pirate could look after the gunpowder supply?

**IGNATIUS PELL** served as Stede Bonnet's bo'sun aboard the *Royal James*. While trying to avoid the hurricane season in 1718, Bonnet was sheltering in the estuary of Cape Fear River. Pirate hunter William Rhett discovered him and attacked. A vicious battle followed and both ships ran aground. Realising they were trapped, Bonnet ordered that the gunpowder magazine should be fired to scupper the ship, but the order was ignored and the crew surrendered.

Brought to trial at Charlestown on 2nd October 1718, Bonnet, Pell and sailing master David Herriot were removed from the rest of the crew, held separately in the provost marshal's house. Bonnet and Herriot managed to escape, but left Pell behind.

Herriot was shot in the ensuing hunt for the escaped prisoners and Bonnet was recaptured. Pell turned King's Evidence testifying against Bonnet and the crew of the *Royal James*. He confirmed various acts of piracy that had taken place, although he went out of his way to excuse Thomas Nichols, claiming that he had been forced into piracy against his will. Nichols was subsequently acquitted. Pell also claimed Bonnet was not the true captain, but that quartermaster Robert Tucker held the command for he was the more competent of the two, and that Bonnet was not to blame for the piracy that the crew had committed. The majority of the men, including Tucker, were found guilty and hanged on 8th November 1718, with Stede Bonnet's execution taking place on 10th December 1718. Bonnet was buried in the marsh below the low-water line.

It is unknown what befell Pell, but he seems to have been acquitted for he did not hang.

**RICHARD WORLEY** was active as a pirate for only six months in 1718. He left New York in a small boat with a crew of only eight men, and their first success was a hoard of household goods in the Delaware River, an act of theft more than piracy but let's not be picky. Their next achievement was the capture of a sloop, which brought in four new crew. Soon after they took another sloop, which was in good repair and fully provisioned. Ah, this was more like it!

They headed for the Bahamas where they took a brigantine and another sloop, again increasing the crew to twenty-five men, along with some extra cannons. He flew a flag of a white death mask against a black background. His crew swore they would rather perish than be taken prisoner.

While careening near Charlestown, South Carolina, the governor sent two Royal Navy sloops after him. Despite their noble vow, Worley and his crew were captured and hanged in Charlestown.

For many pirates, we know nothing except their name and where they were tried, hanged, or very occasionally, acquitted. For a few there is information about where they came from and the ship they sailed in, but it is a sad legacy for the other men who sought only to survive the harsh life on the sea with enough money to live it that all we know is their name and that they were all hanged.

## Stede Bonnet's Crew: all hanged for piracy on 8th November 1718 at Charlestown, South Carolina

Alexander Amand from Jamaica. He was buried below the low-tide waterline as a deliberate mark of disrespect.
Job Bailey from London. No information.
Samuel Booth. No information.
Robert Boyd from North Carolina. No information.
Thomas Carman from Maidstone, Kent. No information.
George Dunkin from Glasgow. No information.
William Eddy from Aberdeen. No information.
William Hewett from Jamaica. No information.
Matthew King from Jamaica. No information.
William Livers – alias 'Elvis'. No information.
Zachariah Long from Holland. No information.
John Lopez from Oporto Portugal. No information.
William Morrison from Jamaica. No information.
James Mullet from London. No information.
Neil Patterson from Aberdeen. No information.
Daniel Perry from Guernsey. No information.
Thomas Price from Bristol. No information.
John Ridge from London. No information.
Edward Robinson from Newcastle-upon-Tyne. No information.

George Ross. No information.
William Scott. No information.
John-William Smith. No information.
John Thomas from Jamaica. No information.
Robert Tucker. No information.
Henry Virgin from Bristol. No information.
James Wilson from Dublin. No information.
Jonathan Clarke. No information. Acquitted.
Thomas Gerrard from Antigua. No information. Acquitted.
James Killing gave evidence against Stede Bonnet. No further information. Acquitted.
Thomas Nichols from London. No information. Acquitted.
Rowland Sharp. No information. Acquitted.

**Blackbeard's crew, killed at the Ocracoke, North Carolina on 22nd November 1718 in a battle against Lieutenant Maynard**
Joseph Brookes Senior. No information.
Joseph Curtice. No information.
Garrat Gibbens, Boatswain. No further information.
John Husk. No information.
Nathanial Jackson. No information.
Thomas Miller, Quartermaster. No further information.
Phillip Morton. Gunner. No information.
Owen Roberts Wales. Carpenter. No information.

**Blackbeard's crew hanged at Williamsburg, Virginia, 1718**
James Blake. No information.
Joseph Brookes, Junior. No information.
Caesar, a Negro. No information.
John Carnes. No information.
Thomas Gates. No information.
John Gills. No information.
Richard Greensail. No information.
John Martin. No information.
Joseph Phillips. No information.
James Robins. No information.
Edward Salter. No information.
Richard Stiles. No information.

James White. No information.

### Edward Lowe's Crew, tried for piracy at Newport, Rhode Island in July 1723

Thomas Child, aged fifteen. Not guilty. No further information.

Doctor John Hincher of Edinburgh, a graduate of the University of Edinburgh. Tried for piracy aged twenty-two. Acquitted; proved he was forced against his will.

### George Lowther's Crew aboard the *Happy Delivery*, hanged at St Kitts, 11th March 1722

John Churchill. No information.

Jonathan Delve. Crew on the *Happy Delivery*. No further information.

Matthew Freebarn. No information.

Andrew Hunter. No information.

Nicholas Lewis. No information.

Edward Mackdonald. Crew, *Happy Delivery*. No further information.

John Shaw. No information.

Henry Watson. No information.

Richard West. No information.

Robert White. No information.

Robert Willis. No information.

Roger Grange. Crew *Happy Delivery*. No information. Acquitted.

### Charles Vane's Crew

Captain Robert Deal mate to Charles Vain, hanged, Jamaica 1718. No further information.

Black Bartlemy was said to be a surly buccaneer who, after murdering his wife and children, fled to sea with a band of pirates. He preyed upon the Atlantic coast plundering, pillaging and murdering, destroying anything and everything that crossed his wicked path. Approaching Nova Scotia, his ship was loaded to the gunnels with looted treasure.

Fog swamped Fundy Bay, and as the ship stealthily approached the harbour, the current hurled it against the rocks near Cape Forchu, gouging a great hole in the hull. Bartlemy was made of stern stuff; he ordered the crew to stow as much treasure as it would carry into the ship's boat. Then he had his trusty first mate, Ben the Hook, murder the men so that the two rascals could keep the loot for themselves. They rowed for the shore, looking for a place to bury their treasure trove and found a cave that would suit their purpose. As Ben the Hook rolled a final boulder into place to hide the cave entrance Bartlemy thrust a blade into his chest and killed him outright. Laughing to himself, he walked along the shore hoping to come across a town where he could eat and rest, and find another ship and crew. Alas, he stumbled into quicksand and only the mournful gulls heard his cries for help and his dying curses.

Many years later, the lighthouse keeper saw a flare go up, and launching the lifeboat went to aid the ship he thought was in distress. He saw only a tattered-sailed galleon, its deck strewn with treasure and a solitary man aboard dressed all in black. The storm-tossed breakers spewed over the ship and took it down into the sea, with only the sound of Black Bartlemy's laughter left behind as a ghostly echo.

And if you believe that story, you will believe anything.

## 50

# Scratch a Stay and No Whistling: Superstitions

Sailors were a superstitious lot. Were pirates as wary of causing bad luck as their merchant and Royal Navy counterparts? Maybe because they led a life where they were in control of their freedom, rituals and taboos were not so important. On the other side of the deck, perhaps they were even more necessary in order to stay alive and catch that next Prize.

Certain days of the week were regarded as unlucky to do things on, particularly in the Western, Christian, world. Friday was a bad-omen day to set sail from harbour. This came from Good Friday, the day when Christ was crucified. The first Monday in April was the day Cain killed Abel, the second Monday in August was when Sodom and Gomorrah were destroyed by God and the last day of December was the day Judas committed suicide. All bad luck days.

Also from the Bible was the fear of a Jonah, someone aboard, either crew or passenger, who was the conduit for bad luck or bad things to happen. There is a Jonah character in the Patrick O'Brian novels, which were made into that excellent movie, *Master and Commander*.

Candlemas Day, celebrated forty days after Christmas Day, was also thought to be a bad day to set sail. In pre-Christian custom, this day was associated with the approaching end of winter and coming of spring, a day to bring as much light as possible into the world to chase away the darkness. There was, additionally, a belief that the weather on this day would predict what the year was to bring:

If Candlemas Day be fair and bright
Winter will have another fight.
If Candlemas Day brings cloud and rain
Winter shall not come again.

If you were a sailor it makes good sense to take note of this.

Roaring waves and rolling clouds also indicated an omen not to set sail – but this was common sense more than superstition.

The belief that a woman aboard would bring bad luck stemmed from the Roman and Greek mythology of the female deities such as Sirens who lured sailors to their death. Given that it is possible several women served as crew disguised as men, this superstition seems somewhat amusing. In some cultures, mermaids and mermen were considered to be lucky as they granted wishes.

Sea birds were lucky omens, the albatross being the prime one, but it was bad luck to kill an albatross. This large seabird can have a wingspan of up to twelve feet and mainly ranges over the Southern

Ocean and the Pacific, although some do stray into the North Atlantic. They are superb in the air, riding the thermal currents and covering huge distances with very little effort. They feed on fish and squid. They are colony nesting birds, making use of remote islands to breed, which may explain their importance to sailors – the birds could indicate a way to fresh water, a haul of fresh fish and even wind direction. It was also believed that birds carried the soul to heaven after death.

For some obscure reason, bringing bananas aboard was a taboo. Maybe because they often had tarantulas or poisonous spiders hiding within the huge bunches?

Whistling on deck was a no-no because it could call up the wrong wind, but maybe the real origin is associated with being confused by the whistles sounded in connection with giving orders. It could also be connected with the legend that mutineer Christian Fletcher used a whistle-call as the signal to rise up against Captain Bligh aboard HMS *Bounty*. One exception was the cook. If he was whistling, then he wasn't sampling too much food.

Renaming a boat supposedly was bad luck, although given that pirates did this all the time maybe it did not affect them? Or could this be why so many pirate ships had the same name? Still, there was a tradition to avert the bad luck: you de-name the vessel in a special ceremony, then officially re-name it. Sounds like a good excuse to have a party to me.

Not all superstition was concerned with ill-luck, there were some good omens, although many were assumed to ward off bad luck ...

Cats. Ashore, in many areas, a black cat was associated with witches and was regarded as unlucky; but for sailors a cat aboard ship was sure to bring good fortune. This one is a practical belief: cats catch rats and mice.

Caul. Babies born with the uterus membrane in place around their heads were believed to be protected from drowning. It is a very rare occurrence. Sailors would often purchase a caul from midwives and mothers to keep as a good-luck charm.

Losing a hat over the side indicated that the voyage could be a long one.

Eggshells had to be crushed into small pieces before tossing them overboard in case they attracted witches.

Wearing gold hoop earrings, typical of a pirate, was to assist the soul to the afterlife if death was by drowning and therefore no formal burial could take place, when a coin would be placed in the mouth, or over the eyes; the gold was there to pay the ferryman the required fee.

Tattoos were often designed to bring good fortune and ward off bad luck.

A red-haired man was to be avoided.

Certain words were not to be uttered aboard: drowned, goodbye and good luck being three of them.

To scratch a stay brought good luck, as did turning three times east to west, the way the sun travelled – woe betide anyone who got it wrong and turned widdershins, west to east.

The Patron Saints of sailors, (they had two) were Saint Nicholas because he calmed a storm with prayer, and Saint Erasmus, also called Saint Elmo. He is said to have continued preaching even though a thunderstorm raged and lightning struck the ground beside his feet. An electrical discharge, which occasionally occurs at the masthead, was believed to be a sign of his presence and was called Saint Elmo's Fire.

51

# Edward England

Edward England was born with the name Edward Seegar sometime around 1685 in Ireland. He changed his name to England when he chose to live the life of a pirate. Prior to that, he served as a privateer – as did most of them – during the War of the Spanish Succession. He was caught by pirates, was forced to join the crew, and ended up in Nassau. There he met Henry Jennings and was one of the men who plundered the Florida warehouses filled with salvaged gold from the sunken Spanish treasure fleet. From there, he sailed with Charles Vane as his quartermaster. When Vane's sloop, *Lark*, was captured by the Royal Navy in 1718, England was pardoned in the hope that other pirates would then come forward to accept the proffered King's Amnesty. That hope was in vain where Edward England was concerned, for he promptly sailed off to Africa in another ship, given him by Vane, taking several ships as Prizes en route. One of them, the *Cadogan*, was under the command of Captain Skinner, who was murdered by England's men because he had failed to pay them their due wages when they had sailed with him on a previous voyage. His death was not pleasant. They bound him to the mast and threw glass bottles at him, then shot him through the skull.

Also aboard the *Cadogan* was Howell Davies, a man not easily swayed into the life of piracy. When he said he would rather die than become a pirate, England was impressed by his bravery and gave him the *Cadogan* to command. Obviously, Davies's principles were not that entrenched when it came to worthwhile reward.

The pirates took ten ships between the River Gambia and Cape Coast. England and his crew remained in Africa for some while, until disagreement arose over the treatment of the native women. Fighting broke out, the town was burned, and the pirates hastily returned to sea.

In 1720, England was prowling the Indian Ocean where he joined with Captain Oliver la Buse and captured a thirty-four gun Dutch vessel, which England made his flagship after he renamed her *Fancy*. The decision was made to try for an East Indiaman, the *Cassandra*, commanded by James Macrae, near the island of Comoros. Both ships, *Cassandra* and England's *Fancy*, ran aground after a protracted and bloody battle in which ninety of the pirates were killed. Macrae and his crew escaped and hid for almost two weeks on the island. But injured and hungry, Macrae surrendered and begged for help from England's consort ship, the *Victory*.

*Cassandra* had been carrying a cargo estimated to have a value of £75,000 and as England was not one to torture his victims, he ordered Macrae's life to be spared. England repaired *Cassandra* and kept her, giving *Fancy* to Macrae.

England's quartermaster, John Taylor, now in command of *Victory*, did not approve of this. However, by cunningly getting him drunk, England managed to persuade him to change his mind. They sailed off, leaving Macrae to see to the extensive damage to the *Fancy*.

When another English ship was later taken as a Prize, her captain boasted that Macrae had completed the task, was back at sea and was assembling a fleet in order to go pirate hunting. Enraged, and led by Taylor, the crew deposed England who was marooned without any provisions on Mauritius with three more of the crew. They managed to construct a small boat during the four months they were there, and sailed across the Indian Ocean to St Augustine's Bay, Madagascar. Living for a while on the charity of other pirates, England died in 1721 of an unknown cause.

Character-wise, England was one of the better pirates because he did not use torture and was known to be lenient with captured prisoners, which was his downfall with the others of his crew. What a pity he had not taken advantage of the King's Pardon. He would perhaps have had a more satisfactory life.

52

# Action and Adventure

An excerpt from *On The Account*, the Fifth *Sea Witch Voyage* by Helen Hollick:

*Jesamiah Acorne is at sea, frantic to track and find Barbary pirates who have kidnapped his wife. Nothing will stand in his way, not even a British Royal Navy Frigate ...*

Jesamiah squinted into the dense mist, sight, touch, smell, hearing alert. He could sense nothing except fog. The smell of damp tar, wet wood, rope and canvas; the cold, clammy touch of the mist on his face and a faint breeze stroking his cheek – but not enough to flutter the bedraggled blue ribbons in his dew-glistening hair, or stir the sails. The creak of the ship, the squeak of rope rubbing against rope. Aware that somewhere to leeward the Spanish coast with its jagged rocks lurked unseen, he listened harder, expecting to hear the sound of the sea slapping against the shore. But all he could hear was the ocean gurgling past the hull, nothing else. Except – except his skin was crawling, the hairs standing up along his arms and at the back of his neck. There was *something* out there ...

~ *Tiola? Are you near?* ~ His mind met the nothingness of blank, empty space. The nothingness of a coffin in a grave. No! He could not, would not, believe she was dead!

He wasn't sure if he heard or saw it first. A flashed glow of light, the *whoomph* of sound.

'Down! Get down!' He leapt towards Maha'dun and brought him down to the deck as a few pounds' weight of a lead shot ball ripped through the taffrail, splintering the wood and sending shards fountaining into the damp air. The ball hurtled forward, smashed through the quarterdeck rail, then, badly made, disintegrated into lumps of shrapnel – a miracle that not a soul had been injured.

'Run out the guns! Alter course three points! Steer sou'east!' Jesamiah roared his orders, hastily patting Maha'dun's shoulder to ascertain he was all right, then running to the rail to bellow more orders. Not that his regular men needed them, these were old-hand pirates, well used to quick action, to do, not to stand and think. A man's life depended on not questioning. Run out the guns meant just that.

The braces were already being hauled round as Skylark put the helm over. The effect was immediate. *Sea Witch* tilted as if she were a child's toy ... A ball ripped in low, scudding across the waves where a moment before she had been, spray hurling upward in a spouted plume. No one on board noticed, all attention was on a ship looming out of the fog not more than 400 yards away. The only comfort, from the shouting and bellowing coming from her, *Sea Witch*'s sudden appearance was causing as much alarm.

'Starboard guns run out!' Jesamiah was shouting as he launched himself down the companion ladder to the deck. 'Run up my personal colours. Let 'em know who they are dealing with!'

A sound like squealing pigs as the gun trucks protested. Men were hurtling from the larboard side to assist the starboard gunners. Jesamiah's black pirate flag with its leering white skull atop a pair of crossed bones flew up the mast, hung there, motionless a moment, then the wind blew, filling the sails, making them crack and rattle, sweeping the flag outward, rippling and fluttering. The fog disappeared as if a magician had waved a wand. The sun shone, bright and apparently carefree, oblivious that two ships were near enough to blast the other out of the water – depending on which one fired a broadside first.

Maha'dun squirmed like a beetle into the protective cover between rail and bulwark. Sense was shouting as loud as Jesamiah to get below, but he had never experienced anything as exciting as this before! Danger awaiting around the corner was always a possibility but this time it had come trumpeting over the threshold with all guns blazing. No way was he going to miss this! The exhilaration, the pounding blood-rush through the veins; the feeling of being so, so alive because at any moment he might be dead.

Jesamiah stood, one leg slightly forward, knee bent, his left hand on the hilt of his cutlass, his right fiddling with the ribbons in his hair – both unconscious actions. Unheeding of the demented sails, the grunts of the men slipping on the wet deck, of *Sea Witch*'s protest at the sudden change of tack, all his attention was focused on that frigate looming closer, most of her deck in shade, none of her sails – as with *Sea Witch* – clewed up for action.

As calm as if he were ordering coffee, Jesamiah called his next order. 'On the down roll – and make every shot count. *FIRE!*'

Maha'dun slammed his hands over his ears as the first gun roared, then a second, a third; each one blowing columns of flame and billows of acrid smoke across the water before hurtling inboard on their tackles from the force of rebound. The gun crews leapt in, working with sponges to clear the barrel of smouldering debris, reloading for a next shot.

Six shots struck below the waterline of the enemy ship as *Sea Witch* rolled downward and the frigate upward exposing a length of her water-sodden hull at the height of her rise. A cheer went up, spread rapidly along *Sea Witch*'s deck. No need to reload, the frigate's crew were running about, leaving their guns, shouting and cursing. The frantic sound of pumps coming into play: she was holed, and rapidly sinking.

'Do we heave to, sir? Give them quarter?' Tearle was at Jesamiah's side, watching the frenzy on the other ship; men hurrying to launch the boats, throwing anything that would float into the sea before jumping in themselves. The Spanish coast was not far away, with help they would live. Without, they would drown.

Jesamiah stared at Tearle as if he had just been awoken from a trance. 'Do you think they would stop for us?' he asked as he pointed upward to his flag contorting in the freshening wind. 'Maintain previous course. Set all sail, we need to make way.'

Skylark, as Jesamiah's second-in-command, cocked his head on one side, brows furrowed. 'To bring the poor sods aboard would give us more crew.'

'Which will take up a lot of time, and who would not want to fight for but against us.'

'T'aint right to leave 'em t'drown,' Finch piped up. 'Don't think Miss Tiola would approve if'n she knew.'

'They are the losers, death is expected,' Maha'dun interjected, his eyes glittering for the blood-rush of excitement.

Finch, Skylark and Tearle were right, but so was Jesamiah and he was desperate to find Tiola. Unless luck was with them it could take days, weeks. He decided on compromise; as he went towards his cabin, ordered, 'Lower the gig for them, that'll have to suffice.'

'And what,' someone called with more than a hint of sarcasm, 'are we supposed to do if *we* sink?'

Jesamiah glared at the sailor. 'I suggest,' he drawled, 'you make bloody sure we don't.'

From the stern windows Jesamiah watched, impassive, as the British ship went down. Perhaps he should have organised a rescue. Perhaps he should never have returned fire – but it was unlikely that the British captain, whoever he was, would have been so considerate. Those first shots had been well aimed with intention behind them, only Jesamiah's seamanship had saved *Sea Witch* from irreparable damage. War had been declared, that made men nervous and inclined to attack first, question later. Perhaps if he had hoisted a British flag, not his one of piracy …?

He poured himself a large brandy. Who cared about *perhaps*? Perhaps if he had not permitted Tiola to go to this blasted party, perhaps if he had gone with her, perhaps he would now be as dead as Rue.

Piracy was in his blood it was how he thought and fought and no, that captain would not have stopped to pick them out the water. He would have left them all to drown, unless he'd possessed a merciful streak and ordered his marines to shoot them.

Perhaps he should have brought the survivors aboard, but beyond all else Jesamiah wanted to find the *Safeena Hamra*, reach Tiola and set her safe. Or failing that, know she was dead and beyond his help.

## 53

# Talking Like a Pirate

Some useful (fun) piratical nautical phrases; you will find a glossary of the serious meanings at the end of this book. Don't forget to have a toy parrot balanced on your shoulder and a pirate-patch covering one eye.

*Ahoy*! – hi there!
*Avast*! – stop or shut up.
*Avast behind*! – look out!
*Aye* – OK.
*Aye Aye* – yes, I heard you the first time or OK, I'm doing it.

*Bilge Rat*– A scoundrel.

*Black Spot* – you are doomed.

*Cap'n* – the person in charge.

*Dead men tell no tales* – as this is a fun thing: keep it secret or else – but strictly speaking, to kill everyone.

*Doldrums* – bored.

*Fire in the hole*! – an exclamation warning before someone farts.

*Hornswaggled* – well, I'm blowed.

*Keep a weathered eye* – keep watch.

*Land Ho*! – nearly there!

*Marooned* – on your own.

*Sail ho* – there it/ he/she is.

*Savvy?* – do you understand?

*Scurvy dog* – a scoundrel.

*Under bare poles* – to go commando.

*Walk the plank* – be gone with you.

*Wet me pipe* – have a drink.

*X Marks the spot* – here we are, or here it is.

*Yo-ho-ho* – I agree.

'*Arrr, shever m'timbers, bud did'n be ye knowim' tha' jist un'er 'alf o'Bartholomew Roberts' crew bist vrom Kernow, Devom an' Zummerzet?*'

That's the West Country accent, where there is a distinct speech pattern made famous and forever associated with pirates because of West Country actor, Robert Newton, who played Long John Silver in the 1950 version of *Treasure Island*. Born in Dorset, Newton was educated in Cornwall and his strong accent, with its rolling rs and clipped vowels, became synonymous as a pirate way of speech.

The 'arrr' appeared for the first time in the earlier 1934 version of the film starring Lionel Barrymore.

However, many sailors and seamen originated from the West Country in the form of fishermen, Royal Navy recruits, smugglers, and of course, pirates. Spanning a variety of ports and harbours from Falmouth, Exeter, Bideford (in the late 1600s and early 1700s the third largest tobacco port in England) to Weymouth and Bristol, not counting all the creeks, rivers and inlets. The West of England was the major sea-faring area. So it does not take much imagination to conclude that the predominant accent, therefore, was West Country.

Sir Francis Drake and Sir Walter Raleigh were noted for their strong Devon accents at Queen Elizabeth I's court, again another reason why the West Country was associated with the sea and privateers.

Wessex, founded by the West Saxons, was an Anglo-Saxon kingdom before the unification of the separate English kingdoms into one realm in the 10th century. The two most famous kings of Wessex were Alfred the Great and Harold Godwinson, who, as King of England fought and died at the Battle of Hastings in 1066. The various West Country dialects echo the spread of the first Anglo-Saxon settlers, with Devon's original Celtic population integrating within these new foreign settlers at a slower rate than the rest of England, and Cornwall falling even further behind to retain much of its own language and customs. The Celtic, or what we now call Welsh – which is a Saxon word meaning 'foreign', dialect and many words were absorbed into the Old English and can still be heard today. A Devonian accent has a slow rhythm, caused in part by a lengthening of the vowels, although the Cornish are the opposite, their speech is quite fast.

'S' becomes a 'Z' sound and 'F' becomes more like 'V', so 'Zummerzet' and 'var' and 'vire' instead of Somerset, far and fire. Rs, especially at the end of a word are stressed (hence the pirate 'Arrr'.) There are also distinct grammar differences.

The male gender is used to describe objects, "*e is in the barn*', instead of 'it is in the barn', and '*put 'e over there,*' instead of 'put it over there', or '*they boots,*' instead of 'my boots'.

While often mocked now as a supposed slovenly or ignorant dialect, as also is the Northumbrian accent, the West Country dialect is, in fact, the last remnant of a more correct pronunciation of English as it is almost directly descended from the 6th century English settlers. As an example, the verb *To Be* has changed in modern times to become *I am, you are, he is, we are, they are*. But in the West Country dialect – Old English – you will hear: *I be, thee bist, he be, we be, they be.*

If you really want to spend some time as a (fun) pirate (yes we know real pirates were a monstrous lot, this chapter relates to the fun fictional ones, not the cutthroats) mark September 19th in your diary. This is an annual date designated as *International Talk Like A Pirate Day*, which according to the website, www.talklikeapirate. com, is an 'original concept created in a moment of temporary insanity by John Baur and Mark Summers'.

The day came into being on 6th June 1995 when Americans, Baur, known as Ol' Chumbucket, and Summers – Cap'n Slappy, were playing a game of racquetball 'not well but gamely' and one of them reacted to a minor injury with a resounding 'arrr!' and the idea for a pirate language day came into being. The concept was originally intended as a joke between the two, but the idea spread after 2002 when humour columnist Dave Barry got to hear of it.

Media coverage and a huge interest in pirates (despite what publishers of fiction say) saw the fun-day spread, helped along because of their sensible policy of not restricting the use of copyright. The intention is for anyone interested to have as much fun as they like doing piratical things on 19th September every year. The idea took off, going viral.

So to Talk Like A Pirate you need to learn some Devonish:

a – as in *jam*

aa – a long sound a bit like a sheep bleating but without the quiver

ai – as in *gain*

d – instead of th: *datch*, not thatch

e – if the first letter of a word, pronounced as *i* so *ivery* instead of every, but in the middle of a word as ai, as in *gain*

f – as v, *virst*: first or *vew*, few

h – often added to a word to give it emphasis: *h*over instead of over, or m'*h*ornin' (morning)

i – instead of u or oi: *jidge* (judge) and *jist* (just)

m – is often used instead of an n, so *Devom*, (Devon) and *dem* (den)

o – sounds like an a, so *Garge* instead of George

oo – similar to the Scot's ui in *guid* (good)

r – a peculiar one. It often changes places with the letter after it, so red is *erd*, run is *urn*, great is *gurt*

s – z

t – occasionally replaces d,

th – is often dropped *is'n 'at* (isn't that)
u – I or ou *joug* (jug)

How about these? (You can almost hear the pirate can't you?)
'*Ark a'ee*' – listen to him.
'*Yer tiz*' – here it is.

Or try slipping these into a conversation:

*Aid* – head
*Anzum* – handsome
*Arken* – harken (listen)
*Awl* – hole
*Back along* – some time ago
*Bain't it?* – isn't it?
Bissle – to make dirty (daw'n 'ee bissle yersel',')
*Blimmer* – a mild swear word
*Boddle* – bottle
*Chillern* – children
*Crackin'* – chatting
*Crame* – cream
*Dashels* – thistles
*Dimpsey* – murky, poor daylight
*Drang-way* – narrow way, an alley
*Drekly* – directly
*Erbons* – ribbons
*Fan-tag* (in a) – in a huff, cross
*Flibberts* – pieces
*Grockle* – a tourist.
*Gurt* – big or great
*G'woam* – going home.
*How be on?* – how are you?
*Hullifant* – elephant
*Jonnick* – correct, honest
*Kerping* – finding fault
*Long-tailed rabbit* – a pheasant!
*Lustree* – to bustle about
*Maunderin'* – grumbling

*Maized* – mad 'yu'm maized as a brish': you are as mad as a brush.'
*Muxy* – muddy
*On-cum-verable* – uncomfortable
*Oozle* – whistle
*Piskies* – pixies
*Popple-stones* – pebbles
*Rucksel* – noise, disturbance
*Shevvers* – small pieces
*Skat* – shower of rain
*Thurdle-gutted* – thin
*Upperds* – upwards
*Viddy* – fitting, proper
*Vuzlin'* – fussing
*Wha' be gwain 'ave?* – what are you going to have (to drink or eat)
*Wommle* – wobble
*Yullery* – yellow
*Zummerzet* – Somerset.
*Zyder* – cider.

Finally, longer vowels are for words like beautiful – *bootiful*...
    And *arrr* of course...

# Drop Anchor

So why *do* we like the bad boys (and girls)? Why the fascination with pirates?

Before I get shouted at for being sexist and talking about the guys, not the gals, it is the heroes – those drop-dead gorgeous actors who usually play the predominant part in movies and TV-series. (O.K so I enjoyed looking for the images of those hunks in the name of research: it was a tough job, but Amberley had commissioned me to do it ...)

It is somewhat amusing that in so many historical dramas, whether for big or small screen, the hero is usually clean, tidy and well-shaven. Didn't they grow beards or sport a five-o'clock shadow in the past? In reality, there is nothing romantic about a ship being boarded by dozens of drunken cut-throat louts bellowing at the top of their voices, '*Death! Death! Death!*' all eager to torture, rape, murder, plunder, loot, and then destroy the evidence by setting the ship on fire. Fictional pirates are rogues; they would as soon cut your throat as cut your money-pouch from your belt, but there is a rugged charm associated with these make-believe scallywags. Pirate tales are a grand adventure romp, usually with barely any historical accuracy. You know the hero will survive the storm and subsequent shipwreck, recover from a near-fatal wound, dodge the gallows, find the treasure, get the girl in the end and sail off into the sunset horizon. That is all a part of the fun of fiction.

We enjoy the adventures of these loveable charmers because they are not real. The danger they get into or create makes our hearts race; the thrill of the chase or the fight, the within-an-inch-of-his-life death-defying scenes. The ability to keep on fighting /

running / bedroom antics even though shot / wounded / kicked in a vulnerable place where real men would be curled up on the floor clutching their nether regions and howling in agony. You know these heroes are in trouble. You also know they are going to get out of it; the thrill, the excitement, is not knowing *how* they do so.

So what role does sexual excitement and a good dollop of *phwor* play in anything pirates? We have already seen that most were drunkards, uncouth, unhealthy and a not very nice lot to be around, yet readers of fiction and viewers of on-screen entertainment love a handsome bad boy made good hero. The sexy guy with the come-to-bed charisma. We are, for some unfathomable reason, drawn to the intoxicated womaniser, the werewolf, the vampire – and the pirate.

Fidelity is a big thing for today's morals but the notion of being faithful to a partner, and the laws of sexuality against under-age sex for instance, came in with the Victorian and Edwardian era. Before then, I would not go as far as saying nobody cared. Well, lots of things were accepted pre-circa 1850s that are not acceptable now.

Being faithful was not strictly adhered to in centuries gone by, especially with the chaps going off to sea or to fight in the army for months, or even years, on end. The wives very possibly preferred the men enjoying the intimate company of other women because of the risk of death in childbirth and no reliable contraception. Lamb's intestine or leather 'cundum' sheaths were worn, but as a barrier against contracting a sexual disease, not to prevent pregnancy. The best way to avoid being 'with child'? Avoid the possibility of getting pregnant in the first place. Because men were absent for great lengths of time, it was accepted that they sought release elsewhere. The only infidelity frowned upon was if the man lived openly with his mistress, thus publicly humiliating his wife; although this is what Eleanor of Aquitaine and several other queens of various nationalities were forced to endure.

In an historical context, men were rarely loyal. Is it only now that we see love and sex as the same thing? The two used to be separate issues. Sex was sex, love was probably not that common for the simple reason men and women did not move around so much, which meant a limited choice of prospective partners. Marriages were often arranged in Medieval times; as in some cultures even today, the first meeting between husband and wife was at the altar. And there were no celebs to drool over, apart from maybe a passing knight, travelling troubadour or exciting pirate with whom to compare your over-corpulent, somewhat flatulent, lazy drunk of a spouse.

How many of us admired the brooding Oliver Reed as Bill Sykes, even though he was horrible to Nancy? Sean Bean's Richard Sharpe in Bernard Cornwell's *Sharpe* series was a no-nonsense soldier who loved his 'bedroom entertainment' with various woman. Clark Gable as Rhett Butler in *Gone With the Wind* was a bit of a cad – even Scarlett was not exactly the good little wife was she? '*Oh Ashley, Ashley!*'

Aidan Turner as *Poldark* is – need I say? In Winston Graham's fabulous novels, the character, Ross Poldark, was rugged, capable and all man – but he had his flaws. The glittery vampires of *Twilight* appeal to many, and Johnny Depp as Captain Jack Sparrow, how we drooled over him! Then there are the characters in *Game of Thrones*, the books and the TV-series with a variety of popular favourites, all of whom you are never certain will make it to the next episode, let alone series! *Black Sails*, as a TV-series has proved more popular in the US than the UK, possibly because of the broadcast network; it was not on prime TV in the UK. Again good characters and bad characters appealed in equal measure, although, being cynical, this depended on the 'hunk' factor of the men, or the size and exposure of the women's 'assets'. Finally, my own Jesamiah Acorne. He often has difficulty keeping his breeches buttoned. I deliberately made him the lovable scoundrel; quick to laugh, formidable when angry, torn between the love of the sea and his ship, and the woman he wants as his own. Yet so easily seduced into straying.

Is it the excitement these characters create, the knowing that they are dangerous? They are usually tall, dark, and incredibly handsome. Would such characters be as interesting if they all fell in love, got married and then stayed at home with pipe and slippers happily helping to do the dishes? I doubt it. That sort of plot does not do much for an exciting storyline.

So, is the sexy hero supposed to be faithful to his wife / woman, or do we mind if he occasionally strays? Do we enjoy the adventures of heroic, bad boy rogue pirates sailing the seas because we know the stories are not real? The life of a pirate in fiction is mere fantasy, enjoyable escapism from humdrum daily life. Let's face it, who wouldn't choose being on deck with Jack Sparrow over trundling round a supermarket for the weekly shop?

Were pirates sexy? To the young women in the filthy cobbled streets of London, yes. Even if the only time they saw a pirate was as he made his way to the gallows. That in itself was exciting – grim and gruesome to us now, but then how many of us sit glued to those violent and bloody horror movies, enjoying the chill of fear and danger from the safety of our comfy settee or cinema seat? How many of us gawp at road accidents, or wallow in the over-dramatic unrealistic tragedies of the soap operas? There is no denying it, we get a thrill from these events, even if that thrill, that rush of adrenalin, is only caused by the relief that we, or our loved ones, are not in danger. That is where the 'safe danger' comes into play. A hanging, or a horror movie, a murder-mystery or a thrills-and-spills adventure where the 'baddies' get killed with no remorse from the one doing the killing – usually the hero who ends up with the cute, scantily clad and somewhat busty blonde. The excitement sets our hearts racing because we are in no danger – apart from a possible nightmare or two.

My pirate novels, the *Sea Witch Voyages* are adult adventures not meant to be taken seriously. I write them for fun, they are meant to be read as tongue-in-cheek Errol Flynn / Jack Sparrow romps. They are entertainment ... even if the real pirates were far from entertaining to the poor souls who met a boatload of them somewhere on the open ocean.

Whatever the fact, whatever the fiction, we enjoy the escapism of dressing up in stripy clothes as pirates, pretending to be the scallywag rascals with a plastic parrot on the shoulder and a black patch over the eye, but the crunch is ... why *are* pirates the coolest guys?

Simple answer?

Because they *ARRRR*!

# Glossary of Terms

Aback – a sail when its forward surface is pressed upon by the wind. Used to 'stop' a ship.

Ahoy! – used to hail a ship or a person. To attract attention.

Air and exercise – a flogging while tied to a cart.

All nations – a mixture of the dregs of alcohol left in bottles.

Aloft – up in the tops, at the masthead or anywhere about the yards or the rigging.

Amen curler – a priest.

Anne's fan – a disturbance or thumbing your nose at the rules.

Apple dumplings – a woman's bosoms.

Avast  – a command to stop or desist.

Aye – Yes or 'aye aye': an affirmation that an order has been heard and understood.

Bagpiper – a long-winded talker.

Banbury story – a made-up tale.

Bar – a shoal running across the mouth of a harbour or a river.

Bark at the moon – to waste your breath.

Batten down the hatches – to cover the hatches leading to the lower decks with canvas during a storm to prevent water seeping below deck, or to prepare for something unpleasant.

Bear garden jaw – foul language.

Before the mast – to take an oath while on deck standing before the commanding officer.

Belay – to make fast or secure. Also: 'Stop that.' 'Belay that talk,' would mean 'Shut up.'

Belaying pin – a short wooden rod to which a ship's rigging is secured, used as a commonly improvised weapon aboard a sailing ship because they are everywhere, easily picked up, and are the right size and weight to be used as a club.

Bell (Ship's bell) – used as a clock, essential for navigation as the measurement of the angle of the sun had to be made at noon. The bell was struck each time the half-hour glass was turned.

Bilge – the lowest part of the ship inside the hull along the keel. They are filled with stinking bilge water or 'bilge'. Can also mean nonsense or foolish talk.

Binnacle – the frame or box that houses the compass.

Boiled man – someone who has bribed the press gang to be left alone.

Bosun – short for boatswain, usually a competent sailor who is in charge of all deck duties.

Bosun's chair – a platform on ropes made to form a chair-like structure, and hauled aboard.

Bow – the front or 'pointed' end of the ship.

Bowsprit – the heavy slanted spar pointing forward from the ship's bow.

Beggar maker – a publican or taverner.

Belly gut – a greedy or lazy person.

Bit of red – a soldier.

Brace – rope used to control the horizontal movement of a square-rigged yard.

Bring to one's bearings – to see sense.

Broadside – the simultaneous firing of all guns on one side of a ship.

Buck fitch – a lecher.

Bulkheads – vertical partitions in a ship.

Bull calf – someone who is clumsy.

Bulwark – the short 'walls' that encircle the deck.

Cable – a long, thick and heavy rope by which a ship is secured to the anchor.

Cackle fruit – hens' eggs.

Calfskin fiddle – a drum.

Cape horned – cuckolded.

Capstan – a drum-like winch turned by the crew to raise or lower the anchors.

Careen – the process of beaching a ship, heeling her over on to her side and cleaning the underside of weed, barnacles and worm; making essential repairs to the part of a ship which is usually below the waterline.

Cast up accounts – to vomit.

Cat sticks – thin legs.

Chain shot – two balls of iron joined together by a length of chain, chiefly used to destroy masts, rigging and sails.

Chanty/shanty – a sailor's work song. Often lewd and derogatory about the officers.

Chase – or Prize. The ship being pursued.

Chatter broth – tea.

Cleat – wooden or metal fastening, to which ropes can be secured; can also be used as a ladder.

Clew – the lower corners of a sail, therefore Clew up – to haul a square sail up to a yard.

Clodpoll – an idiot.

Close-hauled – sailing as close to the direction of the wind as possible with the sails turned almost ninety degrees.

Cold cook – an undertaker.

Cordage – rope is called cordage on board a ship.

Colours – the vessel's identification flag, also called an ensign. For a pirate, the Jolly Roger.

Come About – to bring the ship full way around while sailing into the wind, and to swing back into the enemy in combat.

Crack Jenny's teacup – to pass the night in or visit a brothel.

Crosstrees – horizontal cross-timbers partway up a mast to keep the shrouds spread apart.

Deadeyes – a round, flat, wooden block with three holes through which a lanyard, or rope, can be thread to tighten the shrouds.

Dog's soup – water.

Dutch concert – everyone playing or singing a different tune.

Earwig – a flatterer.

Eternity box – a coffin.

Fathom – a measure of six feet.

Fire a gun – to speak without tact.

Fish broth – saltwater.

Flapdragon – a sexual disease.

Fly in a tar box – excited.

Fore or for'ard – toward the front end of the ship, the bow.

Forecastle – pronounced fo'c'sle; raised deck at the front of a ship.

Fore-and-aft – the length of a ship.

Fother – to seal a leak by lowering a sail over the side of the ship and positioning it so that it seals the hole by the weight of the sea.

Full as a goat – very drunk.

Futtock shroud – short pieces of rope that secure lower deadeyes and futtock plates to the top mast rigging.

Galley – ship's kitchen.

Game pullet – a young prostitute.

Gaol / gaoler – pronounced 'jail' and 'jailer'.

Grapeshot – or grape, small cast iron balls bound together in a canvas bag that scatter like shotgun pellets when fired.

Grog – watered rum.

Grog blossom – a drunkard.

Groggified – very drunk.

Gundiguts – a fat person.

Gunwale – pronounced gun'l; upper planking along the sides of a vessel. 'Up to the gunwales' – full up or overloaded.

Gut-foundered – hungry.

Halliard or halyard – pronounced haly'd. The rope used to hoist a sail.

Handsomely – quickly or carefully.

Hang the jib – pout or frown.

Haul wind – to turn into the wind.

Heave to – to check the forward motion of a vessel and bring her to a standstill by heading her into the wind and backing some of her sails.

Heel – to lean over due to action of the wind, waves or greater weight on one side. The angle at which the vessel tips when sailing.

Helm – the tiller (a long steering arm) or a wheel that controls the rudder and enables the vessel to be steered.

Helm's a-lee – a warning that the ship is about to make a turn, most often used when tacking.

Hempen halter – a noose.

Hog in armour – a boastful lout.

Hold – space below deck for cargo.

Hornswaggle – to cheat, or trick.

Horse's meal – food without a drink.

Hull – the sides of a ship that sit in and above the water.

Hull cleats – the 'ladder' or steps attached to the hull via which entry is gained to the entry port.

Jack Ketch – an English executioner, his name became synonymous with hanging.

Jack Tar – common term for sailors.

Jaw me down – a talkative fellow.

Jolly boat – a small boat, a dinghy.

Jury-rigged – makeshift repairs.

Keel – the lowest part of the hull below the water.

Kiss the gunner's daughter – to be bent over one of the ship's guns and flogged.

Knot – one nautical mile per hour.

Laced mutton – a prostitute.

Landlubber or lubber – a non-sailor.

Langrage – jagged pieces of sharp metal used as shot. Especially useful for damaging rigging and killing men.

Larboard – pronounced larb'd; the left side of a ship when facing the bow (front). Changed in the 19th century to 'port'.

Lee – the side or direction away from the wind i.e. downwind.

Lee shore – the shore onto which the wind is blowing, a hazardous shore for a sailing vessel particularly in strong winds – can easily be blown onto rocks etc.

Live lumber – passengers.

Loaded to the gunwale – drunk.

Look like God's revenge against murder – very angry.

Loose in stays  – specifically refers to a ship that 'misses stays' i.e fails to complete a turn while tacking, but often an expression for slack discipline or a ship that is poorly handled

Lubberly – in an amateur way, as a landlubber would do.

Luff – the order to the helmsman to put the tiller towards the lee side of the ship in order to make it sail nearer to the direction of the wind.

Lumping pennyworth – a bargain.

Marlinspike – a pointed iron tool used to part strands of rope so that they can be spliced.

Marry old boots – to marry another man's mistress or whore.

Mast – vertical spar supporting the sails.

Measured fer yer chains – to be imprisoned.

Molly boy – a homosexual prostitute.

Nelsons folly – Rum.

Nipper – short length of rope used to bind an anchor cable but also a small child.

No quarter – no mercy, no survivors.

On the account – or the 'sweet trade'; a man who went 'on the account' was turning pirate.

Ope – an opening or passageway between buildings.

Painter – a rope attached to a boat's bow for securing or towing.

Paper skull – a fool.

Pipe tuner – a cry baby.

Pump ship – urinate.

Quarterdeck – the highest deck at the rear of a ship where the officers stood and where the helm is usually situated.

Quartermaster – usually the second in command aboard a pirate ship. In the Royal Navy, the man in charge of the provisions.

Rabbit hunting with a dead ferret – a pointless exercise.

Rail – timber plank along the top of the gunwale above the sides of the vessel.

Rake – when a ship sweeps another with a broadside of cannon.

Ratlines – pronounced ratlins; horizontal lines tied across the shrouds to form a rope ladder for climbing aloft.

Remedy critch – a chamberpot.

Rib roast – to thrash or flog.

Ride to fetch the midwife – be in haste.

Rigging – the ropes that support the spars (standing rigging) and allow the sails to be controlled (running rigging).

Rope's end – a flogging.

Round shot – iron cannon balls.

Rudder – blade at the stern that is angled to steer the vessel.

Run a rig – to play a trick, to cheat someone.

Rusty guts – a surly fellow.

Sail ho! – 'I see a ship!' The sail is the first part visible over the horizon.

Salamugundy – a cook.

Scallywag – a scoundrel.

Scuppers – openings along the edges of a ship's deck to allow water to drain back to the sea rather than collecting in the bilges.

Scuttle: 1 – a porthole or small hatch in the deck for lighting and ventilation, covered by the 'scuttle hatch'. Can be used as a narrow entrance to the deck below.

Scuttle: 2 – or scupper – to sink a ship deliberately.

Shark bait – someone thrown overboard

Sheet – a rope made fast to the lower corners of a sail to control its position.

Sheet home – to haul on a sheet until the foot of the sail is as straight and taut as possible.

Ship's biscuit – hard bread. Very dry, can be eaten a year after baked. Also called hard tack.

Shrouds – ropes forming part of the standing rigging and supporting the mast or topmast.

Snail's gallop – to go very slowly.

Spanish trumpeter – a donkey.

Spar – a stout wooden pole used as a mast or yard of a sailing vessel.

Splice the mainbrace  – to issue the crew with an extra ration of rum or grog.

Starboard – pronounced starb'd. The right side of a vessel when you are facing toward the bow.

Stay – strong rope supporting the masts.

Stem – timber at the very front of the bow.

Step to – a command to move quickly.

Stern – the back end of a ship.

Strike – to bring in or down, i.e strike the colours

Swab – a disrespectful term for a seaman, or to clean the decks.

Tack / tacking – to change the direction of a vessel's course by turning her bows into the wind until the wind blows on her other side. When a ship is sailing into an oncoming wind, she will have to tack, make a zigzag line, in order to make progress forward against the oncoming wind.

Tackle – pronounced 'taykle'. An arrangement of one or more ropes and pulley blocks used to increase the power for raising or lowering heavy objects.

Taffrail – upper rail along the ship's stern.

Take a caulk – take a nap.

Tilly tally – nonsense.

Trodden on your/my eye – a black eye.

Wake – the line of passage directly behind as marked by a track of white foam.

Weigh anchor – to haul the anchor up; more generally, to leave port.

Windward – the side towards the wind as opposed to leeward.

Yard – a long spar suspended from the mast of a vessel to extend the sails.

Yardarm – either end of the yard.

# Nautical Measurements

6 feet = 1 fathom
22 yards = 1 chain
10 chains = 1 furlong
8 furlongs = 1 mile
6,116 feet = 1 nautical mile (in modern times this measurement is 6,080 feet)
3 miles = 1 league

4½ gallons = 1 pin
1 pin = ½ firkin
2 firkins = 1 kilderkin
2 kilderkins = 1 barrel
1 barrel = 36 gallons
6 barrels = 1 tun
¼ tun = 1 hogshead
54 gallons = 1 hogshead
½ tun = 1 butt

# Bibliography

| | | |
|---|---|---|
| A General History of Pirates | Captain Charles Johnson | Conway |
| A History of Pirates | Nigel Cawthorne | Arcturus |
| A Pirate of Exquisite Mind | Diana and Michael Preston | Corgi |
| Barbary Pirates | Greg Bak | Sutton |
| Blackbeard | Dan Parry | National Maritime Museum |
| Blackbeard & Other Pirates | Nancy Roberts | Blair |
| Empire of Blue Water | Stephen Talty | Pocket Books |
| Heroines and Harlots | David Cordingly | Pan |
| If a Pirate I Must Be | Richard Sanders | Aurum |
| Jack Tar | Roy & Lesley Adkins | Abacus |

Lasivious Bodies: a sexual history of the eighteenth century

| | | |
|---|---|---|
| | Julie Peakman | Atlantic Books |
| Legends of the Outer Banks | C.H. Whedbee | John Blair |
| Life Among the Pirates | David Cordingley | Abacus |
| Piracy – The Complete History | Angus Konstam | Osprey |
| Pirate Hunter of the Caribbean | David Cordingly | Random House |
| Pirates – Predators of the Seas | Angus Konstam | Thalamus |
| Pirates of Barbary | Adrian Tinniswood | Vintage |
| Pirates of Colonial Nth Carolina | Hugh F. Rankin | Dept. Cultural Resources |
| Pirates of the British Isles | Joel Baer | Tempus |
| Pirates, Ghosts & Coastal Lore | C. H. Whedbee | John Blair |
| Scourge of the Seas | Angus Konstam | Osprey |
| Seafaring Women | David Cordingly | Random House |

She Captains: Heroines and Hellions of the Sea

| | | |
|---|---|---|
| John Druett | Simon & Schuster | |
| The Atrocities of the Pirates | Aaron Smith | Prion |
| The Buccaneers of America | Alexander O. Exquemelin | Dover |

| | | |
|---|---|---|
| *The Georgian Art of Gambling* | Claire Cock-Starkey | British Library |

*The Honourable Company: A History of the English East India Company*
John Keay                                    Harper Collins

*The Pirate Trial of Anne Bonny and Mary Read*
Eastman, Tamara J, and Constance Bond              Fern Canyon
                                                   Press
*The Pirate Wars*                Peter Earle                Methuen

*The Pox: the Life and Near Death of a Very Social Disease*
   Kevin Brown                    Sutton
*The Sea: a Cuktural History*     John Mack              Reaktion Books
*Tobacco Coast*                   Arthur Pierce Middleton   Johns Hopkins
*Under the Black Flag*            David Cordingly        Random House
*Women Sailors and*              David Cordingly        Random House
   *Sailors' Women*

## Fiction

*The Sea Witch Voyages*       Helen Hollick        Silverwood Books Ltd
*Sea Witch*                    *Voyage One*
*Pirate Code*                  *Voyage Two*
*Bring It Close*               *Voyage Three*
*Ripples In The Sand*          *Voyage Four*
*On the Account*               *Voyage Five*
*Gallows Wake*                 *Voyage Six (expected publication date 2018)*


*Frenchman's Creek*            Daphne Du Maurier
*Like Chaff In The Wind*       Anna Belfrage
*Peter Pan*                    J. M. Barrie
*The Black Banner*             Helen Hart
*The Book Ark*                 Janis Pegrum Smith
*The Only Life That Mattered*  James L. Nelson
*Treasure Island*              Robert Louis Stevenson

## Website Links

Helen Hollick                 www.helenhollick.net
Helen Hart                    www.authorhelenhart.wordpress.com

| | |
|---|---|
| John F Millar (Newport House, Williamsburg) | www.newporthousebb.com |
| James Nelson | www.jameslnelson.com/ |
| Janis Pegrum Smith | www.janispegrumsmith.com |
| Cindy Vallar *Pirates & Privateers* | www.cindyvallar.com/pirates.html |
| Colonial Williamsburg | www.history.org |
| Talk Like A Pirate Day | www.talklikeapirate.com |
| Whydah Museum | www.discoverpirates.com |
| Wikipedia | http://en.wikipedia.org/wiki/Piracy |

# Acknowledgements

It has been an enjoyable experience, and a slight challenge, to produce *Pirates: Truth and Tale*, not least because I had the chance to meet new potential characters for possible novels, and to reacquaint myself with some old fictional friends.

For the real people, I have a few thank yous: to the staff of Amberley Publishing for commissioning me in the first place, and for their assistance in producing this book; Cathy Helms, who provided the images and accompanied me on an enjoyable trip to Colonial Williamsburg, where we stayed with John Fitzhugh Millar and his wife (another Cathy). John provided me with the words for most of the sea shanties and told me about the adventures of the men aboard the *Bachelor's Delight*. I have promised him, in return, that I will try to write a novel about Master William Dampier one day, although I'm not sure when time will permit this as I have quite a list of 'Novels to Write.'

Thank you to authors Helen Hart, Publishing Director of SilverWood Books Ltd, Anna Belfrage, James L. Nelson and Janis Pegrum Smith for permission to use extracts from their novels. To

Phil Berry for his information about weaponry, Kelly Stambaugh for her opinion of *Black Sails*, the 'Crew' of the *Faithful Bride* for their thoughts on the *Pirates of the Caribbean* movies. My thanks also for general information gleaned from knowledgeable 'pirate people' such as Cindy Vallar, Roy and Leslie Adkins and a host of authors who have written invaluable and interesting text books.

Thank you to Lynn Harmon for scouting out some pirate text books in North Carolina, to Nicky Galliers for bravely reading through the text, and assisting with various errors, and my son-in-law, Adam, for the occasional helping hand.

Thank you to Johnny Depp for rekindling the fire that brought a passion for pirates alive again for many people, and to my own Jesamiah Acorne for boarding my imagination and becoming as real as a fictional character can become – may adventures and Fair Winds follow him, and all fictional pirate heroes, for many years to come.

Helen Hollick, 2016